The Betrayal of the Church

The Betrayal of the Church

Apostasy and Renewal
in the Mainline Denominations

Edmund W. Robb and Julia Robb

CROSSWAY BOOKS • WESTCHESTER, ILLINOIS
A DIVISION OF GOOD NEWS PUBLISHERS

Book Design by K.L. Mulder

First printing, 1986

Printed in the United States of America

Library of Congress Catalog Card Number 86-71006

ISBN 0-89107-403-1

For David Jessup,
who cared enough to start from scratch

Table of Contents

*"It is difficult to reach you, so very difficult—
much more difficult than to reach God, yet I cannot
remain silent."*

Deacon Vladimir Rusak, from his
1983 open letter to the World Council
of Churches

ONE

Has the Church Been Betrayed?

Has the church been betrayed?

Betrayal is a harsh word, a dangerous word. It is, in some respects, the most serious charge which can be leveled against any person or entity. If the charge is correct the results can be serious. If the charges are frivolous, opinion can turn against the accuser. Therefore, betrayal is not a word to be used often or casually. Yet, sometimes no other term will do.

Has the church been betrayed when many of the church's bureaucracies, both Catholic and Protestant, have substituted political propaganda for God's message of grace and salvation— and implied that the two messages are identical?

Has the church been betrayed when many of its leaders, bishops, and presbyters have used their credentials to transform the church into a political errand boy?

Has the church been betrayed when church boards and agencies pour millions of their members' tithes and offerings into radical political causes?

Has the church been betrayed when much of the clergy have valued loyalty to the system more than faithfulness to their message?

Has the church been betrayed when the thousands in its membership suspect that something is wrong, but have failed to demand change?

The evidence of the last ten years demands an answer.

These are the questions on which this book will reflect and the facts which it will examine: has the church been betrayed, and if so, who is guilty of its betrayal?

It will also explore a related subject—the Religious Left; what it is, how it operates, and what effect it has on the American political scene and on American opinion.

THE CREATION OF THE RELIGIOUS LEFT

When people reflect on the Christian church they generally picture a fellowship of believers whose focus is on spiritual growth, spreading the faith, and good works. These were the church's primary goals until the last few decades. There is a wide gulf, however, between yesterday's goals and today's agenda. The American mainline churches—the most prominent of which are the United Methodists, the United Church of Christ, the Presbyterian Church (USA), the Episcopalians, the American Baptists, many Catholic leaders and orders, and the Lutheran Church in America—have realigned their priorities in a frighteningly political direction.

A growing percentage of Christian leadership has abandoned its role as spiritual shepherd because it no longer considers humanity's spiritual welfare its greatest concern. A great many bishops have rejected winning souls in favor of influencing political issues. Church bureaucracy now neglects traditional mission in favor of lobbying for political causes. In fact, certain sectors of the church now make it their primary business to manufacture, widely distribute, and finance a radical agenda by which they hope to save the world. In doing so, they have created the Religious Left.

Main components of the Religious Left are organizations financed by the church. These organizations, such as Clergy and Laity Concerned (an anti-American, prodisarmament group), lobby the secular world and the American government on behalf of the Religious Left agenda. Unfortunately, church members are rarely aware of these organizations or their denomination's spending practices and would probably disapprove if they did know.

The Religious Left is a result of the cooperation between these church-created organizations and mainline denominational bureaucracies (such as the United Methodist General Board of Global Ministries, the United Church of Christ Board for Homeland Ministries, the Presbyterian General Assembly Mission Board and the Presbyterian Peacemaking Program), mainline church leadership, and the National and World Council of Churches. The cooperation among these groups is not planned, but is the product of mutual agreement among allies on what they consider true and important.

The transformation from classical Christianity to political advocacy has occurred gradually during the last twenty years and is the result of spiritual depletion. Christian leadership, for the most part, no longer believes that eternity is of prime significance. The emphasis is now on this world. The lack of metaphysical religious belief, a belief which was once the hallmark of Christians, is demonstrated in some church literature. Now bureaucrats tout the value of other religions while refusing to assert the uniqueness of Christianity. At the same time historic Christian mission is attacked as one which allegedly corrupted and oppressed native peoples.[1] Mainline literature, in large measure, no longer teaches that the world must be saved for Christ, but from poverty and oppression.

WHAT THE RELIGIOUS LEFT BELIEVES

These new concerns have produced, in turn, a fervent ideological conversion to socialism, pacifism at home, violent "liberation" abroad—the theological expression of which is liberation theology—and a determination to play power politics. Following these beliefs to their logical conclusions, church leadership continually attacks American government for its alleged indifference to the poor and American free enterprise for its alleged exploitation of the Third World. It continuously demands America rid itself of military defenses and seems determined to believe Marxist-Leninist regimes bring the new millennium.

Radicalism has become so strident on these subjects that in 1985 twenty of the fifty-seven Presbyterians in Congress protested to Presbyterian Stated Clerk James Andrews. The signers declared that the church was not "cognizant" of the expanding military nature of the international Communist presence in Central America, and protested the church's "peace" advocacy by admonishing that "peace at any price is not peace."

Charging that leadership is out of touch with its members, the five-page letter criticized the General Assembly and church social action agencies for their liberalism. It also stated that the Presbyterian stance on U.S.-U.S.S.R. relations is "ultimately self-defeating." They charged that the church's position was "based on the inaccurate belief that we can expect perfection of countries," and the idea that the United States is "self-righteous and hypocritical if we denounce even the most atrocious actions of governments who declare themselves our enemies."

This, then, is the Religious Left: a group of allies who are in positions of leadership within the American mainline church and its bureaucracies, or who are leaders and members of like-minded organizations funded by the mainline church. If the Religious Left was only a harmless, loosely knit alliance which advocated far-left positions it would be bad enough. It has, however, caused active damage to the American psyche. Not only are the main issues of the Religious Left—such as the ones which the Presbyterians denounced—untrue and strident, their anti-Americanism directly affects what theologian C. S. Lewis termed part of one of the "four loves," patriotism.

THE RELIGIOUS LEFT AND THE AMERICAN PSYCHE

Lewis saw patriotism as a healthy and necessary attitude in sane, just societies; patriotism is not blasphemy, he maintained, and not idolatry. But the result of the church's attitude toward its country, and its country's enemies, has been the creation of an undue sense of guilt which has helped produce an atmosphere of self-doubt among church membership and the population at large.

A typical statement of this sort was made by United Methodist minister James Lawson in his keynote address to the 1982 National Assembly of Clergy and Laity Concerned. It was later repeated in its newsletter. "We face a time, now as Americans," he pronounced, "where we must either will the defeat of our nation's policies, domestic and international, in order that the human race might have a future of promise, or we will will the chaos of the human family. What seems very clear is that the number one enemy of peace and justice in the world today is the United States."

Lawson repeated the charge to a Methodist Council of Bishops meeting in May 1985, this time going further and stating that U.S. leadership had deliberately chosen, after World War II, to cynically accuse the U.S.S.R. of being an enemy of the U.S. in order to keep up a high level of defense spending. At the same meeting, The Rev. Barbara Green of the Presbyterian Peacemaking Program declared that "The U.S. made the Soviet Union an enemy so it would have a reason to build its arms and have an evil entity it could find itself superior to."[2]

It is interesting that most council members did not openly protest Lawson's remarks, but not altogether surprising; Lawson was one of the people consulted by the bishops while they were gathering information for their pastoral letter concerning American defense and nuclear weapons.

Mainline leadership seeks to justify these sorts of attitudes, as exemplified by Lawson, by demanding "peace with justice," usually in the Third World. However, it seldom demands freedom. Liberty does not seem to have a high priority. The inequities of society disturb churchmen, and rightly so. But as statists, they seem to believe that government should remedy all injustice in this imperfect world. They have discarded the ancient Christian belief that hearts must be changed before societies can be reformed and therefore refuse to recognize that much suffering and poverty has root causes in moral, cultural, and spiritual problems. In Religious-Left thinking it logically follows that since the Third World is not responsible for its problems, some negative force must be in control. The negative force choosen as villain is, most often, the United States.

THE RELIGIOUS LEFT LOBBY, ITS GOALS AND EFFECTS

Perhaps the most injurious aspect of these attitudes is that they cannot be ignored. The Religious Left has become the most vocal purveyor of the above ideas, and the most powerful. It now has disproportionate influence over Central American policy, defense issues, and American perceptions of Marxist-Leninist societies and intentions. Its influence has made itself felt not by suggestions based on realistic political assessment, but by criticism which reflects both its negative view of American intentions and an implied threat from its constituency. Ironically, its shrill demands for a decisive voice in political decision-making has been the identical process which has discredited it with many U.S. government officials.

Otto Reich, the State Department's coordinator of public diplomacy for Latin America and the Caribbean, explained to the authors that the Religious Left has been so politically active that many in the Reagan Administration have concluded they are not religiously motivated at all. "It takes lots of political courage to say we will ignore advice from religious groups," he said, "but people in the administration have become very cynical because they believe many religious groups, such as the National Council of Churches and the U.S. Catholic Conference, are led or manipulated by individuals who have a political agenda and have taken advantage of a convenient cover.

"They have a political agenda there. Their actions appear to be actions of people who want to change this society. They don't like the way it is, they don't like the political, social or economic system. This is opinion, but they appear not to like those structures and that is what they really want to change, using peripheral issues. . . . The strictly political activists have been given a mantle of moral respectability which is not deserved."[3]

Sanctuary for illegal aliens is one example, Reich said, of church activists using an erstwhile religious issue to criticize American policy. Activists in the sanctuary movement (who are often persuaded to take the sanctuary course by church agencies and quasi-religious organizations) ostensibly believe the American government should change its immigration policy toward refugees from Central America, principally those from El Salvador—to accept automatically all such aliens who claim they are fleeing from war and persecution. It is, they say, the Christian thing to do. There are now an estimated forty illegal sanctuaries operated in the United States through approximately two hundred and fifty churches.

Reich suggested, however, that sanctuary workers are interested in refugees primarily as a means of combating U.S. government support for El Salvador's democratically elected government. By publicizing its alleged victims, they hope to gain support for the Marxist-Leninist guerrillas who are seeking its overthrow.

FACTIONS

Reich's viewpoint is confirmed by those in the ranks of the Religious Left itself. In an article for *Monthly Review*, a Marxist magazine,

Sister Kathleen Schultz of the religious order of the Immaculate Heart of Mary declared that the most notable change in the United States over the last twenty years has been the emergence of Christians in radical politics.[4]

Schultz attributed the change to upheaval caused by the civil rights movement and the verbal war over Vietnam. The major concerns of radical Christians now, she wrote, are the antinuclear and disarmament movements and the struggle against American policy in Central America. The Catholic Bishops' pastoral letter on nuclear arms, Schultz declared, is the "frontispiece" of the Christian Left. "The document signals a significant shift and development within the national hierarchy and opens the door to even greater Catholic, and wider Christian, awareness of and dissent against U.S. policy in the same arms race."[5]

The change has been so notable, Schultz believes, that the church has split in half, the church in "solidarity" with the poor and exploited and the "church of the established order." She identifies four factions of the Christian Left. The first faction is "center-center" mainline Christians, who she implies are largely officials of the local church structure who believe in the Left's agenda. The second are center-left Christians whose activities are "based on anti-capitalist critique within a social-democratic framework," but who are "anticommunist." The third category is the "socially committed Christians," who have "begun to develop an alternative ecclesiastical and theological awareness (liberation theology)." Their activities are usually "prophetic denunciation and symbolic resistance."[6]

The fourth category is that of "politically committed Christians" who are "characterized" by "revolutionary left practice and socialist political commitment." These Christians, Schultz said, are Marxists* who, considering the "repression" in the United States, have not yet publicly admitted their political orientation.[7]

This is a revealing statement as Schultz reports that its "analysis of issues and of the role of the churches, along with their organizational capacity, gives this sector an influence disproportionate to their numbers. . . . " In other words, Schultz believes that Marxists have a great, albeit subtle, influence within the Religious Left.[8]

---

*There is a difference between Marxism and Marxism-Leninism. The former refers to the theory of Marxism, the latter to aggressive Marxism, a movement whose adherents attempt to impose Marxism on society by undemocratic means.

BUREAUCRATIC MANIPULATION OF CATHOLIC HIERARCHY

What Schultz did not explain is the way in which the bureaucracies have often manipulated mainline leadership to take Religious Left positions. The Catholic bishops are a case in point. While many Catholic bishops are more conservative than their Protestant counterparts, their political activism has been, as Schultz noted, a "frontispiece" for the Religious Left. The Catholic pastoral letter on defense and nuclear war, "The Challenge of Peace: God's Promise and Our Response," effectively advocated nuclear pacifism by declaring that not only was the use of nuclear weapons wrong, but even the threat of using the weapons was wrong. The letter on the American economy which followed is a model for leftist thinking on economic matters.

These developments do not signify a sudden radicalization of most Catholic bishops. What they do signify is the abdication of responsibility by the bishops and their subsequent dependence on their more radical bureaucracy. Even in instances when the Catholic hierarchy seems to be leading, publishing letters on national defense or on the U.S. economic system, they are willing prisoners of staffs (largely of the United States Catholic Conference) who do the initial studies and recommend the consultants.

Edward Doherty, one of the Catholic Conference staffers who had great influence on the bishops' pastoral letter on defense, is an excellent example of Religious-Left thinking. He wants the bishops to advocate immediate unilateral disarmament in favor of conventional defense. If that is not enough to deter the Soviets, Doherty believes that it would be "preferable" for the United States to be in the position Afghanistan is currently in (occupied by the Soviet army) than for it to retain its nuclear weapons. This is all based on Doherty's conception of morality. If the Soviet Union occupied America it would be good from a moral point of view, he believes, because "it would force people to defend themselves on an individual, human level rather than ask their governments to take care of them by building more missiles."[9]

HIERARCHICAL OBSOLESCENCE

In his excellent article "The Catholic Bishops, Public Policy, and the New Class," James Hitchcock traced both the attitudes which allowed staff members like Doherty to manipulate the bishops and the effect it has had on the decision-making process. Because the bishops found the world of the late sixties "daunting and bewildering," and because their education did not seem adequate to help them cope, many bishops began to defer to the "experts."[10]

"In most dioceses," Hitchcock wrote, "activities like religious education became semi-autonomous, for example, the bishop rarely 'interfering' with the work of people whose competence in a particular area he estimated to be superior to his own. Before long some bishops found themselves unable to act decisively in any area of church life where some definable competence could be claimed, since certified experts had staked out those areas for themselves.[11]

"Bishops have tended, in the midst of this predicament, to define their own rules in two opposite ways—on one hand continuing to exercise ultimate budgetary authority in their dioceses, and on the other hand presenting themselves merely as kindly grandfathers, holding the diocese together by bonds of personal affection."[12]

Hitchcock's observations are just as valid for the Protestant hierarchy. The United Methodist bishops decided in 1984 to write a peace letter. They used Alan Geyer of the Churches Center for Theology and Public Policy and listened to James Lawson's views. Lawson's political position has already been explored. The Center for Theology, as demonstrated by its own literature, is far left of center. The resulting letter was, unsurprisingly, left of center.

OF BISHOPS AND ISSUES

Further, many Catholic bishops seemingly do not understand the issues in which they are supposedly guiding their membership, making them even more vulnerable to manipulation.

After being picked at random by a writer of a conservative magazine, some Catholic bishops were asked their viewpoint on various questions which related to their pastoral letters on the economy and American defense. Bishop Edward O'Donnell of St. Louis admitted, among other things, he doesn't know what percent of the national budget is spent on defense. He said he wants an "adequate non-nuclear defense" to protect Europe, but he is "alarmed at the information that conventional weapons cost more than nuclear weapons."[13]

Bishop Maurice Dingman of Des Moines, one of the most radical bishops, told the writer that he is "going more and more pacifist" because of his realization, "Why can't we win wars without ever lifting a gun?"[14]

"Confronted with the magnitude of the Soviet buildup and asked to explain it," the writer said, "Bishop Dingman is not flustered. '*Megatrends* gives me the answer,' he says, in reference to the best-selling book. 'Both we and the Soviets have hierarchical systems that are outdated. We have to move into networking.'"[15]

It would seem that men whose ideas are so vague would be ignored by the public. If it were only bishops speaking, that would probably be the case. But much of the time the bureaucracies who speak for them provide the bishops with statements containing seemingly authoritative arguments. Those bureaucracies then reach out to millions of church members. They urge them to get involved with issues for which they supposedly, as Christians, are responsible; issues such as America's involvement with anti-Sandinista forces in Nicaragua and defense spending for weapons systems. The church-financed organizations, at the same time, preaching the same issue, reach millions in the secular world and are doubly effective because they wear the cloak of religious respectability.

WHERE THE MONEY GOES

They are also very well financed. Most mainline churches, as well as the National Council of Churches, now use a large percentage of their national income to finance the Religious Left. An analysis of Presbyterian grants for the year 1983, done by *The Presbyterian Layman*, revealed that 60 percent of Presbyterian Hunger Funds sent outside the United States ($1.9 million or 38.8 percent of the total) were used for direct hunger relief and agricultural support, but 55 percent allocated for use in the United States ($2.2 million or 82.6 percent) were directed to nonagricultural political action projects.[16]

Either because church bureaucracies could not fund their mission programs at former levels and still spend great amounts on Religious Left projects, or because church agencies simply lost interest, many denominations now spend almost as much on political projects as on missionary programs. In 1968 the United Methodist General Board of Global Ministries had fifteen hundred career overseas missionaries. The mission force in 1985 was less than a third of its former size, with only four hundred and sixty career missionaries left in its ranks. This does not include short-term missionaries or foreign nationals. Between 1972 and 1981, the United Church of Christ nearly doubled the amount they spent on non-UCC projects—from $6.5 million to $12.1 million. According to UCC dissidents, rebellious UCC churches have become so disgusted at official church spending that they gave $800,000 more in 1981 for projects outside the church than they gave to the church itself. Unlike other mainline denominations, the United Church of Christ does not require its local congregations to support any of its bureaucracies.

The Methodist mission board spent only 16.9 percent—a little over $10 million—of its 1981 expenditures for missionaries. But they spent $29.9 million on grants, much of which went to politically active, ideologically committed organizations.

The largest recipient in 1981 was the World Student Christian Federation. It received a total of $120,900 and almost $170,000 more in the next two years. The amount dropped to $50,000 in 1984. The organization describes itself as an ecumenical Christian student organization with affiliates in ninety countries.

In August 1981, however, the Federation proved itself something more than a Christian organization. It passed resolutions supporting Cuba, the Nicaraguan Sandinistas, and the former Marxist-Leninist government of Grenada. The gathering decided that the Palestine Liberation Organization is the "sole representative" of the Palestinian people, supported a violent Marxist-Leninist organization (SWAPO), and said Puerto Rico should be freely allowed to determine its status (as if it had not been allowed to do so).

In 1984 the United Methodists gave Clergy and Laity Concerned $30,500. They also gave over $37,000 to Agricultural Missions, a program of the National Council of Churches so radical that in 1985 its officials were refused admittance to the island of Antigua.

Officials of the Antiguan government later told the authors that the organization is not "compatible with government interests." Unofficially, the Antiguan government indicated it did not appreciate Agricultural Missions' intention of having Tim Hector, a well-known Caribbean radical and reported friend of Fidel Castro, as speaker at its annual board meeting. Nevertheless, Mr. Hector's organization, the American-Caribbean Training Institute, has received approximately $10,000 to $15,000 from Agricultural Missions since 1980.[17] Agricultural Missions gets its money from other denominations who are members of the National Council of Churches and the National Council itself. Apparently a great number of people who know nothing about Mr. Hector's organization are contributing to his annual budget.

It is also a comment on United Methodist priorities that while the church was funding over $18 million in non-Methodist projects, it was announcing severe financial shortages. In April 1985, the United Methodist General Board of Global Ministries announced funding of its overseas missionaries was in a "significant crisis." A special appeal in 1984 for $2 million for additional missionaries had been virtually ignored, the agency said, adding that United Methodist membership had given only $17,000. In order to support missionaries in 1986, the agency said, it would pass a "faith" budget because it was dependent on United Methodists giving $1 million more, a 20 percent increase, toward missionary salary.

When the appeal was launched in 1984, the agency said the $2 million would put fifty more missionaries in the field, but they later revised those figures to say that the $2 million would only insure a three-year salary for about twenty missionaries, due to increased costs. Furthermore, Global Ministries official Peggy Billings said a full 25 percent of the money had been designated for nonpersonnel projects overseas. As of 1984 the Board was spending $18.6 million for non-United Methodist projects and organizations and $20.4 million for persons in mission.

STRATEGIC LOSSES

The church's tilt toward the radical agenda has had two disastrous consequences: real damage done to the nation's strategic position, and the growing gap it has created between the church's hierarchies and church members, resulting in a loss of millions of members and potential members.

The strategic damage has been sustained by the Religious Left's creation of an atmosphere in which it is much harder to justify defense spending, thus making it more difficult to maintain a balance of power. Literature—churned out by the ream—claims that the United States does not need a military buildup and blames the United States for the arms race. This activity has had a decided effect on the weapons debate by making it appear to the public, the media, and Congress that a vast section of American citizenry favor disarmament.

The most common tactic used to defeat proposed defense spending is a massive mail-out of literature which urges concerned Christians to protest to their legislators. Readers are urged to concentrate on "swing votes," congressmen and senators whose vote will pass or kill legislation.

Most mainline denominations have passed endless resolutions calling for a nuclear freeze, a repudiation of the MX missile, and a halt to the Strategic Defense Initiative. Some resolutions have called for a halt to the placing of Pershing missiles in Europe; most mainline denominations have demanded President Reagan withdraw economic aid from El Salvador and financial support from Nicaragua's anti-Sandinista rebels.

To be sure, most of the resolutions considered by the church conventions and bishops' councils are drafted and introduced by the bureaucracies, but they are meekly passed by delegates and leadership. The resolutions are then forwarded to Congress.

Worse still, however, has been the stance the church has taken against American influence throughout the world. Mainline leadership has actively worked against it, while piously stating they are only working for "peace." A typical example of this sort of hypocrisy is the National Council for Churches' effort to establish a "nuclear-free Pacific." The NCC is allied in this campaign with the Australian Council of Churches and a Dutch church group, as well as several Communist-controlled labor unions. They have now partially had their way because New Zealand, in Spring 1985, banned American ships carrying nuclear weapons from its harbors.

It does not appear disturbing to either New Zealand, the National Council, or other American church leaders that the Pacific swarms with Soviet submarines carrying nuclear weapons. Methodist bishops positively rejoiced in New Zealand's actions. In May 1985, they sent letters of support to New Zealand's prime minister and to Methodists and Presbyterians who had worked against American interests in the Pacific.

THE CHURCH TOUTS TOTALITARIANS

It is tragic enough for the church to adopt general anti-American attitudes, but it has compounded the tragedy by becoming a public relations firm for the Soviet Union, China, Nicaragua, Angola, Cuba, and a host of others. Since those regimes are among the most repressive and the most anti-Christian the world has ever known, it could be argued that the church (as Lenin predicted the Western businessman would do) is supplying the rope with which it—and the rest of the world—can conceivably be hanged. By showering its approval on these regimes, the church has also discredited itself with persecuted Christians in other parts of the world.

After returning from Cuba in 1977, former United Methodist Bishop James Armstrong, past president of the National Council of Churches, and seven other church leaders made the remarkable assertion that there is a "significant" difference between situations where people are in prison for opposing governments which practice inequities and ones in which people are jailed for opposing governments which attempt to remove inequities. The latter, of course, was a reference to Cuba.[18]

Such statements sound particularly ironic after hearing Cuban poet Armando Valladares recall his years in Cuban prisons. When his captors wanted to taunt him and the rest of Castro's political prisoners, Valladares said, the "communist indoctrinators" repeatedly used the statements of support for Castro's revolution made by representatives of American Christian churches.[19]

If greater or lesser culprits can be identified, the World Council of Churches should easily come to mind. When officials of the Ethiopian Orthodox Church—many of whom had been members of World Council committees—began to disappear after the 1974 Communist takeover of their country, no World Council official even protested. When the church patriarch, a man who had attended every World Council meeting since its founding, a man who in 1971 hosted the World Council Central Committee Convention in Addis Ababa, disappeared into the prison system, no World Council official even murmured a public protest.

Ethiopian Aradom Tedla attended the World Council convention in Vancouver in 1983 and begged ex-World Council General Secretary Philip Potter to help the patriarch. Potter, however, limited himself to investigating the patriarch's whereabouts. Then, putting his arm across Tedla's shoulders, he said, "Well, I have good news for you, the patriarch is still alive." He did not offer to mediate the patriarch's release from prison, nor did he seem particularly upset by the situation, Tedla said.[20]

In 1976, Soviet dissidents Father Gleb Yakunin and Lev Regelson pleaded to the Nairobi Assembly for help against religious persecution. They charged the Council had been silent when "the Russian Orthodox Church was half destroyed" in the early 1960s. The Assembly responded by voting to scrutinize religious freedom more closely. The resolution, however, did not mention the Soviet Union. The Council subsequently sponsored a low-key human rights program, but never spoke out openly against Soviet repression.[21]

At the 1983 Vancouver Assembly Potter again received appeals from Yakunin and from Russian Orthodox deacon Vladimir Rusak. This time Yakunin was pleading from a prison camp in the Soviet Ural mountains. He was sentenced to that unpleasant fate for his temerity in cofounding the original Christian Committee for the Defense of Believers' Rights. This time the Assembly was given little information about the appeals and "WCC spokesmen blandly explained that any action by the assembly would have amounted to intervention in the internal affairs of a member church."[22]

Christian activists are also some of the last defenders of the Nicaraguan Sandinistas, one of the few groups which has not admitted the regime is totalitarian and anti-Christian. In this particular instance, it is difficult to tell which of the pro-Sandinistas are part of the Religious Left and which are simply naive, in view of the Religious Left's policy of leading idealistic Christians to Marxist-Leninist societies and introducing them to miracles of Christianity-in-Action that no one else has discerned. Maryknoll nun Peggy Healy, a longtime resident of Nicaragua, has been extremely influential in persuading Christian tourists that the Sandinistas are true democrats.

THE OPINION GAP

Religious radicalism might not be such an affront if it were representative of church membership as a whole. Such is not the case. The gulf between the political and religious opinions of mainline church leadership and the political and religious opinions of membership is wide;

polls also reflect a difference in opinion between members and local clergy as well. This widening gap has resulted in a devastating loss of members and potential members.

The ideological disparity between bureaucrats and membership was underlined by a 1980 study of the attitudes of National Council of Churches membership. "Profiles By Faith," or "Surveying the Religious Landscape," prepared by the National Council of Churches' Office of Research, Evaluation, and Planning, asserted that members who thought of themselves as "liberal" constituted a group smaller than any other category. Labeled "confidential," the Planning Office asked that the study not be disseminated to the public because some people might use the findings to prove the National Council is "out of step" with its constituency "and censure us for it. To those who are hunting for such ammunition we need not supply a silver bullet."

The study was prepared using social indicator data researched by The National Opinion Research Center of the University of Chicago. The data was based on seven surveys conducted between 1972 and 1978. Since the country has become more politically conservative since the midseventies, it is possible that the disparity between attitudes of NCC bureaucrats and NCC member churches might now be even sharper than when the surveys were originally conducted. The Robert Johnson Company was later commissioned for a study, but that too was never released.

Episcopalians and Presbyterians have both made it clear they do not want their church involved in politics. A 1985 Gallup poll commissioned by the Episcopal Prayerbook Society found that 76 percent of Episcopal laity oppose the church acting as an agent of political change in the U.S. However, a majority of Episcopal clergy disagreed.[23]

The Presbyterians regularly conduct polls through their research unit, and those polls usually indicate a wide gulf between member views and the views of clergy and bureaucracy. A February 1985 poll, for instance, revealed that while 74 percent of Presbyterian members either strongly agreed or agreed that the security of the United States depends on its military strength, only 48 percent of clergy agreed or strongly agreed. The disparity was even more marked between membership and bureaucrats, religious workers and clergy assigned to special advocations.[24]

Although Catholic bishops have made their political views well known, their parishioners apparently disapprove by a wide margin. A recent poll proved that only 39 percent of Catholic membership believe their bishops should become involved in political issues. Catholic priests, however, disagree. Eighty percent of them are in favor.[25]

MEMBER EXODUS

Most rank-and-file membership suspect something is wrong. There have been numerous articles criticizing the Religious Left, small books written for esoteric circles, exposés printed in *Reader's Digest*, and a "CBS 60 Minutes" documentary detailing World and National Council of Churches funding of Marxist-Leninist organizations. Mainline church membership as a whole, however, has not been transformed into a tidal wave of indignation. That is not to say that indignation does not exist. For the most part, church members have voted with their feet.

According to a study by Harvard divinity professor William Hutchison, the percentage of U.S. Protestant membership represented by the mainline churches has fallen 30 percent in the last sixty years. Mainline churches constituted 76 percent of the U.S. Protestant population in 1920. In 1984, mainline bodies only represented 49.2 percent.[26] Further, the membership remaining in mainline churches is disproportionately made up of people above age fifty. Young adults comprise only 21 percent of United Church of Christ membership and 28 percent of the United Methodists. These figures are significant when it is considered that 40 percent of the nation's adult population belongs to the eighteen to thirty-four age group.[27]

Some experts predict that the United Methodist Church, already more than a million and a quarter members down from its 1968 level, will lose another 3.5 million by the year 2000, bringing its membership rolls below six million.

Figures from a recent National Council of Churches census showed the United Methodists losing 11 percent membership since 1970, the Lutheran Church in America 6 percent, the Episcopalians 15 percent, the Presbyterians 23 percent (*The Presbyterian Layman* magazine places the figure at 27 percent), and the United Church of Christ 13 percent. During the same time period, the conservative Southern Baptist Convention gained 22 percent, the strait-laced Mormons 41 percent, and the evangelical Assemblies of God an astounding 85 percent. Unlike the mainline churches, these congregations are made up of a disproportionate number of young adults.

The Presbyterian Church in America, a conservative group which split from the Southern Presbyterian Church (now the Presbyterian Church U.S.A.) in 1973, has doubled its size in its first ten years (it now has one hundred and fifty thousand members), and is expected to double again by 1991. The church originally split from the Southern Presbyterians due to its scheduled reunion with the Northern Presbyterian Church, which was considered more liberal.

It becomes clear where many of the lost mainline members are going when one considers that the Presbyterian Church in America has added more than three times as many members through transfers from other churches as it has through new congregations. It has gained membership through its mergers with the Reformed Presbyterian Church, Evangelical Synod and the Orthodox Presbyterian Church; but thirty-four thousand people transferred from other churches with which they felt an obvious dissatisfaction.

FUTURE DECLINE

Hutchison does not believe his figures necessarily indicate that Protestant liberalism is "enervated," nor that the growth of conservative churches and decline of the mainline church are related, nor that liberalism will continue to decline. Most of the professors and sociologists who have recently studied mainline membership loss strongly disagree. Wade Clark Roof, a sociology professor at the University of Massachusetts, has predicted the decline will continue into the next century. He believes low birthrates among liberal Protestants, gains among conservative denominations, and an increase in the number of people growing up outside any religious tradition will keep the mainline churches from regaining their former numbers and influence. Conservative Protestants have a far higher birthrate than liberals. Methodists made up 16 percent of all Americans born at the turn of the century. By 1965 they made up only 7.7 percent.[28] The other prominent mainline churches suffered a similar decline.

Some of the mainline decline can also be attributed to a growing number of people who do not belong to any church. A 1978 study seemingly proved that 41 percent of the American population is "unchurched." Most of those, the study said, are in some way religious, but have not chosen to become members of a denomination.[29] It can be considered a major failure of the mainline churches that they have not been able to touch this group.

Some of the most radical activism has sprung from Roman Catholic clergy, and that church has also suffered a great decline. There has not been as much controversy about the activism among church members, but the quarreling between Catholic clergy and the Vatican over who will interpret doctrine has had its effect. Young men and women no longer opt for religious orders as they once did, and attendance at weekly Mass has dropped 23 percent in America since 1958.[30] Although the number of Catholics has continued to grow because of a higher birthrate and because of immigration, younger Catholics do not attend Mass in the numbers their elders do.

The breakdown of authority on moral issues, such as abortion, contraception, and ordination of women, has also been an apparent factor in the Catholic decline, as well as the changes brought on by the Second Vatican Council. Discarding the ancient Mass which Catholics had used for centuries was a jarring experience for many. Nonetheless, the traditionally conservative anti-Communist American Catholic has been further alienated by theologians and priests who openly espouse a quasi-Marxist liberation theology, with some missionaries going so far as to take up arms with Marxist-Leninist guerrilla groups.[31]

RELIGIOUS ATTITUDES AND LOST OPPORTUNITY

One of the real tragedies in religious radicalism has been the loss of opportunity. A 1984 Gallup poll proved that religious belief and importance of religion in individual lives has increased dramatically in the last few years. A majority of 56 percent told Gallup that they are more reliant on God than they were five years ago, and as many as four in ten said their spiritual well-being has improved.[32]

Religion for youth has taken a dramatic upturn, with the percentage of college students who say religion is very important in their lives increasing from 39 percent in 1975 to 50 percent in 1984. Gallup also reported that the proportion of college youth today who say their religious commitment has become stronger since they have been in college is twice the percentage of those who said it has become weaker.[33]

The authors of *All Faithful People*, a sociological study of religion in Muncie, Indiana, took Gallup one step further and proved, by comparative studies, that religion in America is actually stronger than in the 1920s. They suggested that religious upswings occur on a regular basis. If that is so, it is a fact that has not been capitalized on by the mainline church. If church leadership had encouraged godliness instead of participation in politics in the last two decades, it might have tripled its membership.[34]

It might have also revitalized morality in America. The Gallup poll showed that although religion was growing in importance in America, morality is losing ground. There is little difference in behavior between the churched and the unchurched, the poll said; it recommended that religious leaders channel people's new interest into "not simply religious involvement but into deep spiritual commitment."[35] As long as mainline leadership stresses social awareness over spiritual commitment, that change will probably never occur in their denominations.

MEMBER REACTION TO CONTROVERSY

Given the gap between mainline church leadership and the people in the pews, one would think that the latter would be outraged by the radical stance their leaders have taken. It would seem that members who faithfully give to support their church and its Christian mission would react angrily when they find out where much of the money has gone. To a certain extent this is true; the church *has* lost many members. But it is not true of those who stayed. Many were angered enough by "60 Minutes" ' "The Gospel According to Whom?" to demand an investigation into the funding practices of the National and World Council of Churches. But the furor soon died and the status quo has remained unshaken.

In September 1983 the United Presbyterian Council on Church and Race, obviously determined to defy negative opinion, voted $3,000 for the World Council's Program to Combat Racism. The child of that program, the Special Program to Combat Racism, funds the African National Congress (of South Africa) and the Southwest Africa People's Organization (of Namibia): both are Marxist-Leninist terrorist groups. The Presbyterians reasoned that the Council's "commitment to a cause" had come under attack from *Reader's Digest* and others who publicized what kind of organizations the WCC supported. The $3,000 was the Presbyterian Council's way of throwing down the gauntlet.

LEADERSHIP REACTION

Church leadership, including most pastors, supported the Council's decisions from the first, blindly defending them and maintaining that the charges were not true. The Council of Bishops of the United Methodist Church named a blue ribbon commission (the Conciliar Review Committee) to study the charges directed at the National and World Council of Churches. The resulting report was largely a whitewash of the Councils. The report did include an inquiry into the United Methodist Board of Global Ministries which did contain criticism of that agency. The district superintendents of the Southeastern Jurisdiction of the denomination subsequently petitioned the General Conference (governing body) of the church to name a commission to study the allegations. By a narrow vote, the Conference refused.

Moreover, the defense of funding practices and attitudes by mainline officials has been blindly hostile. Defensiveness has been so automatic that not only has nothing changed, there apparently is no suspicion that it should. Critics are often accused of not only being wrong, but evil to make such outrageous accusations. James Armstrong, then a United Methodist bishop and president of the National

Council of Churches, protested the media exposure, charging that part of it "had been 'exploited' by right-wing forces bent on destroying the ecumenical voice for justice of the world."[36]

Ironically, the controversy itself has fueled organizations which are angered at the church's lack of response. A separate mission board has been created by conservative United Methodists, in response to frustration felt over the seemingly immovable Board of Global Ministries. Presbyterians, United Church of Christ, and Episcopalians have also created organizations designed to spur reform in their churches; the Presbyterian Lay Committee, Presbyterians United for Biblical Concerns, The Prayerbook Society of the Episcopal Church, United Church of Christ's Biblical Witness Fellowship, and Good News, a United Methodist organization, are all having an impact.[37] But these organizations only involve a small percentage of people. Most mainline church members have either left or ignore the situation.

Excuses can be made for the general lack of action by membership in responding to the radical transformation of their church. Most of the demands made by the Religious Left are made in the name of the church as a whole. The National Council of Churches also advertises itself as the voice of mainline Christian America and the World Council as the voice of world Christianity. It must seem difficult to oppose such intimidating numbers. It is unfortunate that such pretentions to representation should be believed because most of the grass-roots National and World Council membership has little knowledge of those institutions' activities and of the activities of their own National and World Council representatives.

Further, lay persons often do not feel competent to deal with such issues because the problem seems far away. If things are going well in their local church, they are hesitant to disturb the status quo. They hesitate making their pastor or priest unhappy and do not want to be thought rabble-rousers. But much of membership's obvious passivity can be attributed to a reluctance to get involved in battles that can get unpleasant and have no happy end in the foreseeable future. Some members also seem to want religion to be their comfort, but not their challenge. They want to attend church on Sunday mornings and feel they have done their duty toward God, but do not want to be accountable for action taken in their name. Knowledge is responsibility, and responsibility demands energy and commitment.

It is also possible that some members, who are not involved in charity work, or who feel guilty they are able to live in a safe, prosperous society, actually feel the church is their surrogate, fighting battles they abdicated long ago.

Pastors, on the other hand, often understand the issues, but many are more concerned about their professional careers than being honest with their congregations. To be sure, many are concerned about the unity of their church and seek to protect the members from disillusionment; but they are all too willing to overlook what they disapprove in order to keep the peace.

It is easy to understand why members and clergy have kept silent. But if they do not demand change, the American mainline church will wither into a small, ineffective organization devoted exclusively to secular concerns. It will become only another failed political party devoted to pacifism, socialism, anti-Americanism, and allegedly favorable aspects of Marxist-Leninist societies. Those are the ideas which the Religious Left now preaches. This book will explore this thesis and examine these ideas. It will attempt to prove them wrong. It will, most of all, attempt to warn about the dangers of continuing this course.

Alexis de Tocqueville, that most astute observer of American democracy, observed one hundred and fifty years ago that it is extremely dangerous for clerics to become involved in politics of any persuasion. When they do, he said, they are identified with their politics instead of their faith. One of America's great strengths, he thought, was that the ecclesiastics had not compromised their belief by acting out their secular opinions. As a result, ". . . . belief has remained unshaken." The church in Europe was not as wise, he pointed out, and has "allowed itself to be intimately united with the powers of this world. Now that these powers are falling, it is as if it were buried under their ruins. . . . "[38]

The trend that Tocqueville observed has played itself out in Europe today where only a small percentage of people attend church or even believe in God. But Tocqueville had a solution, one which was never implemented in Europe. It is not too late for America.

He wrote: "A living being has been tied to the dead; cut the bonds holding it and it will arise."[39]

The Religious Left and Disarmament

"Our heroes," "God bless Uncle Sam," "Thank God for America," the graffiti said, sprawled over the sunbaked walls.[1] It was Grenada, and the people were glad we had come on October 25, 1983. On that day the United States destroyed a dictatorship and later arranged democratic elections, earning a lasting gratitude from the Grenadians. The last American soldiers, sixty of the 82nd Airborne, left the island twenty months later.

Nonetheless, most American denominations, the National and World Council of Churches, and a host of leftist organizations financed by the church began a deafening diatribe when the first soldiers landed. They called the invasion illegal and immoral. Included were the Presbyterian Church U.S.A., the United Methodists, the president of the United Church of Christ and its Board of World Ministries. The churchmen and quasi-churchmen did not wait to see what the Grenadians themselves thought or to hear what Grenada's government had done to deserve American intervention. There was, at once, an absolute conviction that the United States was wrong.

Sadly, this is typical behavior by the Religious Left, which has apparently decided that the inequities it perceives in American society have put it into the oppressor category. Therefore, it seems to feel, since the United States is an oppressor, nothing it does to defend either itself or democratic values elsewhere in the world is morally justified. This is very unfortunate for both the churches and the United States. It is unfortunate for the church because that unreasonable attitude helps alienate Christians who do not agree; and the resulting alienation speeds the denominational decline. It is unfortunate because the Religious Left is using psuedo-Christianity as an excuse for political action. Doctrinal Christianity does not discourage self-defense. It is unfortunate for the country at large because there is a great need for military strength in this dangerous world.

The Religious Left, however, does not share the same viewpoint. It has spent much of its time and money campaigning against weapon and defense systems: the neutron bomb, the MX missile, the placement of Pershing missiles in Europe, and now the Strategic Defense Initiative. It has also spent vast resources of time and money in campaigning for a nuclear freeze or, one of its favorite tactics, "nuclear-free zones."

Typical of this type of activity was the $132,000 spent by the Presbyterian Church in 1981 for its "Peacemaking Project." The commission, which is still in existence, did every conceivable thing it could to influence Presbyterian membership to support the nuclear freeze movement. For example, it mailed a nuclear freeze resolution—which had been endorsed by the 1981 General Assembly—to every Presbyterian pastor, and five copies to every clerk of session, published a collection of eleven peacemaking sermons by Presbyterians and prepared a study guide on the freeze for congregations.

Campaigns of this type have been partially effective because they seem to represent the legitimate political and theological viewpoint of a large number of people. After all, church leaders and agencies represent their denominations. If Congress suspects that they represent only a minority of their membership, or that only a minority of their membership is malleable, church leadership still manages to help shape the debate by the virtue of its endless, shrill lobbying. If credible people shout murder long enough, they do get attention, at least to the point where someone is eventually forced to look into the matter or prove there has been a mistake. If Congress suspects that the Religious Left organizations represent a minority, they are still somewhat influenced by its constituencies.

TYPES OF DISARMAMENT ACTIVISTS

Unfortunately for both the country whom it addresses, and for church membership which is both its captive audience and its pawn, the Religious Left has not forthrightly expressed the real reasons behind its hostility to national defense. It cloaks its real feelings in two primary rationalizations and thus can be classified in two categories. The first rationalization against direct military action and/or defense spending is that the United States is wrong in any given situation. It either denies that any regime in the world is a threat, claims that the United States government is actively persecuting those whom it foolishly considers a threat, or charges that the U.S. government is wrongfully attempting to control other countries.

Pacifists, who compose the second category, base their arguments on their interpretation of Scriptures. There are three main schools of pacifist thought. The first school seems to believe that God will take care of Christians and therefore there is no need for military defense. The second believes that God may not take care of believers physical-

ly, but pacifism is the "right" attitude despite any possible consequences to themselves or others. The third, the nuclear pacifists,
sometimes believe in conventional defense, but believe nuclear war is
too costly to indulge in for any reason. But instead of calling for a
stronger deterrence, they call for disarmament.

AMERICA THE VICTIMIZER

The invasion of Grenada is a perfect example of the first category.
Outraged church leadership charged the Reagan Administration had
no reason to take action against the island's Marxist-Leninist regime,
was evil to do so, and that Grenada was no threat to the United States.
"The United States is adopting the same immoral policy which Soviet
Russia is following in Afghanistan and Poland," Dr. Alan Walker,
director of world evangelism for the Methodist World Council,
charged. The General Assembly Mission Board and the Program
Agency of the Presbyterian Church said in a joint statement that they
were "profoundly disturbed by the precedent-setting conception that
the request of several neighbors can legitimate armed intervention by
the United States in the affairs of another country. . . . We call upon
the American people to question the image of the powerful United
States acting as judge, jury and enforcer in world events . . . and we
call upon Presbyterians to hold constant in prayer those that have been
victimized."[2]

After condemning the invasion as illegal, United Church of Christ
officials said they affirmed their "solidarity with the people and
churches of Grenada in this time of anguish and oppression."[3] Most
statements from religious groups accused the United States of violat-
ing international law. Not one, of course, mentioned that the Bishop
regime had been forced on the Grenadian people against their will
when Bishop led a coup against Sir Eric Gairy in 1979, nor that
Bishop himself was murdered—and his government overthrown—by
a rival (an even more extreme Marxist-Leninist) two weeks before the
invasion.

Bishop, among other things, had suspended the country's constitution, refused to hold early elections, and turned to "revolutionary
democracy" with the help of nine hundred Cuban military advisors.
Habeas corpus was also abolished for political detainees, and by 1982
there were about ninety-five political prisoners. Freedom of the press,
of course, was abolished. There was no improvement by Bishop's
successor.[4]

A few days after the invasion a press conference was held in New
York by the Committee in Solidarity with the People of Grenada
(which had the same phone number as the Methodist Office for the

United Nations); speakers included spokesmen from the National Council of Churches and various other church and "peace" groups. *New York Daily News* columnist Bill Reel, who covered the event, reported that the speakers refused to criticize the Marxists-Leninists who murdered Bishop. It was the U.S. who was accused of "butchery."[5]

It should not surprise anyone that the Solidarity Committee has also sponsored national campaigns to raise money for the Marxist-Leninist guerrillas in El Salvador.[6]

Protest over the invasion was then included in the November 1983 march on Washington, sponsored by the most prominent radical leftist, religious, and quasi-religious organizations in the United States. Prior to the invasion, the main cause for the march had been dissatisfaction over the Reagan Administration's Central American policies.

The furor eventually died, but there has never been an apology or a retraction from U.S. churches for their stance on Grenada. That they have not done so makes it very clear they are more interested in political rhetoric than facts. If they had been interested in understanding what had happened on the island, they were welcome to read over twenty-five thousand documents captured by the U.S. Army and released to the public. They should have been interested. The documents proved that the Grenadian regime, with Cuba's help, had meant to destroy the Christian church.

CHRISTIANS UNDER FIRE

In a memorandum drafted by the chief of the Grenadian security forces, Major Keith Roberts, dated July 12, 1983, Roberts said the Party must begin infiltrating the churches. He declared that they must be watched and that the government had to build up the Communist mass organizations as alternatives. Point 7 of the memorandum recommended the removal of all deeply religious head teachers from the primary schools and replacing them with more "progressive elements." It also called for eliminating religion from the media, beginning with the Sunday morning radio mass.[7]

Other plans called for bringing liberation theologians from Nicaragua to the island and creating "progressive churches." After the notation about starting progressive churches ("people's churches," apparently like those in Nicaragua which support the government and teach Marxist theory), Roberts wrote in parentheses, "Talk with Nacar . . . and Cubans." Several documents reveal that the government was very concerned that 4,365 copies of the *Jerusalem Bible* had been imported by the church. They were apparently worried the Bibles would influence the people.[8]

By the time American troops landed, the regime was in the first stages of its assault on Christianity. The government was taking the young people away on Sundays and placing them in work crews, and children were being taught to hate the church. Work crews would sometimes drive earth-moving machines close to the churches during Sunday services, apparently as a way to express the regime's hostility to Christianity. Cubans, it was later revealed, would gather near the entrances to churches on Sunday and create distractions.[9]

When the island was captured, American troops found almost nine hundred Cuban, Soviet, North Korean, Libyan, East German, and Bulgarian personnel, including military advisors. They found warehouses full of weapons, five secret military assistance agreements (three with the Soviet Union, one with North Korea, and one with Cuba), documents and notes proving an attempt to transform Grenada into an instrument for Cuban and Soviet objectives.[10]

American intelligence believes the Soviets wanted to control Grenada because of its strategic importance to the United States. More than half of all U.S. sea trade and oil imports pass through the Caribbean, and strategic planning for the navy requires free movement of ships and ports on the Gulf of Mexico. In addition, the Port Salinas airport was scheduled to open March 13, 1984. When the 9,700-foot airport runway became operational under Cuban-Soviet control, MIG-23s would have been able to cover the whole Caribbean.[11]

The runway could also have helped Cuba support its forty thousand to fifty thousand troops in Africa and assisted Libya and Soviet flights to Central America. According to the Pentagon, Libyan planes which were detained in Brazil in 1983, while taking military supplies to Nicaragua, could have refueled in Grenada instead.[12]

REJECTED LESSONS

There were obvious lessons to be learned from the Grenadian experience: that events proved the Reagan Administration had sufficient justification to take action; that sometimes populations do need help and welcome it when it comes; that physical force can lead to good ends when it is used wisely and for pure motives. But the leaders and activists in the mainline churches have rejected these lessons and instead stepped up their criticism of America's military and defense establishments. Corporations have been under increasing attack from denominations and Catholic orders which oppose defense contracts. In 1984, for example, twenty-six Catholic orders announced they would divest themselves of all General Electric stock due to the company's defense contracts. The Presbyterians announced in 1982 they would withdraw their stock from twenty-one defense-related companies, and the United Methodists in 1985 voted to limit their future investments to companies whose defense-related contract income does not exceed 15 percent. These are just a few of many examples. Church-related agencies and orders also use their privileges as investors to protest defense contracts through resolutions.

The disinvestment and resolutions have minimal effect on the defense industry. They do, however, have an effect on the American defense debate because they question the morality of those who produce weapons. By inference, it also questions the morality of those who approve the spending and the people from whom the money is obtained—that is, the American public. In other words, the implied culpability extends to most of the nation except those righteous who agree with the Religious Left.

It is difficult to tell whether the above-mentioned denominations and orders are in the first category (who fight the good fight against America the aggressor) or the second (pacifism). Many of the church agencies who practice disinvestment and attack by resolution would probably agree that nations need some kind of defense; but they just have not found one they could support. On the other hand, pure pacifism has been given an effective voice by Protestant bishops and Catholic bishops and archbishops. Many of these admit this is a dangerous world, but base their resistance to defense on the premise that defense spending is just another way to cheat the poor. The Episcopal Bishop of Newark, John Spong, gave a good example of this type of thinking when he called for restraint in the arms race because the poor and needy were carrying "a disproportionate amount of the burden."[13]

SCRIPTURAL PACIFISTS

A second category of pacifists are more fragmented in their beliefs. They base their pacifism on their understanding of Scripture, but not all agree what Scripture says. As was already stated, some apparently believe that God takes care of those who have faith He will do so and some believe that enlightened Christians are pacifists no matter what is done to them (or others). Many bishops, the most prominent and influential of which are the Catholic, have now deviated from their traditional belief in the "just war" theory as regards nuclear weapons: they now believe that the United States should never use, or even threaten to use, nuclear weapons no matter what the situation.

Archbishop Raymond Hunthausen of Seattle took the most extreme position in 1981 when he declared that "failure to achieve mutual disarmament leaves us with only one moral position in this tragic situation, the position of unilateral disarmament with trust and reliance on the Lord as our security." Hunthausen defended his position by stating, "I believe that a stand like mine reflects a love for our country because it reflects a belief that it is responsive to challenge for moral growth. In a question like the nuclear arms race, I believe it is God Almighty who is calling us to take such a stand." The bishop apparently did not want to concede anything to possible critics. He added that "any nation which makes as first priority the building up of armaments, and not the creative work of peace and disarmament, is immoral." The bishop added a suggestion—that as a means of "protesting the nuclear arms buildup individuals could withhold 50 percent of their taxes."[14]

That attitude has been carried one step further by bishops such as Catholic Bishop L. T. Matthiesen, who have urged their parishioners to quit jobs in the defense industry. Matthiesen suggested that Catholics who worked in a neutron bomb plant in Amarillo, Texas, stop doing so.[15]

Perhaps the ultimate in masochistic advice was offered by Bishop Thomas Gumbleton, when he told an audience that they should "surrender to the invader. Let yourself be dominated." The use of force, in self-defense or in the defense of others, is "unChristlike. . . . We must defend against evil by goodness . . . if that seems contrary to human reasoning, reasoning has to go by the boards."[16] Gumbleton, the auxiliary bishop of Detroit, is also the president of Pax Christi-U.S.A. and on the advisory committee of Witness for Peace, a pro-Sandinista lobby.

THE BISHOPS ASSUME EXPERT STATUS ON WEAPONRY

Bishops, obviously not satisfied to merely lead their flocks, have also claimed expertise on American weaponry. Some of the Catholic bishops involved in the 1983 pastoral letter on nuclear arms and defense told a House Foreign Affairs Committee meeting in 1984 that they did not approve of the MX missile or the Strategic Defense Initiative. They maintained that the MX would not provide protection and the Strategic Defense Initiative would not work. Since trained scientists are still debating the merits of the Strategic Defense Initiative, it is strange that the bishops seem to have informed knowledge on this highly technical subject.

Still, they are taken seriously. Subcommittee Chairman Dante Fascell (D-Florida) said he agreed with the bishops and added that religious groups "have been doing the best job in peace making."[17]

Just the mere suggestion that the U.S. discard its nuclear weapons seems to put leaders of all denominations into a state of mind that allows clerical posturing to overcome orthodox Christian teaching. A

United Methodist Council of Bishops meeting in 1981 was addressed by a former bishop to Bolivia, Mortimer Arias, who decried the "ideology of national security." After Arias's speech, Bishop William Cannon (of North Carolina) asked what would happen if the democratic countries succeeded in abolishing nuclear weapons but the "totalitarian nations" kept theirs.[18]

"Responded Dr. Arias: 'It is a call for a decision of faith. Somewhere we will have to make our own option.'[19]

"'I don't think the issue is unilateral disarmament,' said Bishop John B. Warman of the Harrisburg (Pa.) area. 'The issue is what weapons we choose. We can take the nuclear armor of Goliath. Or we can take the five smooth stones' of the gospel of peace. 'There are other ways to defeat Communism—to defeat evil. If anyone is to disintegrate the earth, let it be someone else.' Bishop Warman paused and then pleaded, 'Don't let it be us.'"[20]

True to their beliefs, the United Methodist Council of Bishops, in 1985, one day before the U.S. Senate vote on the MX missile, wrote a letter stating, "Chances for a nuclear war will be increased by the production and deployment of the MX missile." The letter was hand-delivered to senators.[21]

PASTORAL LETTERS

They later wrote a poor imitation of the Catholic bishops' 1983 pastoral letter about defense, titled "The Nuclear Crisis and the Pursuit of Peace." In it the bishops, like the Catholic bishops, opposed not only the use of nuclear weapons, but also said even "nuclear deterrence" could not "receive the churches' blessing." The bishops did not even attempt to justify their positions with thoughtful, in-depth studies of theology, but largely depended on waving the concept of "shalom"— which they misinterpreted as "harmony between humanity and all of God's creatures" on this earth—and using half-pietistic, half-trendy rhetoric. "But we write also in gratitude for the swelling chorus of those who cry No to nuclear weapons, No to poverty, No to racism, No to sexism—and Yes to the things that make for peace," the letter said. The study document also used the concept of "shalom."

Both the letter and the study document which accompanied it assumed a moral equivalency between the United States and the Soviet Union. They suggested that the nuclear arms race is a disease which afflicts both countries. In doing so they totally ignored the differences in American and Soviet political systems, in effect putting totalitarianism and democracy, and American and Soviet foreign policy, on the same moral level.

The Presbyterians wrote similar statements in a 1982 resolution titled "Confronting Idolatry." The title itself is shrewd because it suggests that those who disagree with its viewpoint are guilty of a sin against God. The resolution stated that "the arms race" (known as our national defense in more rational circles) is a reflection of our disobedience to God because it places our security in weapons and not in God's hands.

CHRISTIAN PACIFISM IN HISTORY

These theologies of "peace" are particularly hard to counter since they are based on emotionalism, not logic. But they are old philosophies and have always had a pernicious effect on whomever they impressed. Pressure from the Christian church prior to World War II was one reason for the success enjoyed by pacifists who vehemently opposed American rearmament. Many of those clergy believed that it is not Christian to kill or to go to the defense of others, but resist passively. Others believed we should not interfere in European affairs and some even questioned whether the Nazis were, in fact, as bad as they were depicted.

French theologian Jacques Ellul wrote about the consequences of those beliefs in *False Presence of the Kingdom*. Christians should have been aware of the nature of Nazism before 1937. Yet they were not, and the results were disastrous. "That was when the clarity of vision was essential. After 1937 it was already too late. The fate of the world was already sealed for thirty years or more. But in those years the Christians, full of good intentions, were thinking only of peace and were loudly proclaiming pacifism. . . ."[22]

Although America's lack of preparation for war cost the nation dearly in lives, there were very few churchmen who afterward admitted they had been wrong, despite even the clear object lesson provided by the Nazi death camps: unchecked evil has no limit on the destruction it can impose.

It is one thing piously to exclaim that we should use "five smooth stones." It is quite another thing to defend the notion that these platitudes will stop the bombs, tanks, and machine guns. God never promised to deliver us from evil in this world, but to judge it in the next. Theologian Reinhold Niebuhr agreed with this viewpoint and tried to stem the tide of Christian pacifism in 1940 with a book of essays called *Christianity and Power Politics*. In it Niebuhr said that Christian pacifism is an effort to make the Kingdom of God into a simple historic possibility, which Jesus never said it would be. *He* was to bring the Kingdom, not man.[23]

GOD'S PEACE AND MAN'S PEACE

Dr. Allan Parrent, an associate dean of the Protestant Episcopal Theologian Seminary in Virginia, has pointed out that there are two ways of thinking about peace. One is pax, which is the peace of the well-ordered political community, and the other is shalom, the peace of God who is author of peace. Parrent interprets shalom as more than the absence of conflict; it is a "right relationship involving self, fellow creatures, the creation, and God . . . the establishment of peace in this full sense will coincide only with the realization of the messianic kingdom at the end of time."[24]

Parrent said the church often fails to make a distinction between the two kinds of peace, which leads to "confusion about the church's witness and to the undermining of its credibility in the public debate." While we can, and should, contribute to both pax and shalom, Parrent said, the fullness of shalom is a divine gift.[25]

Parrent also divides the duties of a Christian into God's alien work and God's proper work. The former is what Martin Luther termed "civil righteousness," maintaining peace, order, and justice. God's proper work (the morality of perfection) is self-giving to others and building the Kingdom of God. God has given us duties to perform within our society, Parrent said, which cannot be carried out solely in the grip of love because it involves maintaining order through force. "The morality of perfection is needed to keep us honest, and the morality of duty and station is needed to keep us alive . . . but one cannot be substituted for the other."[26]

Niebuhr, Parrent pointed out, said justice without love ceases to be justice, and degenerates into mere balance of power. Love without justice, however, ceases to be love and degenerates into vague sentimentality.[27] Love is not the same thing as indulgence and does not require surrender in order to prove itself. Ellul pointed out that "To allow oneself to be damned out of love for the other person could eventually result in two damned people, never in one saved person!"[28]

THE STATE AS GOD'S PRESERVER

While it is true that the only ultimate security is in God, Parrent points out that God provides temporal security through the state. God sustains His creation by providing temporal security as part of His divine work in history. Christians who help with this task are cooperating in God's work of preservation and protection and are also being good stewards of a world which God placed under their dominion.[29]

While Parrent did not say Christians should avoid questions of national security, he did warn against ecclesiastical bodies overstepping the boundary between giving unambiguous direction to public policy and issuing precise directives for legislative and administrative action. "The institutional church must remember," he said, "that the more specific it becomes, the less can be its degree of certitude; the more its judgments are based on political prudence, the thinner will be the theological ice on which it can claim to stand, and the greater the probability will be of honest and legitimate disagreement within the church."[30]

NUCLEAR PACIFISM

Most church leaders, like the United Methodist bishops, seem to believe that nuclear weapons complicate the defense debate, changing the rules that Christians have used about war for centuries. The Catholic bishops, in their pastoral letter on defense and nuclear war—titled "The Challenge of Peace: God's Promise and Our Response"—argued just this point. The bishops did not demand unilateral disarmament, but came close when noting that not only is the use of nuclear arms and the "declared intent" to use them wrong, but the threat of attack as part of a strategy of deterrence is wrong. They based these arguments on the "just war" theory.

JUST WAR THEORY

That theory was partially developed by St. Thomas Aquinas in his *Summa Theologica*. In it he cited the three things that are required for any war to be just. The first was the authority of the "sovereign on whose command war is waged. . . . Secondly a just cause is required . . . one that avenges wrongs. . . . when a nation or a state has to be punished either for refusing to make amends for outrages done by its subjects or to restore what has been seized injuriously . . . thirdly, the right intention of those waging war is required . . . they must intend to promote the good and avoid evil." Aquinas concludes that a just war can never be waged for its own sake, but to bring peace.

Other theorists, such as Anglican theologian John Macquarrie, cite further conditions for a just war, some of which are the use of violence as the only means left for making change and a means which must be appropriate to the end. The latter is usually referred to as the principle of "proportionality." The Catholic bishops used this point, noting that "A nuclear response to either a conventional or nuclear attack can cause destruction which goes far beyond 'legitimate defense.' . . . . Such use of nuclear weapons would not be justified."

They also added probability of success—"its purpose is to prevent irrational resort to force or hopeless resistance when the outcome of either will clearly be disproportionate or futile."

As pious as a condemnation against nuclear weapons sounds, it is a sterile denunciation when made in a reality-free vacumn. The bishops neglected to explore the very real dangers and options which face the United States today. Author George Weigel has pointed out that weapons have very little to do with war: war is caused by a strategy that either works or does not work. An arms race helped bring on World War I, but weakness in the face of a German threat encouraged World War II.[31]

NUCLEAR SURRENDER

The bishops stated that possession of nuclear weapons could be tolerated only if "meaningful" arms negotiations were in progress, but the church's attitude would have to shift to "uncompromising condemnation of both use and possession" if that hope were to disappear. The bishops obviously did not think this through. The logical end-result of this attitude would be unilateral nuclear disarmament in the face of evil. If the bishops did consider the possible results of their attitude, should anyone take it seriously, they apparently believe that the world is better off slave than dead, a "survivalist" attitude which Weigel calls "an abandonment of faith . . . it is acquiescence to neopaganism."[32]

It could also be argued that advocating defenselessness in the face of a great evil is, in itself, immoral. It is the "ethics of intention" as opposed to the "ethics of consequence."[33] Evangelizing for a position which, if enacted, would adversely affect the lives of millions, without truly considering those consequences and explaining them to your audience, is highly irresponsible. It is one thing to persuade mankind to pledge its soul to righteousness and quite another to ask them to submit their physical beings to tyranny. Especially if you infer, as Hunthausen has done, that God will be a shield in this life.

Furthermore, prostrating before evil in order to escape harm is not a correct Christian attitude. That posture can only be justified by a non-Christian who does not believe in God's judgment and eternal life. Christianity teaches that this world is a battleground between God and Lucifer, and that survival is definitely not the greatest good. If it had been otherwise, Christians would not have willingly perished in Roman arenas, devoured by lions, all murdered for their faith.

THE MORALITY OF DEFENSE

The bishops' view (and that of most of the Religious Left) suggests that we must not, under any conditions, become aggressors ourselves lest we lose our Christian principles. Noted Christian thinker Francis Schaeffer believed that it is "nothing less than lack of Christian love, to not do what can be done for those gripped in the power of those who automatically and logically oppress."[34] He was not a pacifist,

Schaeffer wrote, because pacifism in this fallen world means desertion of those people who need the greatest help. Unilateral disarmament, considering the Soviets' antipathy to God, would be "totally utopian and romantic and lead, as utopianisms always do in a fallen world, to disaster."[35]

One of the most practical arguments against Christian pacifism has been offered by Michael Novak. Novak, a lay Catholic theologian, has noted that Christ said, "Blessed are the peacemakers," not "Blessed are the peacesayers."[36] U.S. disarmament would not necessarily deter nuclear war. If the world fell into the hands of Marxist-Leninist factions, Novak said, there is still the possibility they would fight among themselves. Surrender to the Soviets would not encourage the kingdom of peace and love and those that desire it, "or with passionate intensity permit it, know not what they do . . . "[37]

Moreover, pacifism as church doctrine was firmly repudiated by Pope John Paul in 1983 when he said that a just Christian "has the courage to intercede for others who suffer and he refuses to surrender in the face of injustice, to compromise with it—and likewise, however paradoxical it may appear, the person who deeply desires peace rejects any kind of pacifism which is cowardice or the simple preservation of tranquility."[38]

THE PEACE CHURCHES

Of all the churches which insist on disarmament, the "peace" churches (such as the Mennonite Church and the Church of the Brethren) have been the most vocal. Like the United Methodists, the peace section of the Mennonite Central Committee has blamed America for the arms race, stating that people just do not understand or do not "take seriously" the historical and current perceptions and fears which the Soviets have of the U.S. The Mennonites seemingly doubt that the Soviets really want to dominate anybody else. They believe Soviet foreign policy and military decisions are simply the result of their fears.[39]

That very common viewpoint has no basis in reality. It is the product of a refusal to see things as they are. That refusal is often the result of a deep-seated reluctance to abandon the familiar, easy route and actually take action against an evil situation. This denial of reality both eases the mind and allows righteous inaction at the same time. It is easier to project evil on benevolence (the Mennonites have often blamed the arms race on America's alleged urge to dominate world affairs) than it is to face the danger of an uncontrollable system that threatens not only our lives, but civilization itself. Nonetheless, this sort of willing blindness is dangerous because it both distracts us from the real menace and saps our faith in our ability to do good.

IGNORING SOVIET FRUITS

It is this inability to forthrightly evaluate and discuss the nature of Soviet totalitarianism which is the greatest weakness of the religious "peace" lobby. It is not just the Mennonites who have this weakness. It is common. The Catholic bishops urged mutual trust between the United States and the Soviet Union, a statement which infers that the Soviet system poses no real cause of alarm. The United Methodists made similar statements in their pastoral letter. But Christ gave wise advice in evaluating the human heart, an injunction which is just as sound when dealing with governments; "By their fruits, ye shall know them." That advice is usually ignored by peace activists, although Soviet fruits are so publicly bitter that it takes a real strength of will not to notice.

One of the most prominent Soviet fruits has been its deception concerning "peace." It is an idea that they incessantly promote. But it is also an idea they only want discussed in the West—which makes them both liars and cynics. Soon after independent peace activist Oleg Radzinsky began his work, he was arrested by the KGB. When Alexander Shatravka and Vladimir Mishchenko marched for peace, they were arrested, tried, and sentenced to hard labor in Siberia.[40]

Documents from the official legal examination have made their way to the West. According to emigré Sergei Batovrin, once an independent Russian peace activist himself, the "representatives of Soviet political science" gave their official evaluation of the "crimes against the State." The commission took the view that the very idea of a citizen's struggle for peace, independent of the government, is a crime.[41]

SOVIET PEACE ACTIVISTS PERSECUTED

Batovrin noted that the two accused had not sat on railroad tracks to block trains carrying radioactive materials, or gone out in boats to try to stop the progress of nuclear submarines, as has been done in the West. "In the U.S.S.R., a train carrying nuclear materials would simply run over any demonstrators who happened to get in its way . . . the civil disobedience of the imprisoned Soviet peace activists in the U.S.S.R. is the very fact of their independence . . . they did not want to play a game where posters scream that 'the struggle for peace is everyone's business,' but where, in reality, people only have the choice of saying yes. . . . "[42]

Facts about Soviet attitudes, however, are ignored by Western peace groups (which include a large segment of the Religious Left). In May 1983 the Institute for Policy Studies sponsored a "U.S.-USSR Bilateral Exchange Conference," which was to have focused on disarmament. Twenty-seven Soviets and a larger group of Americans, leaders of peace and disarmament groups, attended.

The Soviet delegates consisted of a Russian Orthodox priest who said that freedom of religion was in the Soviet constitution, a teacher who stated the Soviet educational system was better than that of the U.S., "journalists" who insisted that Soviet citizens were better informed than Americans, and academics who study the U.S. American delegates were largely anti-U.S. government and included Episcopal Bishop Paul Moore, William Sloane Coffin, Cora Weiss, Policy Studies officials, and various other radicals.[43]

Peace is the goal of all their people, the Soviets insisted. *Izvestia* columnist Vikenty Matveev maintained that millions of Soviets participate in independent peace committees. But citizens who had launched a nongovernmental peace group and were subsequently sent to labor camps were dismissed as a group of young people who wanted to emigrate to Israel. Matveev said their names had been forgotten in the Soviet Union. "They cease, so to speak, to exist."[44]

Young martyrs for peace got no help from the clergymen present. When supporters of Jewish "refuseniks" and Soviet and Eastern European emigrés asked hard questions about human rights at a public forum, then jeered at Soviet answers, the Soviets (and the American apologists) were furious. Bishop Moore said he was "deeply ashamed" and "deeply humiliated." Sloane Coffin, whose Riverside Church leads the most radical disarmament and anti-American campaigns of any American religious body, said when there were restrictions in armaments, dissidents in the Soviet Union would fare better because the Soviet Union would feel "less threatened."[45]

A VIEW FROM THE TOP

A far more sober picture of Soviet leadership has been drawn by defector Arcady Shevchenko. The former diplomat, the highest ranking Soviet to defect since World War II, was privileged to observe the Politburo firsthand. In his best-selling memoirs Shevchenko wrote, "I saw how easily they' called vice virtue, and just as easily reversed the words again. How their hypocrisy and corruption had penetrated their lives, how isolated they were from the population they ruled. (Andre) Gromyko had not set foot in the streets of Moscow for almost 40 years. Almost all the others were no different.

"The falsity of these men was everywhere, from their personal lives to their grand political designs. I watched them playing with détente. I saw them building military strength far beyond the needs of defense and security, at the expense of the Soviet people. I heard them express with cynical jokes, their willingness to suppress freedom among their allies. I witnessed their duplicity with those who follow the Soviet line in the West or in the Third World, extending even to participation in conspiracies to kill 'unsuitable' political figures of other countries. They avidly sought hegemony and were infected with the imperialistic sickness of which they accused others."[46]

THE SLAUGHTER IN AFGHANISTAN

Afghanistan is the best example of the Soviets' real nature. The Soviet army invaded Afghanistan in 1979 and is still busy slaughtering peasants, freedom-fighters, and children while talking about peace in Moscow. As of 1985, 40 percent of the Afghan population has been murdered or is in exile. One out of two refugees on this planet is an Afghan.[47]

According to Soviet soldiers who have defected to the Mujahedin, Soviet atrocities have been so horrible they have decided to fight against their own people: chemical weapons are used, they said; retaliation against civilian populations is doctrine; they air-drop booby-trapped toys that maim children, use saturation bombing of villages, and violently torture those suspected of guerrilla activities.[48]

THE SOVIET USE OF FIRE

In order to get an idea of the barbarity inflicted on the Afghans, we will examine just one method of atrocity—burning. "They (the Soviets) burn people easier than wood."[49]

- A Paris *Match* reporter saw 153 Hazari tribesmen bound back-to-back thrown from a truck on the outskirts of Kabul and set ablaze with gasoline. The atrocity was repeated a few minutes later when another truck arrived with human cargo. There is no doubt that this story is true because an Afghan photographer took pictures of the bodies. The next day the scene was put on the front page of *The New Times*, the English-language Afghan government newspaper. The caption said the victims were rebels who had committed brutalities.[50]

- Soviet soldiers fighting for the Mujahedin have testified that Afghans have been burned to death with flame-throwers.[51]

- The U.S. Helsinki Watch Committee reported the case of a twelve-year-old whose right arm was so badly burned he could hardly move it. The doctor in charge of the case said, "They told me that Russian soldiers came to their village and held their son's arm over a fire while they asked about the Mujahedin. . . ."[52]

- Mike Hoover, a CBS television producer, said he had filmed an interview with an Afghan who had formerly worked as a translator for the Soviet army. "He was extremely disturbed," Hoover said. "He told how he translated questions the Russians were asking about the Mujahedin while they held a child over a fire."[53]

- A French doctor tells how the Soviets punished an entire village after some Afghan troops defected: "They tied them up and piled gasoline over them and burned them alive. They were old and young, men, women, and children. Many, many people were telling this story. They all said forty people had been killed. . . . " Another such report says, "My name is Shir Dal, I am from the Kats area. . . . When the Russians came, the children were hiding in a cave. One Parchami Communist man was with them, and helped bring the children out, and they burned them to death. . . . The children who were killed, their parents could not recognize them, because they were burned. They made fires with wood, and put the children in them or put kerosene on children and burned them. Sometimes they killed children and burned them and sometimes they burned children alive. They were taking children out to the fields and burning them alive, and they put them in the rushes and burned them alive. Burned alive."[54]

- In May of 1985 freelance journalist Rob Schultheis interviewed survivors of an atrocity campaign carried out by Russian troops in the Laghman Valley in Eastern Afghanistan. In a single district, he found nearly eight hundred people were killed, from pregnant women and newborns to the elderly. They had been shot, *burned alive*, hanged, bayoneted, tortured to death, killed with grenades, decapitated and beaten to death. The Schultheis interviews were carried on public radio in June 1985.[55]

Meanwhile, in the cities the Khad (the secret police) are in firm control. There are branches of the Communist party in every neighborhood, office, and school. Thousands of children, as young as five and six, have been sent to the Soviet Union for a proper ideological education; twelve thousand Afghans are now studying at Russian universities.[56] Thousands more children have been sent to the Soviet Union, not only for a proper ideological education, but for intense training as guerrillas and terrorists. According to children who have received this training, they were to have become the Soviets' best antifreedom-fighters in Afghanistan and were to have also been sent to other countries to commit terrorist acts.[57]

These are some of the Soviet fruits which Christians, no matter how sincere, ignore at great peril both to themselves and others.

ANABAPTISTS AND PACIFISM

Finally, there is a newly influential pacifism. It is a kind of theology of the radical reformation, and it is now being touted by the Sojourners community in Washington, D.C., and its publication, *Sojourners* magazine. These modern Anabaptists not only believe that no defense is permissible for a Christian, they advocate refusing to pay taxes in order to protest American defense. They frequently demonstrate against American foreign policy, using civil disobedience to gain attention.

Sojourners magazine—which has a readership of about sixty thousand, a great many of whom are Catholics—is widely read on college campuses. The community of about fifty members, including children, live and work with the poor in Washington's inner city. Those wishing to join must spend a year as novices, then must donate all their property to the community and share expenses. They live on about $5,000 a year each.

It is difficult to argue with *Sojourners* on subjects such as whether it is Christian or un-Christian to pay taxes, because the community's reasoning is based on ambiguous Scripture. For instance, the traditional call for Christians to pay taxes, Mark 12:13-17 (Christ said, "Render to Caesar the things that are Caesar's, and to God the things that are God's"), has been interpreted by Sojourners to have the opposite meaning.

It is not difficult to argue with, however, or understand such statements as "The Reagan Administration remains the chief obstacle to the first step in stopping the arms race." Or, "For us, nuclear weapons are an intolerable evil, and as Christians we cannot tolerate their production or use. . . . We are the new abolitionists." Or, "It is sometimes difficult to remember how the Russians became our enemy. . . . At each step in the cold war, the U.S. was presented with a choice between very different but equally plausible interpretations of Soviet intentions, each of which would have led to very different responses. At every turn U.S. policy makers have chosen to assume the very worst about their Soviet counterparts."[58]

It might be easier to understand these statements if we know that Richard Barnet, of the Institute for Policy Studies (see Appendix), is a contributing editor. Barnet once wrote an article for *Sojourners* which strived to "demythologize" the Russian threat. It was titled, "Lies Clearer than Truth."

Sojourners' real position can be better understood as pacifism at home and revolution abroad. Although editor Jim Wallis touts himself as a pacifist, he has allowed CISPES (the public relations arm of the Marxist guerrillas in El Salvador) to participate in many Sojourners activities, such as the "pledge of resistance," a threatened occupation of American public buildings in case of military invasion of Nicaragua.

A SOJOURNER RETURNS

Clark Pinnock, Canadian theologian and a former *Sojourners* contributing editor, explains the Anabaptist perspective as one in which you "couldn't be a Christian simply by being a citizen of the state. Being a Christian puts you over against the power. The Anabaptist theology has a sharply drawn dualism of the light and dark in the moral realm. Counterculturalism is basic Anabaptist thinking about the world." Pinnock went on to say, however, that *Sojourners* has broken with historic Anabaptism on pacifism.[59]

In the early days of Vietnam *Sojourners* was opposed to the war on the grounds of pacifism, that any war is unjust. But Pinnock said *Sojourners* soon moved away from expressing a general distaste for violence and began to believe there "was a just cause and it was not ours. They were really hoping that the Vietcong were going to win, to beat the might of American imperialism. When Saigon fell there was great rejoicing. Normally a pacifist wouldn't rejoice in a victory as bloody as that one. . . ."[60]

Nicaragua is one example, Pinnock said, of *Sojourners'* peculiar mixture of utopian idealism and hypocrisy. The *Sojourners* community believes the Sandinistas are reformers because they were "100 percent in favor of the Nicaraguan revolution," and because "they hope it is true."[61]

Pinnock explained the *Sojourners* follower as one who was deeply alienated from American reality on issues like Vietnam, the alleged plastic character of modern life, and racism and sexism in America. These causes made them feel America was a very evil place, Pinnock said, engendering sympathy in them for revolutionary governments which claimed they were making efforts to do away with "these deficiencies."[62]

Sojourners has been given a voice in the left-liberal mainline church, Pinnock said, because *Sojourners* says the same thing as the Left, but by way of a "hermeneutical ventriloquism. . . . When they are feminists, the Bible has to be feminist or they can't be feminist. They have to think the Bible says it, even if it is necessary to make the Bible say it by way of ventriloquism."[63]

FALSE PROPHETS

More worrisome than the evangelical leftists are antidefense programs obstensibly emanating from a Christian church (as opposed to organizations financed by the church), but which are, in reality, cynically using the church for political purposes—such as Riverside Church of New York City. Riverside officials are so blatantly leftist and have erected such secular, ideological, anti-American programs that the church cannot be properly considered simply a church anymore.

Although Riverside sponsors many special projects, such as the war crimes trial that put the United States in the dock (see Appendix), its major project is the "Riverside Church Disarmament Program." The project presents conferences on disarmament (with seminar titles such as "teaching disarmament," "economics of militarism," "mobilizing the religious community"), coordinates demonstrations around Washington, and gives extreme leftists—including Richard Barnet and many associates of the Institute for Policy Studies—a platform at various functions. The disarmament program director is Cora Weiss.

Weiss, wife of Peter Weiss (see Appendix), has come very close to openly treasonous activities. During the Vietnam War she was a leading member of Women Strike for Peace, which a Congressional study termed "a pro-Hanoi organization," which from its inception "has enjoyed the complete support of the Communist Party." During the actual fighting, Weiss traveled to Hanoi and Paris to meet with North Vietnamese. Those activities culminated in her organization of the victory celebration of Vietnam's 1977 admission to the United Nations. After the war she became a director of Friendshipment, an organization that was established to coordinate aid (much of it provided by the church) to Vietnam.[64]

Pacifists are obviously of several different stripes. Most of them do not operate from the same premise. Yet they affect American opinion and national defense in much the same way. The public is influenced to believe that national defense is either not necessary or less necessary than the facts warrant. A guilt complex regarding the possession of nuclear weapons is also insinuated into the public's consciousness. Thus America's strategic planners have a much harder time obtaining the weapons and consensus they need to protect the nation.

The impression pacifism makes on enemies of democracy is probably just as similar. "Their conquerors," Michael Novak wrote, "will not overlook the fact that such brave persons failed to lift a finger to help the five million persons now in the Gulag Archipelago; that such persons bowed docilely to 'the tide of history,' and that such persons abandoned their Christian obligation to come to the defense of innocent peoples already suffering from unjust aggression. Faced with the naked power of the executioner, what further principles will they now betray? Will they not assist the authorities in urging the captive population to remain non-violent? . . .[65]

"Those brave pacifists who counsel surrender and imagine glorious martyrdom do not imagine themselves as quislings. No one does. Confident in their own virtue, they betray not only their own country but their Christian faith. It is nowhere commanded that Christians must join in complicity with Pilate's armies in crucifying Christ."[66]

THREE

The Attack on Free Enterprise

The baby is pitiful; no more than nine months old, he is already dying. His bony, starved body is so emaciated that his head looks oversized, too large a burden for such frailty. A baby-bottle is lying by his side. The caption on the picture reads: "This is wrong."

Distribution of this heartbreaking picture was a typical tactic of the Infant Formula Action Coalition (INFACT), which during its boycott of Nestlé products had the support of the Presbyterian Church U.S.A., various Catholic orders, the National Conference of Lutheran Women, the Unitarian Universalists, the National Council of Churches, and agencies from most major denominations. Ten million Third World babies were starving because of the heartless, money-hungry activities of powerful multinational companies, INFACT charged.

Thanks to the aggressive, greedy advertising tactics of Nestlé, INFACT claimed, poor women who knew no better bought infant formula and misused it for babies like the one in the picture. They mixed it with dirty water, or otherwise created death and disease because they did not understand hygiene. Or they spent their small incomes unnecessarily. Worse, Nestlé infant formula stopped mothers from breast-feeding, a practice that everyone knows is healthful and one of the few benefits of being born poor in the Third World.

Due to the intensive campaign against Nestlé—which is only one of the infant formula companies operating in undeveloped countries—the Swiss firm was thoroughly humiliated. That, as we shall see, was a major point in INFACT's, and the church's, campaign. If the anticorporate activists had only been working to stem an evil which they believed harmed helpless babies, they could be commended. But churches not only used anticorporate activism irresponsibly, but as a weapon to punish the free market system. The real mission of anticorporate activists was not only to save babies, but to replace the free market with socialism or a welfare state. Since the free enterprise system has not succeeded in providing every person with material comfort, much of church leadership has apparently decided that it must be discarded for something which it considers superior.

It is important to understand this attitude because it is one of the primary foundations of Religious Left thought. This is not to say that disapproval of free enterprise is the reason the Religious Left originally developed or persists. But disapproval of free enterprise is a primary component of its political thesis.

A preference for government intervention in economic life is a legitimate political opinion worthy of debate. Corporations sometimes do act irresponsibly, from greed or ignorance, and cause harm. It is therefore one of the necessities of democratic capitalism that political parties, organizations, and labor unions force the government and business to compromise, or to correct their course. Without these opposing bodies even the most democratic of governments, and well-meaning of companies, would become tyrannical or mendacious. But it is not a proper function of the church to attempt to force a change in democratically established economic systems. It is especially not proper when facts are distorted in order to serve a political bias.

Further, it is not only improper, but extremely harmful to the church for its bureaucrats to back causes a great majority of its membership does not support. Most American Christians, as we shall see, overwhelmingly support free enterprise. A great many mainline church bureaucrats and the anticorporate activists they support, do not.

Moreover, Religious Left attitudes completely overlook how well free enterprise works. Democratic capitalism is generally a condition of political liberty and creates prosperity where it is genuinely practiced. It is also possible that with its emphasis on welfare (or socialism) as a necessity for economic equality, the church has obscured and hindered the real debate on the causes and cure of poverty.

CAPITALISTS ATTACK CAPITALISM

Statements made by INFACT chairman Douglas Johnson and a United Church of Christ study group on economics reflect both the real motives of many anticorporate activists and the Religious Left's feelings about the free market. Johnson admitted he was using the Nestlē issue to hurt the "profit system." He said he saw the issue as a precedent for legislative control of multinational corporations.[1] The study group document, originally drafted in 1984, declares that the "U.S. is launched on a love affair with death and destruction. . . . We are, in a fundamental sense, necrophiliacs . . . choosing life means choosing new economic and political systems."[2]

These are not lone statements and lonely ideologues. It may be one of the world's great ironies that some of America's wealthiest institutions are some of the system's greatest enemies. The total wealth of all churches in the United States, as of 1982, was estimated at $200 billion. About three hundred and sixty thousand Protestant churches hold approximately $22 billion in securities and about 5 percent of the churches' annual income is from the earnings of endowment funds, a source of important income. The Episcopal Church alone owns approximately $1 billion in corporate securities, and the United Methodist pension fund assets were reported in 1983 as about $1.5 billion. The churches are so financially well-off that they are second only to the federal government in monies received and distributed annually.[3]

THE NESTLĒ CAMPAIGN

Yet the same institutions who profit from the system characterize it, or its components, as exploitative, unfair, and unjust. The Nestlē boycott is a typical case-in-point. Company profits were not affected, but INFACT succeeded in unfairly painting Nestlē as a greedy monster who was unconcerned that its product was a baby-killer. The controversy reached such proportions by 1978 that when Egyptian health minister Dr. Mamduh Gabr asked the U.S. Agency for International Development for $5 million in infant formula—for Egyptian babies who could not breast-feed—his offer was rejected. The U.S. government explained that the donation could "subject the entire U.S. AID assistance program to undeserved debate and criticism."[4]

INFACT's charges subsequently led to Senate hearings hostile to Nestlē. When Nestlē executive Oswaldo Ballarin, a Brazilian, told Senator Edward Kennedy's subcommittee on health that the whole infant formula issue was "an indirect attack on the free world's economic system," he was "all but laughed out of the room."[5] Ballarin, however, was just repeating Nestlē's conviction that the objectives of the organizations involved in the boycott were "only a cover for conflicts and goals distinctly different from the issue of infant health."[6]

American understanding of Third-World problems could have been broadened had there been a reasoned public debate. But INFACT's charges were so inflammatory that the media become more interested in repeating the charges than they were in judging the issues. In the first six months of 1981 *The Washington Post* ran ninety-one stories, editorials, or columns critical of Nestlē, including a Brazilian study which alleged that the company was responsible for the deaths of thousands of Brazilian children. After Nestlē deluged the paper with scientific studies about infant formula, the *Post* backtracked and ran an editorial stating that the controversy had been overblown. It is a fair assumption that more people read the stories than read the editorial.[7]

During the same time period, *The New York Times* and other newspapers, magazines, and television stations also ran stories or editorials condemning the company. Nestlē's public relations office began to measure its pile of anti-Nestlē clippings "by the pound."[8]

The constant publicity, fueled by INFACT, was so far-reaching that it had repercussions beyond the infant formula controversy itself. Ernest Lefever, director of the Ethics and Public Policy Center in Washington, believes that his defense of Nestlē hurt his chances of being confirmed as assistant secretary of state for human rights in 1981. Lefever's think-tank had reprinted a *Fortune* magazine article critical of INFACT and had written an article on the issue for *The Wall Street Journal*. Because Nestlē had previously given the Policy Center $25,000 dollars, Lefever said he was accused of acting as a paid company representative.[9]

THE CASE FOR INFANT FORMULA

Had INFACT and its supporting groups been interested in examining the issue on an unbiased basis, they would have found that infant formula is needed in the Third World. Poor mothers in developing countries often do not produce enough milk for complete nutrition. Numerous Third-World pediatricians have warned that additional feeding is needed after the third month and to withhold it produces babies with poor growth and the possibility of severe malnutrition.[10]

As for disease, there is more possibility of severe diarrhea and gastrointestinal infections when mothers use native weaning or supplementary foods than when they use infant formula. The most common native supplementary-weaning food in developing countries is cereal gruels of millet or rice, but the nutritional value of native gruels is low and microbiological contamination of the traditional foods is a fact of life in most poverty-stricken, Third-World homes.[11] The research studies on which these statements are based were made in African settings where commercial baby food had not been used.

Further, studies have proved that infant death rates are generally higher in undeveloped, rural areas of developing countries where infant formula sales are at a minimum. Breast-feeding has dropped "dramatically" in Singapore, and its infant mortality rate is lower than that of the United States.[12] It is true that Third-World mothers have misused the formula, but it is also true that Nestlē had tried to offset that possibility by a staff of about two hundred Nestlē nurses (worldwide) whose job it was to teach mothers how to use the formula correctly. Nonetheless, INFACT charged that the company solicited customers by giving doctors and hospitals samples to distribute and claimed the nurses' sole function was to act as sales representatives.[13] The nurses did act as sales representatives, as well as performing their other functions. Nestlé may not have gone far enough in emphasizing the correct usage of, and possible dangers in, the use of infant formula. But INFACT did its best to portray the company as completely indifferent to both and mercenary to the exclusion of all other considerations.

One of the most ironic aspects of the situation was that INFACT and supporting church groups assumed they knew what was best for Third-World women, despite their never having been consulted. This sort of patronizing is closely akin to racism. When women in developing countries were asked by Nestlé Audit Commission staffer Jack Greenwald what they thought of the boycott, they were outraged. Greenwald said that the women were angry that "Americans assumed they understood the situation and would try and control whether or not they breastfed their children."[14] The commission is an independent organization chaired by former senator Edmund Muskie.

Many women in developing countries now work and are unable to breast-feed, Greenwald said, and the formula is a blessing for them.[15]

At one point, spokesmen cooperating with the antiformula campaign declared they wanted to "demarket" infant formula. In testimony before Congressman Jonathan Gingham's subcommittee on foreign trade, in 1979, Edward Baer, a staffer with the Interfaith Center for Corporate Responsibility (funded by the churches), explained demarketing by citing Socialist Algeria. Algeria is a country in which the importing and distribution of infant formula is in the hands of a state monopoly, and there is no brand competition. Baer did not disclose that imports of infant formula in Algeria rose from two and a half million half-pound cans in 1976 to twelve million in 1979.[16]

According to author Herman Nickel, when asked about the rise in imports, Baer said that it did not bother him because it took place under government control."This reduces the controversy to the absurd but revealing proposition that capitalist formula kills babies, but socialist infant formula does not," Nickel wrote.[17]

NESTLÉ BOYCOTT ENDS

On January 26, 1984 the Nestlé boycott was ended when the company agreed to strictly abide by the World Health Assembly code (to which they had already been adhering for some years) and:

- curtail free infant formula promotions in Third World countries;

- stop providing benefits to doctors who promote the product;

- place warning labels on infant formula packages;
- include warnings and explanations on the benefits of breast-feeding in promotional literature.

Nestlē has been so eager to prove the worthiness of its intentions that it has given a block grant of between $100,000 and $500,000 dollars every year since 1982 to support the Nestlē Infant Formula Audit Commission. The Commission was created to check Nestlē's continued compliance with the agreement it made with INFACT. The commission has no plans to discontinue its work as of 1986.

Nestlē claims its sales have dropped since making the changes. They believe several infant formula companies have taken advantage of its pacifism and are busy trying to corner the infant formula market in developing countries. As much formula is being sold, Nestlē believes; just not by them.

And what is INFACT up to these days? Although many companies who market in developing countries are not living up to the World Health Code standard, INFACT is not declaring boycotts. They claim that low-level pressure is more useful against American Home Products, Roth Laboratories, Bristol-Myers, and seventeen infant formula companies which are not based in the United States. INFACT's primary interest now is crusading against the nuclear arms race; for which they blame . . . corporations.[18]

The Religious Left does not always use confrontational tactics against free enterprise. A commission established by the National Council of Churches recently helped mediate an end to a farm dispute involving Campbell Soup. The dispute involved workers' health conditions, wages, and the recognition of workers' rights to collective bargaining. The NCC subsequently called off a threatened endorsement of a boycott against Campbell products. This victory for moderation might signal a permanent change in attitude. However, the church's more familiar stance has been one of condemnation and confrontation: although the seven-year Campbell boycott was called off, it had had the endorsement of seventeen major religious organizations. These negative attitudes have most often been acted out by the Interfaith Center for Corporate Responsibility, a sponsor-related movement of the National Council of Churches.

THE CHURCHES SPONSOR ANTICORPORATE ACTIVISM

The Center takes a very dim view of multinational corporations. Formed in 1974, the Center is a coalition of twenty-two Protestant boards and agencies and twenty-two Catholic religious communities and archdioceses. It has seven subgroups, some of which focus on "militarism," international justice, and domestic equality. Ironically, churches which belong to the Center's coalition have over $7 billion invested in the same institutions which they regularly take to task.

Among the member agencies are the Mission Responsibility Through Investment committee of the Presbyterian Church U.S.A.; General Assembly Mission Council, the American Baptist Churches in the U.S.A.; the Church of the Brethren Pension Board; the Committee on Social Responsibility in Investments of the Executive Council of the Episcopal Church; the Reformed Church in America; Church Women United; and one hundred and seventy Catholic orders, provinces of orders, congregations within provinces, dioceses and archdioceses.

Four United Methodist agencies are involved, including the General Board of Church and Society and three divisions of the General Board of Global Ministries. The Methodist Church thus has sixteen representatives on the Interfaith governing board.

Although the number of religious organizations which are members of the Center seems impressive, it would be a mistake to believe they truly represent U.S. churches. Most local congregations have no idea their representative agencies are members of the Center, or are even seriously involved with anticorporate activities.

This is especially true of the Catholic orders because the Catholics are fragmented organizationally. Most orders are divided regionally and into separate congregations. Thus, it is possible for the Dominican Province of St. Albert the Great, based in Chicago, to belong to the Center but for most Dominicans in the United States to be completely unaware of corporate activism and the Interfaith Center.[19]

Despite the lack of knowledge about corporate activism among a majority of church members, Interfaith income comes principally from annual contributions of member agencies; the minimum for voting privileges is $1,000 or $1,500 for coalitions. The 1982 budget was $478,839, $326,967 of which came from member agencies, $45,000 from foundations, and the remainder from individual gifts and other sources. The United Methodist General Board of Global Ministries gave, from 1981 through 1984, $248,887 dollars.

The Center does not own stock and files no shareholder resolutions; it claims it is only an arena for ecumenically coordinating strategies. Members send representatives to Interfaith working groups, and on the basis of mutual agreements the Interfaith staff does research and drafts shareholder resolutions. It also assists in arranging delegations to discuss or negotiate with management in the solicitation of proxy support for resolutions or the coordination of presentations at annual shareholder meetings.

ANTICORPORATE TACTICS AND ATTITUDES

The Center initiates and coordinates strategy on behalf of its members, and it is also responsible for researching issues: therefore it directly influences member response. The research may sometimes be flawed, but its political instincts seem to work well. After the Center became involved in an antinuclear energy campaign, Scientists and Engineers for Secure Energy (SE2) (an organization which includes five Nobel Laureates) charged that the Center was presenting an "inaccurate picture of the safety and long-term feasibility of nuclear energy." It recommended that the Interfaith Center base its conclusions on scientific data instead of on "transient political pronouncements."[20]

The Center uses the same tactics with subjects other than nuclear energy. The North American Congress on Latin America, one of the most radical church-funded organizations (see Appendix), wrote a report in 1976 on the Del Monte corporation; it was titled "Del Monte: Bitter Fruits." Being entirely compatible with the Center's philosophy, it was soon incorporated in its Agribusiness Manual. The report claimed that "Del Monte and the banana multinationals . . . will certainly be a major obstacle to the socialist revolution necessary to meet people's needs in the Third World . . . finally, whatever economic benefits producer countries do obtain are not likely to benefit the majority of people, but rather the ruling class groups that control the government."[21]

In the manual, however, a Center representative admitted that Del Monte wages are "almost always above the minimum," and that it is commonly held that Del Monte is one of the better places to work in developing countries. But the representative complained that although the company provided housing, schools, stores, recreation facilities, and hospitals, Del Monte did not provide food or clothing. In what must be one of the decade's more glaring ideological contradictions, the representative then complained that "the worker and family become wholly dependent upon the corporation to provide their livelihood."[22]

Further, Interfaith staffers are not exactly unbiased in their individual viewpoints. Sister Marilyn Uline of the Adrian Dominicans, who worked for reform of infant formula companies, related an encounter with Leah Margulies, the Interfaith Center's director of the infant formula campaign. "But, Marilyn," Margulies reportedly said of businessmen, "they're all bastards. If they weren't they'd be living like we're living and doing what we're doing."[23]

The Center, which is also antidefense, coordinates strategy with organizations such as the Institute for Policy Studies and the American

Friends Service Committee (see Appendix). At a three-way conference of these groups held in Washington in 1984 (and paid, in part, by grants from churches), they meditated on "Meeting the Corporate Challenge." As expected, transnational corporations were labeled "the most dynamic, yet destructive agents in the world economy." The triad then laid plans to establish a worldwide clearinghouse on corporate activities at Policy Studies headquarters.[24]

THE REAL AGENDA

The reform of corporations is only part of the anticorporate agenda. According to Methodist theologian Thomas Oden, a professor at Drew University, the principal aim is the "creation and intensification of a sense of guilt."[25]

This attack against corporations, Oden said, seeks to make "Westerners feel guilty about production and profit, to make corporations feel guilty about bigness and technology, to make church members feel guilty about their political impotence, to make the rich feel guilty about their wealth, to make whites feel guilty about their whiteness, to make males feel guilty about the plight of females, and so on."[26]

Of course, cultural guilt is psychologically useful to people who desire radical change. The less confident a people feel about their system, the less resistant they are to those who seek to replace it. One of the primary ways in which this guilt is inserted into public discourse is through claims, from both Religious Left leadership and its corporate activists, that the poor in America are getting poorer and nobody cares and that the First World's wealth is based on the exploitation of the Third. Presbyterian, Roman Catholic, and United Church of Christ officials have used this technique, not only through their support of corporate activism, but by producing papers on free enterprise which claim precisely these things.

CHRISTIANITY AND FREE ENTERPRISE

"Christian Faith and Economic Justice," produced by the Presbyterian Council on Theology and Culture in 1984, expressed "solidarity" with Third-World revolutions, stating the developing world is poor because its people have been "colonized, dominated, drained of their surpluses, locked into bondage in which they are poor. . . ." The denomination's General Assembly agreed to distribute copies of the document to all Presbyterian congregations.

Authors of the United Church of Christ paper—which as of 1986 is still in the draft stage and has not yet been submitted for church approval—complain that the Presbyterians have not gone far enough. The first draft of their study document states that the hope that basic human needs can be met by the U.S. and world economy, as it is, is a "dying dream."[27] They also suggest that all affluent Americans who profit by the free enterprise system are committing a sin.[28]

The paper claimed that the premodern economy was a better one because it was an extension of the decision-making process of individuals. The modern economy, it said, is based on scarcity and is left to the workings of the market. There is no mention of the fact that the economic condition of people, even those in the Third World, has dramatically improved in the last two hundred years precisely because of free enterprise.

United Church of Christ authors believe that "God and economics must be brought together," but reject the view that individuals can be God's agents. They assert that the word "steward" is "an outworn word." The authors maintain that the economy must be managed like a "household," include everyone, and provide everyone with the "necessities of life."[29]

In other words, we return to the familiar Socialist philosophy that people cannot care for themselves and society itself is responsible, not the individual. More alarming is the author's assertion that God does not endow people with humanity, but people endow themselves by fulfilling a "task." This philosophy denies, by inference, that humanity is created in God's image.

As part of their recommendations for change, the authors urge that United Church of Christ seminaries be transformed to assure that its clergy emerge with similar economic views. They also suggest developing exchanges with such well-known economic successes as Nicaragua, the Soviet Union, China, Cuba, North Vietnam, Eastern Europe, and North Korea, countries which the authors obviously believe would help America to "envision a more equitable economic order than now prevails."[30]

The first draft of the 1984 Catholic Bishops' "Pastoral Letter on Catholic Social Teaching and the U.S. Economy" was more moderate than the United Church of Christ paper, but it endorsed the welfare state. It endorsed the concept of "economic rights," the right of every person to food, shelter, and employment of what is otherwise "necessary to live with dignity." The letter further stated that the "distribution of income and wealth in the United States is so inequitable that it violates the minimum standard of distributive justice." In exploring how all these needs could be fulfilled by the government, without bankrupting the nation, the bishops suggested that employees buy out firms, especially those that are scheduled to be closed. But they also suggested that the government subsidize the takeover.[31]

Blaming an "Atlantic-denominated" economy for the ills of the Third World, the bishops suggested that the profits of transnationals be "reconciled with the common good that governments and the multilateral agencies they have created must seek." The bishops apparently believe corporations have only profit at heart and governments only good.[32]

Contents of the pastoral letter came as no surprise to those who followed the process in which it was created. Only left-of-center economists addressed the bishops directly on issues concerning the creation of wealth. Gar Alperovitz, codirector of the National Center for Economic Alternatives, told the bishops that America has what it takes to provide a decent life for all its citizens, but it does not choose to do so. Alperovitz argued for a more planned economy as a way of making such decency possible.[33]

Although the pastoral letter was produced by the Catholic bishops and their staffs, it was heavily influenced by Protestant bureaucratic staff members. Rev. J. Oscar McCloud, director of the Presbyterian Program Agency, Rev. Fred Allen, former associate general secretary of the United Methodist Board of Church and Society, William Diehl, a management consultant to the Lutherans, and representatives from the Episcopal and United Church of Christ all testified in committee hearings.

McCloud told the bishops that the Presbyterian Church "has turned significant energy to ideas such as shared ownership, community control of industry, and the hope of a social and political process that would do as many European countries have already done." Allen read a statement which he had earlier presented to the United Methodists in the form of a resolution which they had rejected—a fact that he did not disclose at the hearing. It vigorously criticized capitalism as it exists in the United States.[34]

The letter's second draft, released in October 1985, was generally considered less radical in its condemnation of free enterprise than the first and placed more emphasis on community and individual responsibility. Nonetheless, it did not retreat from its basic belief that it is the government's "moral function" to bestow economic rights on its citizens. Archbishop Weakland of Milwaukee made the most accurate comment on the second draft when he said, "The language has been toned down a bit, but the ideas haven't."[35]

FREE ENTERPRISE IN CHRISTIAN HISTORY

As politically biased as the letter seemed, it was probably just a logical extension of Catholic economic thought. The Roman Catholic Church has traditionally favored mercantilism and has frowned upon free enterprise as a system which is subject to abuse. Weakland, commenting on the second draft, said that endorsing unfettered capitalism would violate Catholic teaching because "the glorification of rugged individualism can often lead to a neglect of the common good, that the profit motive of self-interest can often lead to greed and exploitation. . . ."[36] There is nothing wrong with this idea. There is a lot of truth in it. It needs, however, to be balanced with the recognition that free enterprise also encourages freedom among peoples. When the balance in ideas is absent, the bishops' pastoral letters are politically useful to those who are more dedicated to politics than they are to charity.

Michael Novak believes Catholic social teaching errs in that it is closer to a "mild form of socialism, than to democratic capitalism. It has little to say about markets and incentives, the ethics of production, and the habits, disciplines, and organization necessary for the creation of wealth. It seems to take the production of wealth for granted (as if wealth were as limited and static as in medieval times) and preoccupies itself with appeals for redistribution. The discoveries of modern economics seem to have affected it hardly at all."[37]

Novak gently points out that Catholics could be "more modest in speaking of development" because the record of wholly Catholic countries in the "history of economic and social development is not entirely laudable." Novak did not list these countries, but the most typical examples are in South and Central America, regions not known for their modern economic advancement.[38]

Protestantism, however, does not have the excuse of historical distaste for capitalism. Instead, Protestantism was partially responsible for the rise of capitalism, and capitalism, in turn, was responsible for much of the Protestant success in Europe. When Catholicism, and its emphasis on mercantilism, was discarded in Northern Europe, capitalism flourished. The loosening of social ties as a result of Protestantism created a drive in humanity to prove itself by work, and not simply define itself by its relationship with God or social level.

The Protestant approach to economics, therefore, was based on the assumption that if business is not perfect, it is a legitimate and necessary part of the social order. Sometimes sectors of the Protestant church have supported labor's efforts to improve conditions, sometimes they have not. However, Protestantism has never before questioned the legitimacy of free enterprise. Only in this century have Protestants begun to question that assumption. Unfortunately, both the assumption and the doubt have rarely been examined logically or on a theologically sound basis.

Now most church social thought is based on advocacy for the poor and the rejected (seen in terms of "Christ's standing beside us as intercessor . . ."), self-determination and self-development of peoples (the precursors of liberation theology), and "enablement, or later empowerment." These ideas generally imply that systems are basically evil and must be changed, rather than the older belief that systems need to evolve and people to change.[39]

THE POLEMICAL CHURCH

Not only do churches now produce papers on economic matters which claim free enterprise is evil (or at least not a positive system), but church speakers, church literature, and resolutions often claim the same thing. They almost never offer proof of their claims, but depend on emotional rhetoric about the poor, and use Biblical references about Christian responsibility which are taken out of context.

A typical example involves remarks made by a Garrett Evangelical Theological Seminary professor to a preaching clinic in Nashville, sponsored by the United Methodist Publishing House in cooperation with Vanderbilt University Divinity School. Rosemary Radford Ruether charged that the affluent (capitalists) "can no longer run to the private worlds of therapy and health food . . . for the time of exploitation is running out. . . ." In another address she said that "Redemption overturns the present world order. It changes social systems which create and perpetuate inhumanity."[40]

Much church literature does not even bother with Scriptural references. It proceeds directly into political pronouncements. *3rd World Sermon Notes*, a Presbyterian publication which offers sermon suggestions for ministers, published "Stones of Violence" in 1984. Written by United Methodist minister Jim Sessions, the article maintained that "Like colonies of the Third World, Appalachia was appropriated by economic interests in Europe and the Northeastern U.S. for use with the active collaboration of the government. . . . The antidote for all this is not distance, or even charity for the poor but active solidarity with the poor." Presbyterian ministers were urged to tell their members not to waste their time on charity but to work against "systemic" evils.[41]

THE WORLD COUNCIL COMBATS FREE ENTERPRISE

The World Council of Churches is blatantly and unashamedly opposed to the free market and makes full use of its U.S. funds to combat the free enterprise system. It channels money from U.S. churches to the Christian Conference of Asia, the Urban Rural Mission, and other foreign programs. The Conference and Mission share offices in Hong Kong. They evidently do not stress trade union values.

A meeting of the Christian Conference-Urban Mission committee in February 1983 in Bangladesh discussed the "economic domination and exploitation by TNCs (transnational corporations)." They also approved an annual budget of $345,000 for 1983 and the same for 1984, to be provided by non-Asian churches.[42]

The World Council's Program on Transnational Corporations in 1982 adopted a report which states that "This system (world market system) and TNC's operation within it are incompatible with our vision of a just, participatory and sustainable society. . . ." The document was accepted at the 1983 Vancouver World Council of Churches Assembly.[43]

Yet, when the literature is examined in depth, it is clear that the World Council feels as much enmity toward the U.S. as it does transnational corporations. The World Council almost always links transnational corporations with America despite the fact that American corporations make up only 44 percent of the world's largest firms and Third-World transnationals are becoming much more common. For example, South Korea's Samsung Group, a general trading company, operates in twenty-nine countries in products such as hotel construction and sugar refining. Hindustan Machine, an Indian company, sells machine tools to Algeria, and SGV, a Philippine firm, does public accounting and provides management services in every Asian capital.

In its battle against free enterprise, the World Council and the denominations have sometimes called for a world economic order or have advocated some sort of international control of the earth's economies. Typical was the U.N. Law of the Sea Treaty, a project for which the United Methodist Board of Global Ministries alone spent $203,449 between 1981 and 1983. Had it been signed by the United States, the treaty would have authorized the U.N. to equally distribute sea products (minerals, oil, etc.) regardless of who did the work or made the investment. Poor Third-World countries would have undoubtedly found this a profitable treaty; however, it is not a fair treaty and it is unlikely that a bureaucratic, totally political institution such as the U.N. could have been impartial or efficient.

Why the World Council and mainline denominations advocate such quixotic schemes is not really a mystery. Every ideology needs an appealing belief system or it cannot gather adherents to its cause. Therefore, the Religious Left puts forth the notion that the fortunes of the world's disadvantaged would improve if the world's economic system were under a gigantic bureaucracy. Another such assumption—which is constantly repeated—is that America's poor face a deteriorating economic situation. It is also asserted that the free enterprise system is not fair to the poor and they need more help from the callous U.S. government. The former assertion is false, and the latter is highly debatable.

THE PLIGHT OF THE POOR IMPROVES

First, the economic situation is not deteriorating for a majority of America's poor. Author Ben Wattenberg has pointed out that there has been a definite improvement during the last thirty years for Americans on the lower economic scale. In 1950 the U.S. Social Security Administration found that 22.4 percent of Americans were below the poverty level. Thanks to massive efforts by the government to improve the situation, and to a growing economy, by 1979 only 11.6 percent were below that level.[44]

Although the U.S. Census Bureau said in 1983 that there were about eleven million more in poverty than in 1979, a report issued by the Joint Center for Political Studies declared that the increase was due to a downturn in the economy and not the cutting of government programs, as has been claimed by the Religious Left.

The Center's claims were verified in the summer of 1985 when it was announced that 1.8 million people climbed out of poverty in 1984—nearly a full percentage point—thanks to economic recovery. The drop in poverty, the Census Bureau said, was the largest since 1976. Those in poverty now (1986) comprise 14.4 percent, and that figure should improve if the economy continues in a growth pattern.

HIDDEN COSTS IN GOVERNMENT WELFARE SPENDING

There is an often repeated claim that America (and its government) cares less about the poor than in former years. The figures prove differently. The United States now spends about 5 percent more on its social welfare expenditures as a percentage of its Gross National Product than it did in 1950. In 1970 a total of $1,354 dollars per person was spent on social and welfare spending, but the figure rose in 1980 to $2,140, a total amount in 1980 of $492 billion.[45] Overall, "civilian social welfare costs increased by twenty times from 1950 to 1980, in constant dollars." During the same time period, the population of the United States only increased by half.[46]

Poverty figures are also suspect because statisticians do not include benefits received from government agencies. In 1982 the federal government spent $10.2 billion dollars for food stamps for over twenty-one million people, but the value was not included in poverty statistics. The same is true for Medicaid and public housing, legal services, day-care programs, transportation programs, counseling, energy assistance, educational programs, and earned income tax credit.[47]

In-kind transfers, such as the ones just mentioned, went from $5.8 billion per year in 1965 to $98.5 billion in 1982, in constant 1982 dollars. Federal statisticians did not count those transfers in deciding how many were over and under the poverty line. When a Congressional Budget Office study counted in-kind benefits in 1976, the poverty rate dived from 11.8 percent to 6.4. Further, the social programs have not been cut from 1979 levels, but have only had their planned increases cut. Social spending is still going up. In 1970, 6.8 percent of the GNP went to social "safety net." In 1985 the total was 11.3 percent.[48]

Everyone does not agree on the poverty figures or why there is less poverty. Author Charles Murray claims that 30 percent of the population was in poverty in 1950 and it declined to 18 percent by 1964. It dipped to 11 percent in 1973, but then began rising again. Poverty figures, he said, stopped declining during the years in which the government spent its greatest amount of money.[49] No matter which argument is correct, there is less poverty and there is no evidence that a great many people will slide under the poverty line in the foreseeable future. And it is clear that American society, through its government, has done what it could based on the knowledge it has.

WHAT CAUSES POVERTY?

Therefore, the real argument about poverty does not lie in whether it is getting better or worse, but what causes poverty in the first place. The Religious Left has either ignored this question or attributed the cause to the government or the free enterprise system. In ignoring the real causes of poverty, the church has done the poor a disservice. Sociologists are now charging the very welfare system which has done its best to defeat poverty in this country with creating a system of dependency. This dependency has allegedly led, in turn, to the creation of a poor underclass of about three million blacks who have had no incentive to improve themselves.

In *Losing Ground: American Social Policy 1950-1980*, Charles Murray argues that the welfare programs created in the 1960s have made it easy for the poor to behave in ways that are destructive to their character and their lives. One vivid example lies in the damage done to black families. In 1980, 48 percent of all live births among blacks were illegitimate, and that figure has continued to rise. This compares to only 17 percent in 1950. Among black teenagers from ages fifteen to nineteen, 82 percent of all births are illegitimate. This is one of the highest illegitimate birthrates in the world.[50] Let us not forget what illegitimacy means. It means that some child does not have a father. Many babies born to these poor teenagers are also underweight and tend to have medical problems. It also means that the mother will have a much more difficult time climbing out of poverty and giving her children the ability to do so. Almost 70 percent of the black poor live in homes in which there is no responsible adult male.[51]

Respected black scholars such as Thomas Sowell, Walter Williams, and Glenn Loury agree with Murray. They believe the welfare system is responsible for a growing class of people who are chronically dependent, many of whom are children. There are also very few black scholars among the group concerned with welfare dependency who believe it is free enterprise that is to blame for poverty. Robert Woodson, head of the National Center for Neighborhood Enterprise, has called the welfare system "welfare colonialism." His answer to the problem is to "rekindle the entrepreneurial spirit" in black communities.[52]

Arguments for and against welfare are obviously worthy of debate. However, nothing that Murray or any other social critic has said concerning welfare has had an effect on the views of church leadership and bureaucracy—they have not even been considered. It is simply taken for granted that the poor must be supported and the public is selfish if it does not do so. This obdurate attitude can either be attributed to lack of flexibility, or to people who find their arguments too politically useful to consider change. Whatever the reason, it does not help the poor to ignore the real debate concerning their problems. Moreover, the Religious Left has yet to explain why they believe in a socialism from which Great Britain, Ireland, France, and China are retreating.

As for the claim that free enterprise is to blame for poverty, that claim is wrong. But the Religious Left is not totally to blame for its antipathy for capitalism. American enterprise must take part of the blame on itself that so many of those who participate in the system do not believe in its moral legitimacy. The system has not taken the time to defend itself or to produce an apologia for its existence. It has left ideology to the Marxists.

THE SPIRIT OF DEMOCRATIC CAPITALISM

That situation recently changed when theologian Michael Novak produced *The Spirit of Democratic Capitalism*—a well-reasoned defense of a system Novak explains as a merger between a market economy and a political system respectful of individual rights; a system of "cultural institutions moved by ideals of liberty and justice for all." Novak asserts that a political democracy is compatible in practice only with a market economy because both systems spring from identical historical impulses: to limit the power of the state, and to liberate the energy of individuals and communities, both of which are nourished by a pluralistic liberal culture.[53]

Economic liberties without political liberties are inherently unstable, Novak maintains, because citizens with one soon demand the other. But on the other hand, he says, "the state which does not recognize limits to its power in the economic sphere inevitably destroys liberties in the political sphere." Novak also points out that "democratic polities depend upon the reality of economic growth.[54]

"No traditional society—indeed, no society in history—has ever produced strict equality among individuals or classes," Novak writes. "Real differences in talent, aspiration, and application inexorably individuate humans. Given the diversity and liberty of human life, no fair and free system can possibly guarantee equal outcomes. A democratic system depends for its legitimacy, therefore, not upon results but upon a sense of equal opportunity.[55]

"Such legitimacy flows from the belief of all individuals that they can better their condition. This belief can be realized only under conditions of economic growth. Liberty requires expanse and openness."[56]

CAPITALISM IMPROVES LIVING CONDITIONS

Capitalism, Novak maintains, has rescued the world from the poverty in which it was captive prior to 1776. Until two hundred years ago the world practiced mercantilism, based on national policies of accumulating precious metals, establishing colonies (which were exploited for their natural resources) and merchant marines, and developing industry and mining to attain a favorable balance of trade.[57]

Instead of prospering, most of the world was trapped in poverty. Every generation famines descended on the civilized world; in the 1780s, four-fifths of French families devoted 90 percent of their incomes to buying bread (and only bread) to feed themselves. Life expectancy in 1795, in France, was 27.3 years for women and 23.4 for men. In 1800, fewer than a thousand Germans had income as high as $1,000. In 1800, there were more private business corporations in the United States than in all of Europe combined.[58]

Noting that under mercantilism society was so static that there had been few advances in conveniences, Novak cited the almost unknown state of hygiene in both the civilized and uncivilized world prior to the market society. People excreted wherever they could, and the streets were used as public sewers. Successful medicine did not exist, and entire populations were illiterate. In Africa, the wheel had never been invented.[59]

"The invention of the market economy in Great Britain and the United States more profoundly revolutionized the world between 1800 and the present than any other single force," Novak wrote.[60]

Yet this is the system that church leadership finds profoundly flawed.

LATIN AMERICA'S POLITICAL MYTHOLOGY

Luis Burstin, a Costa Rican doctor and journalist, calls claims that the northern nations are responsible for the poverty of Latin America "political mythology." Burstin points out that hunger, political turmoil, instability, terrorism, and corruption are the oldest stories in Latin America and did not begin with American investment in the region.[61]

"Why is it," Burstin wrote, "that the so-called Fourth World, the least developed countries of the Third World such as Afghanistan, Chad, Bhutan, Burundi, Nepal, and Sikkim, did not until very recently have any external economic contacts, and how is it that most of them were never Western colonies?"[62]

Burstin also pointed out that while Latins have claimed that Latin American dependency on the United States has produced backwardness, in Canada, a country more "dependent . . . to a degree that has no equal in this world, this relationship has not produced backwardness but a modern, progressive, and rich country?" Hong Kong, Taiwan, Singapore, and South Korea were poor and backward nations three decades ago, Burstin said, but they are now some of the most prosperous and vital in the world.[63]

"They were invaded by foreign capital and technology; they became dependent on Western imperialism and markets; and yet in just three decades they left all their backwardness behind and are now jumping into the era of the highest technology," he wrote.[64]

Bishops, denominational groups, and ecumenical bodies who plan to write papers on our economic system would be advised to find out what people want, instead of telling them what they need. When the world is actually asked what it wants, the evidence suggests it wants a free market. Gallup conducted a poll in 1976 to find out what mankind thinks of itself. The study concluded that people in developing countries want more industry by ratios exceeding 20 to 1. In short, they want to develop like Western societies and need jobs and investment capital to do so.[65]

THE OPINION GAP ABOUT FREE ENTERPRISE

The real questions concerning contrasting political views, however, are not whether the Interfaith Center is truthful in its claims, or whether the anticorporate activists are also anticapitalists, or even whether church leaders are Socialists at heart, but whether grass-roots church members approve of their activities and approve of funding organizations which are determined to replace the present economic system. Presbyterian membership, for one, does not approve of all that is done in its name, although it does not seem able to curb its bureaucracies and leadership. A Presbyterian Task Force investigated the church's attitudes toward corporate activism and admitted in its report that the church's general assembly had not affirmed the legitimacy of the U.S. economic system and had "dwelt at length on the flaws and imperfections of our system and its institutions."[66]

The task force report concluded that the Presbyterian Church's anticorporate activities revealed a serious imbalance in the church's mission activities; that they had challenged and condemned the legitimacy of "necessary" economic activity and thus weakened the church.[67] ". . . this imbalance oversimplifies the world of ambiguous choices and trade-offs found in all economic life, and forgets that all economic development carries significant costs . . . when the church's approach to the transnational corporation loses its sense of balance, it risks the constant polarization that leads to counterproductive alienation. We acknowledge that faithful action requires criticism and conflict, but the church must not separate the prophetic action demanded by the gospel from the support and affirmation that are also demanded."[68]

The report further stated that according to a poll taken of Presbyterian membership in 1981, the clergy and church members disagreed to such an extent on economic matters that more than a majority—up to 60 percent—of all Presbyterians had passed beyond disagreement to "genuine polarization." They also significantly disagree on the approach the church should take when dealing with questions of economics and transnational corporations. Church professionals "by training and inclination" focus primarily on the just distribution of wealth, the report noted, while membership is occupied with the tasks related to its production.[69]

About one-fifth of Presbyterian pastors and one-fifth of the lay members are at opposite poles on economic issues, the report said. "This is not surprising when we note that thirty-nine percent of members believe that corporations are overly regulated by government, while only sixteen percent of pastors do."[70]

As a whole, poll findings "further illuminated the increasing tension among us," pointing out that most Presbyterian pastors approved of using pressure tactics, such as stockholder initiatives and boycotts, and membership disagreed to the point that the issues had become "visible opposition."[71]

It is a telling point that when church membership does become involved with issues involving corporate activism, there is often a predictable halt in the propaganda. The United Methodists sensibly set up a task force to study the Nestlé boycott after several of its agencies had indicated support for INFACT. The task force report recommended that the United Methodist Church, its boards and agencies, not endorse the boycott.[72]

They went further than that, however. While endorsing church involvement in social issues deriving from corporate policy, they pointed out that two of their general boards and agencies had persisted in the boycott despite cooperation by Nestlē in ending alleged abuses. They recommended that the church work with business instead of immediately resorting to sanctions. They stated that the church could not let itself be used in these issues by "persons and groups who may not fully share the church's deeper theological and ethical commitments."[73]

Finally—and most importantly—the task force decided that it could not "resolve issues on a purely ideological basis. . . . As a Task Force we recognize that the great debate between capitalism and socialism is important . . . at the same time, it seems clear that multinational corporations, such as the ones with which we have been in dialogue, will be a part of the international scene for a long time to come."[74]

The Task Force report was a victory for Nestlē and for democratic capitalism in general.

FOUR

Attitudes Toward Democratic Capitalism and Totalitarianism

W hen the Ethiopian famine was well underway a few years ago, and mothers were walking hundreds of miles looking for food for their hollow-eyed children, Ethiopia's Marxist-Leninist rulers had a celebration. It was a one hundred million dollar extravaganza marking the tenth anniversary of their regime.

Monuments were erected, parade floats were constructed, the government financed bands and ordered shiploads of Scotch and cream sherry from Great Britain.[1] When the famine was finally acknowledged, relief ships carrying desperately needed food supplies were forced to delay unloading because Soviet ships loaded with concrete for army barracks took first priority.[2]

Aid was so unimportant to the Mengistu Mariam regime that army units were initially forbidden to distribute food. Instead, the units were used to keep starving peasants out of the cities. Using the catastrophe as an excuse to garner revenues, the government charged an import tax of $12.50 per ton for gift food, plus handling and trucking charges of $165 per ton.[3] Moreover, despite the famine, the regime shipped large amounts of food supplies to towns that house army garrisons and surpluses were sold to the Sudan.[4]

Not everybody was indifferent. Beginning in 1984 the Western world and its relief organizations began a massive rescue campaign. The U.S. government alone sent more than a quarter of a billion dollars worth of emergency supplies to Ethiopia, more than a third of all relief. In an article for the *Los Angeles Times*, Ethiopian Dereje Deressa acknowledged the help, expressing his "deepest appreciation" to the American people. Without the food and medicine, he said, the famine would have been much worse.[5]

Yet, officials of Church World Service, the relief arm for the National Council of Churches, blamed the famine on the United States. "Racism" in the U.S. is responsible for the "devastation in

Ethiopia," Church World Service director Willis Logan said. Such a famine, he explained, would not have been allowed to happen in the United States or in Europe.[6]

After a visit to Ethiopia in late 1984, Norma Kehrberg, chief staff executive of the United Methodist Committee on Relief, said she was impressed with the country's "openness and accessibility." Kehrberg said she would correct "misinformation" distributed by U.S. government officials.[7] But the officials to which Kehrberg was referring had correctly charged that the Ethiopian government was exceedingly reluctant to transport, or help transport, relief supplies to the rebel provinces of Tigre and Eritrea, a policy designed to conquer by starvation.

It was later disclosed that peasants in those and neighboring provinces had been forced to relocate in government-controlled territory, a process that killed anywhere from one hundred thousand to three hundred thousand people. A French organization which provides medical help for the starving later claimed that the resettlement had killed more people than the famine. Other organizations testified that many peasants were taken against their will, "sometimes at gunpoint," to land that had not been cleared for cultivation. They were not left with food.[8]

After his visit to Ethiopia, United Methodist bishop Roy Clark commented that the U.S.S.R. had done more to help Ethiopia than had the United States.[9] What the bishop neglected to explain was that the Soviet Union has given almost no food to Africa's starving. If Clark had been interested in really investigating the situation, he should have talked to Angolan Methodist bishop Emilio de Carvalho. De Carvalho said in 1984 that the Marxists have exported food for money to buy arms from the Soviets—not to feed their people; they exported food to bolster their military power.[10] Ethiopia now owes from $2.5 to $4 billion to the Soviet Union for weapons.[11]

Unfortunately, the uncritical opinion of Ethiopian policies entertained by representatives of Church World Service and the United Methodist Church is not an isolated case. It is typical of mainline leadership's attitude toward totalitarian countries in general. Church bureaucracy and leadership automatically make excuses for the shortcomings of Marxist-Leninist regimes, ignoring or denying their terrible excesses. These delusions are expressed by our churches in everything from statements that ignore those governments' responsibility for famines and oppression (Ethiopia, Angola) to the view that concentration camps in some Marxist-Leninist regimes are actually benevolent to the inmates (Vietnam).[12] The worst, more harmful, and most common kind of delusion has been the one in which different Marxist-

Leninist societies are either proclaimed tolerant to Christians, or active persecution is ignored (Nicaragua, the Soviet Union, China).

CONTRASTING ATTITUDES

What makes these sympathetic attitudes even more striking is that they are inevitably opposite to those the Religious Left has of the United States. Whereas Marxist-Leninist regimes are supposedly benevolent, attempting to provide for all, America is supposedly cruel to its poor through economic neglect, insisting on an inherently unjust free enterprise; whereas the Marxists-Leninists are only trying to defend themselves, the United States is militaristic and imperialistic; whereas the United States is uncompassionate, the Marxists-Leninists are passionately committed to human rights. The Religious Left has even helped create the ingenious myth that the reason so many totalitarian societies lack the human rights to which they are supposedly committed is because the United States has made them feel threatened. Many church leaders actually used this excuse in behalf of Nicaragua's Sandinistas.

JESSE JACKSON VISITS CUBA

Cuba, however, is the best illustrated example of these attitudes as it has been the most revered "political pilgrimage" of both the religious and secular Left. Consider the Rev. Jesse Jackson's 1984 pilgrimage. He ostensibly made the trip as part of a vague "mission for peace," during which he spoke at the University of Havana, toured the Isle of Youth, and hobnobbed with Fidel Castro and a swarm of reporters. Jackson's speech was consistent with the rest of his attitudes toward his country as opposed to the Third World. "Industrial powers purposely and consciously structured their relationships with weaker societies in such a way that the 'natural' operations of this structure would reproduce and exaggerate an already asymmetric relationship," he said. In other words, the United States has exploited the Third World. Castro later called Jackson's speech "profound."[13]

Jackson also appeared at a Martin Luther King memorial service—which was attended by about three hundred representatives of U.S., Caribbean, and Cuban churches—accompanied by Castro. According to reports on the service, Jackson, who spoke, criticized the United States for interfering in Nicaragua. He also praised what was being done for children on the Isle of Youth.[14]

One hopes Jackson was ignorant about the Isle of Youth because it is an indoctrination center for children from anyplace where Cuban troops "have reached a critical mass."[15] The children are also used as forced labor in Cuba's sugarcane fields. There are six thousand children there from Angola alone, most of whom had no choice but to go. Obviously, Mr. Jackson thinks well of Cuba, despite overwhelming evidence of Castro's oppression. It is also evident Jackson does not think well of the United States.

CHRISTIAN LEADERS CONFESS ANTI-IMPERIALISM

The King memorial service was interesting in itself. It was included as part of a seminar on Martin Luther King and was attended by Tyrone Pitts, the director of the National Council of Churches' Racial Justice Program, Rev. Benjamin Chavis of the Commission for Racial Justice of the United Church of Christ, and dozens of other American and Cuban church officials. Various Cuban church-related organizations were supposedly the cosponsors as well as the U.S. Black Theology Project. The Prague-based Christian Peace Conference, which has been labeled as a Soviet-front organization by the West German and U.S. governments, was represented.[16]

The seminar was a bizarre tribute to a man committed to nonviolence. Topics included "liberation struggles" in North and Latin America, theology and Marxist analysis, black liberation theology, and seminars on present-day Cuba. When the seminar was concluded, delegates attended a reception at the Cuban Institute of Friendship with the Peoples. The host was Rene Rodriguez—a man infamous for his indictment by a Miami federal grand jury for his alleged role in smuggling drugs into the United States.[17]

Castro was probably gratified by the statements delegates gave to the Cuban press. A theology instructor from Chicago Theological Seminary said, "The presence of Fidel in the church and among Christians with Rev. Jackson and his acknowledgment of the Catholic Church is an outstanding occasion—the recognition that God is at work in Fidel and Jesse's work in both contexts. I personally feel at home in Cuba and feel that Cuba is a sign of hope that God is still on the move in the world."[18]

Pitts said, "This seminar has given me greater insight into the Church's struggle for peace with justice in the U.S.A., and against those 'principalities and powers' in the world that promote war, hunger and oppression."[19]

Chavis went further, acknowledging the Cuban church's collaboration with the Cuban government, then stating that the history of a majority of the church in the U.S.A. "is a history of supporting counterrevolution and imperialism of the capitalist class interest."[20]

The seminar produced a remarkable "final declaration" with a "confession" of "anti-imperialism." "We confess . . . that our churches have not condemned strongly enough the blockade of the

United States against Cuba; we have learned . . . about the Cuban revolution and the positive role played in the revolution by Christians . . . about the importance of Rev. Jesse Jackson's efforts to bring the peoples of the world together for justice and peace."[21]

Unfortunately, Jackson and company's attitude concerning Cuba reflects views which pervade church bureaucracy. The World and National Council of Churches have never passed a resolution condemning Cuban human rights violations. They have many times, however, called for normalizing relations with Cuba, and delegates have made numerous trips to that country—and inevitably returned praising it as a model of one thing or another.

CUBA THE GREAT

The hero worship accorded Cuba has, at times, been obsequious to the point of embarrassment. A report on Cuba's "thin, healthy church," for instance, published in the World Council of Churches' *One World* magazine, related the writer's arrival at Matanzas Evangelical Seminary and his finding no one there. The professors and students were harvesting tomatoes on a state farm. "For us the tomato harvest became a symbol of evangelical action," the writer joyfully gushed, "of state-church collaboration, of the church side by side with the working people."[22]

Friendship Press, the National Council of Churches' publishing house, has treated Cuba the same way in its *People and Systems* study guide on other countries. Author Mary Lou Suhor suggested Fidel Castro is a hero; that the revolution freed the Cuban people and Castro gave them economic and social justice. One example and the reader can surmise the rest.[23]

After the Cuban revolution, Suhor wrote: "A Marxist analysis is (was) applied, with emphasis on the role of the working class. Agrarian reform is ordered to break up the hugh latifundios, and land so expropriated is turned over to the peasants. Then Law Number 135 lowers all rents by 50 percent. The revolutionary government declares that ultimately all social services—education, health care, hospitalization, sports facilities, transportation and telephones—will be free or virtually free. Later on the leaders are to call that socialism. The poor people call it great."[24]

CUBAN REALITY

In contrast with the National Council's positive view of Cuba are the facts. Cuba has one of the world's more repressive regimes. Block committees spy on their neighbors and report any suspicious meetings, the reading of forbidden books, listening to forbidden American radio broadcasts. Children are taught to inform on their parents. Worst of all, Castro sends his young people, especially black young people, to fight in wars of "liberation" for the Soviet Union, most notably in Angola and Nicaragua. In other words, he sells his own people in order to insure Soviet financial support for his system.

Another tool for financing Cuba's disastrous economy is drug smuggling. The federal government has "strong evidence," President Reagan said in 1983, "that high-level Cuban government officials have been involved in smuggling drugs into the United States." The drug smuggling charges were not voiced lightly. Evidence was gathered during five Congressional hearings and via reports by the Departments of State, Justice, and the Drug Enforcement Administration.[25]

Not only is the Cuban government "directly involved in the production and trafficking of narcotics with the goal of promoting addiction, violent crime, corruption, and obtaining hard currency," it also uses the money to "finance and promote terrorism throughout the Americas."[26] The federal government later charged that the government of Nicaragua is—in cooperation with Cuba—also smuggling drugs.[27]

Ironically, the Christians who spoke so highly of Cuba during their 1984 seminar were speaking of a country where religious believers are persecuted. Those who practice religion are excluded from the Communist Party and thus from positions in the government and military. They also face discrimination in employment, housing, and schools. All the Catholic schools have been closed, and the church is forbidden to educate its young people. Christmas has been repressed, and even the "smallest of Christmas trees is looked upon as counter-revolutionary." People have been sent to prison for translating Scriptures for friends, and prisoners have been beaten for reading the Bible.[28]

Voting with your feet has been so common in Cuba that over one million have left the island, more than 10 percent of the population. About two hundred thousand more have tried to emigrate even though those who apply often suffer persecution: for example, losing their jobs, their ration cards, and their housing, and having their children barred from school. There are at least one thousand political prisoners, some of whom have been in jail since 1959. These jails are not simply dungeons for dissenters; torture and arbitrary murder are employed for even minor offenders.[29] Solitary confinement and starvation are also used to break prisoners, and psychiatric hospitals are common tools, as they are in the Soviet Union.

DE SOSO'S ORDEAL

Eugenio de Soso, a former journalist, is a living example of what can happen to Cubans who resist the power of the state. He was jailed in

1960 in the Combinado del Este Prison in the province of Havana. In 1977 he was suddenly taken to State Security headquarters in Villa Marista. There he was interrogated regarding information he supposedly passed to the "counterrevolutionary" exiles in 1963. Soso said that his jailers told him he would be shot; they kept him naked and isolated in a totally dark cell and slipped hallucinogenic drugs in his food (he found a partially dissolved capsule and stopped eating). One of their favorite techniques was to put him in a completely soundless room for a long period of time, then subject him to extremely loud noise.[30]

After various other tortures, he was taken to the National Psychiatric Hospital, the Carbo-Serba Ward, which he referred to as the Chamber of Horrors. There were about eighty men in the ward, he said, all violently disturbed. "The smell of urine and excrement was sickening." One night a team of four men entered the ward, and six patients were grabbed and rubber pieces stuffed in their mouths. They were thrown to the floor, and electrodes were applied to both sides of their heads and electric shock given. Six more men were captured, and the same thing was done to them. Soso had the shocks applied to his testicles instead.[31]

Several boys were brought into the ward one day, the oldest not more than sixteen. They had been caught writing antigovernment graffiti on walls. Before the first day was over, all of the boys had been gang-raped by more than thirty patients. "To this day," Soso wrote, "I can hear their cries for help and see their bloody bodies as I stood by in impotent rage. Not a single staff member intervened. This nightmare, this terrible episode, lasted for five months. It took place, I repeat, in 1977, not at the beginning, but in the 18th year of the revolutionary government of Cuba."[32]

China has been another revolutionary society which the Religious Left has traditionally glorified (until it introduced capitalism back into its economic life), and it has persecuted Christians with greater vigor than Cuba. Eugene Stockwell, director of the National Council's Division of Overseas Ministries, said in 1979 that his visit to China had not led him to abandon his Christian faith but forced him to ask himself "whether Christian nations can provide nothing better than injustice while an atheist nation struggles mightily to secure a fair modicum of justice."[33]

Stockwell must have a unique definition for justice. Mao Tse-tung expelled all missionaries after he took power in 1949 and forced the Protestants to dissolve their separate denominations and unite over the Three-Self Patriotic Movement. The union was designed to separate the churches from their partner churches in Europe and America. The Catholics were forced to break their ties with the Vatican in 1957. Then came the Cultural Revolution of the sixties and seventies. All religious organizations were subsequently forbidden, and thousands of Christians were sent to labor camps. Many were executed.

THE NATIONAL COUNCIL EXTOLS CHINA

Nonetheless, the National Council of Churches published a 1977 study guide on China which made the Marxist-Leninist government look like its savior. The writer's hero was obviously Mao, and the whole book is a paean to him and to China's version of Marxism. The writers even extol the Cultural Revolution, which the West now knows was a destructive nightmare for the Chinese people.

"China's Communist revolution has propelled a backward, poverty-stricken, virtually medieval society into the modern world," the booklet gushed. "It has brought about the end of such feudal traditions as ancestor worship, arranged marriages and the foot-binding of women. Starvation, epidemic disease, drug addiction, prostitution and illiteracy have been eliminated." The writer attributed several more exemplary virtues to the "Chinese Communists" before declaring that "serving the people" is their "dominant social value."[34]

Some of those claims may be true. China no longer allows women's feet to be bound, and there is probably less starvation and epidemic disease. But that does not compensate the millions of Chinese who have been murdered by the government in Peking through the years, nor does it compensate the Tibetans whose homeland and traditions have been destroyed by the Chinese as well as hundreds of thousands of their people. Nor does it compensate the Christians who are persecuted. Oddly enough, the booklet does not mention that China's Christians are persecuted. "The Chinese official view of religion today is one of supreme disregard." Going even further, it hints that Marxists-Leninists are the real Christians. It quotes the Reverend Hosea Williams: "Is it possible that Christianity is too important to be left in the hands of today's so-called Christians?"[35]

CHINA AND CHRISTIANITY

In the late seventies, when Stockwell and the National Council was busiest extolling Chinese justice, the persecution of Christians in China was at a modern all-time high. It reached new levels of intensity in 1983. Over three hundred and forty Christians were arrested (including Catholic priests) and two Bible couriers were killed. Government officials have also used torture to gain information about the activities and identities of other Christians. The Sixth Session of the National People's Council of China in September 1983 created six new categories of capital punishment offenses. One was for individuals who use "feudalistic superstitions" (religion) to evoke antigovernment sentiments—a law created specifically to punish Chinese house-Christians.[36]

House-Christians meet in homes to avoid government regulations, monitoring, and Chinese efforts to stifle evangelism. One warrant against a house-church Christian claimed the evangelist "deceived" four hundred people into converting to Christianity and also "disturbed the social order" by organizing a rally at a sports field.[37]

Roman Catholics also have a difficult time. Priests who are loyal to the underground church are forced to "roam the countryside" offering clandestine Masses. In 1983-1984 dozens of these priests, and several bishops, were jailed, including Bishop Joseph Fan Xuevan. He was sentenced to ten years in prison for communicating with the Pope. Catholic bishop Peter Fan and his vicar general, the Rev. Huo Pin Chang, were reportedly sentenced to ten years in prison for secretly ordaining priests and communicating with the Vatican.[38]

According to the Chinese Church Research Center in Hong Kong, there are currently an estimated total of thirty million Christians in China, none of whom has been helped by the silence of the American church regarding their persecution.

As this book goes to press, the Chinese government is reportedly easing its persecution and allowing more freedom of religion. Roman Catholic bishop Ignatius Gong Pinmei was paroled in July 1985 after thirty years in prison, and the Chinese government did not require him to denounce the Pope. Groups of Chinese Catholics have also been allowed to meet with Catholic authorities in Hong Kong, and the government has allowed bishops to be ordained who are not members of the officially sanctioned church organization, the Catholic Patriotic Association. Protestants have also been allowed to invite American evangelicals to speak in Chinese churches.

On the other hand, the government has made it clear that although they want aid in social action projects, the money sent to China (by Protestant groups such as the National Council of Churches) for such programs cannot be used to support churches or make converts.

THE REASON WHY

It is difficult to understand how the Religious Left could make positive statements about totalitarian systems like China and ignore the many abuses. It would seem that reasonable people, raised in freedom themselves, would be horrified by the oppression and religious persecution. But the late Arthur Koestler, former Communist and author of *A Darkness at Noon*, offered an explanation: "Faith is not acquired by reasoning. Reason may defend an act of faith—but only after the act has been committed."[39]

Koestler, then, would probably explain the glorification of Marx-ist-Leninist societies by American Christians as their worship at a new shrine. Christians are an idealistic people who have always concentrated on humanity's plight and its need for salvation. This is as it should be. But the same altruistic state of mind which creates compassion and commitment also creates a vulnerability to utopian schemes, the quintessence of which is Marxism. Utopianism is based on the visionary, the possibility that society can be perfected through a system. Marxism reflects that vision as well as a system in which it can allegedly be brought to fruition. Flaws in both systems are overlooked because the belief is based in faith, and is therefore not subject to logical examination.

The attraction seems even more natural when each creed's psychological attitudes are examined. Koestler points out that "There is little difference between a revolutionary and a traditionalist faith." He argues that all true faith is uncompromising, radical, and purist; "hence the true traditionalist is always a revolutionary zealot in conflict with pharisaian society . . . thus all true faith involves a revolt against the believer's social environment. . . ." Devotion to utopia (which can be viewed as the Kingdom of God) and revolt against a "polluted" society, he said, are the two poles of all militant creeds.[40]

Christianity certainly fits Koestler's description of a militant creed. It is uncompromising, radical, and purist. It is in revolt against the values of this world. But it offers no solutions for the problems of this life outside of faith and spiritual values. Seen in this light, it is not difficult to understand why Christians, once they abandon the substance of their traditional faith, would seek a new one which also is "in conflict with pharisaian society," but which offers the added bonus of societal solutions.

Marxism even resembles Christianity in its doctrinal creed. According to author Klaus Bockmuehl, it is a "heretical" form of Christianity. Bockmuehl points out that Marxism has a creation doctrine (historical processes as creator) and original sin (division of labor). Marxism provides a doctrine of salvation in its belief of the proletariat. It also has a doctrine of the church which manifests itself as the Communist Party.[41]

Faith in this utopianism, Christianity's doppelganger, is so deeply ingrained in the Religious Left that facts, observed firsthand, are not accepted. It is obviously possible for the faithful to observe persecution of Christians in Cuba or China and still not accept what they have seen. Paul Hollander, writing of modern American intellectuals, asked, "How can sensitivity to social injustice and indignation over the abuses of political power so abruptly give way to the cheerful acceptance, or denial, of comparable flaws in other social systems?"

He answered: ". . . intellectuals, like most other people, use double standards and . . . the direction of their moral indignation and compassion is set and guided by their ideologies and partisan commitments."[42] This could just as easily been said of the Religious Left.

Malcolm Muggeridge documented this will to believe in his sardonic observation of visitors to the U.S.S.R. during the 1930s. "They were unquestionably one of the wonders of the age," he wrote, "and I shall treasure . . . the spectacle of them travelling with radiant optimism through a famished countryside, wandering in happy bands about squalid overcrowded towns, listening with unshakable faith to the fatuous patter of carefully trained and indoctrinated guides, repeating like schoolchildren a multiplication table, the bogus statistics and mindless slogans endlessly intoned to them. . . ."[43]

". . . earnest clergymen who walked reverently through anti-God museums and reverently turned the pages of atheistic literature, earnest pacifists who watched delightedly tanks rattle across the Red Square and bombing planes darken the sky, earnest town-planning specialists who stood outside overcrowded ramshackle tenements and muttered 'If only we had something like this in England!'"[44]

Hollander points out that even when the partisan understand what they see, they invariably make excuses for the facts. Simone de Beauvoir defended the use of informers in China by stating they were necessary because "counterrevolutionary" activities included "arson, the sabotage of bridges and dikes, and assassinations."[45] Of course, most people in Marxist-Leninist societies who are victimized by an informer are not saboteurs, but have simply made the wrong remark to the wrong person about the wrong thing.

AMERICA THE GUILTY

As has been noted, the Religious Left has coupled its promotion of Marxist-Leninist societies with attacks on the United States. This is not surprising. Those who believe in the utopian society naturally feel enmity toward societies which refuse to acknowledge its superiority or change their policies in order to reach its goals. And since belief in utopia is illogical, attacks on its "enemies" are skewed and emotional. The technique most often used is to take a genuine problem and blow it completely out of proportion, ignoring the fact that most of the rest of the world has the same fault to a greater (or lesser) degree and overlooking any potential for reform. This method is designed (probably unconsciously) to produce guilt and dissatisfaction with democratic capitalism.

These pietistic attacks are so vicious that not only have they completely misrepresented America and its institutions, they have even alienated non-Christians. Paul Gottfried, editor of *Continuity*, has charged that the constant denunciation has heightened Jewish distrust of Christianity. "Guilt-ridden self doubt which organized Christianity shows," he wrote, "may have deepened Jewish mistrust of Christians. If Christians have been as wicked as the National Council of Churches would have us believe, then why should non-Christians trust them?"[46]

It is difficult to be tolerant of these sorts of attack because they are, among other things, so sanctimonious. The rhetoric is ostensibly based on the speaker's religious beliefs, and is sometimes passed off as being "prophetic." Using this concept is egotistical at best. Prophesy is traditionally considered a message from God delivered through human beings. Staffers at Church World Service offered an explanation of the prophetic point of view when they wrote: "American Christians are awakening to the fact that God is bigger than any state and will stand in judgment against any and all states or national leaders. It is God who bids us cease our idolatry of any state and restore the creation to justice and righteousness."[47]

Perhaps the Religious Left has misunderstood this concept because it has also misjudged the sovereignty of God. Instead of simply acknowledging that God judges all nations, the Religious Left has taken it to mean they should judge nations for Him. Unfortunately, when the Religious Left mentions ceasing idolatry and restoring righteousness, it is always the United States to whom it refers.

A perfect example of this guilt-inducing technique is an article by Peggy Billings, the associate general secretary of the United Methodist General Board of Global Ministries. Billings asked her readers, "Isn't it better to lance the boil and let the poison out? Let the descendants of the settler people of England and Europe face up to the fact that we took most of the land from its original peoples, that we built a powerful economy on the unpaid labor of African slaves and the indentured servitude of the refuse of England's jails, that we have started wars and overturned governments not to preserve liberty but to preserve markets, that a strong strain of fascism, American style, almost won out in Watergate."[48]

THE WORLD COUNCIL AND CHRISTIAN PERSECUTION

As distorted and misleading as this rhetoric is, it is still not actual lying. The World Council of Churches, on the other hand, seems unable to tell the truth about what they see during their official visits to totalitarian societies. Ethiopian Aradom Tedla (the same man who unsuccessfully petitioned Phillip Potter to help him obtain the release of the patriarch of the Ethiopian Coptic Church) said in 1984 that after the Marxists took power in his country many World Council executives came to visit. None of them, Tedla said, seemed interested in the fate of dozens of Ethiopian Christians and Coptic bishops who had disappeared into the prison system—or simply disappeared. Instead, they seemed content to be feted by government officials; and none of them returned to the West demanding that the regime stop its persecution.[49]

Similar testimony has been given by Jonas Savambi. Savambi is head of the anti-Marxist-Leninist rebels in Angola. He has charged that World Council representative John Fisher visited Angola at the end of 1976 and reported that everything was going very well for the church. "We were stunned," Savambi said, "because at the same time cries were coming to us all over the country—from Protestants as well as Catholics—that the MPLA (the Marxist-Leninist government party) was destroying everything that had anything to do with the Church![50]

"At the same time Fisher did his report, the MPLA was in the process of transforming churches into military barracks and warehouses all over the country, but Fisher said that everything was going smoothly, and that the MPLA was helping the churches, guaranteeing the freedom of religion—and that is when we knew that he was simply lying. His report was a premeditated lie, and it shocked us that a man who was working for the Church, would do this thing because he was not misinformed—he did it deliberately to help the MPLA. . . . The MPLA's harassment of religion is a deliberate and systematic policy."[51]

It is a tragedy that the World Council aids a nation's oppressor, but it is not surprising. The Council no longer mentions democracy. It speaks of participation, a word sometimes used by Third-World dictators to describe their system. It is especially tragic because for more than a decade after its formation the World Council viewed democracy as "the responsible society." At the founding assembly the World Council adopted a statement which defined the "responsible society" as a place where the ruling authorities are responsible to God and their people.

"Moving Toward Participation," however, the issue paper prepared by World Council staff for the 1983 Vancouver Assembly, moves very far away from the original concept of democracy. It ignores the fact that genuine participation means the right of people to freely choose government officials. Participation now means "a determined effort to promote self-reliance and an economic policy aimed at social justice, as in China. . . ."[52]

The concept of participation was probably created as a concession to the Eastern European and the Third-World governments of churches that were admitted to the Council in the sixties. The World Council as a whole apparently believed that if those churches were admitted, they would also gain an influence over their governments. It has had the opposite effect. The Eastern Bloc and Third-World governments have seduced the World Council into making the changes. Some of this can be attributed to the World Council's reluctance to anger member churches and risk their withdrawing from the Council. Much of it, however, stems from the conviction that Marxist-Leninist societies are superior to those which practice free enterprise.

One of the changes which this attitude has produced is the World Council's refusal to publicly support persecuted Christians in Marxist-Leninist countries. Council officials claim they often speak for the persecuted with "silent diplomacy," in an effort to spare dissidents further harassment. That statement seems to be a rationalization. The Council has no compunction in speaking out for political dissidents (by name) in South Africa or South Korea. Religious dissidents themselves, especially in the Soviet Union, have said that publicity in democratic countries helps them because they are then too well-known to jail or murder.

AUTHENTIC MARXISM

Ironically, if it is Marxist goals—i.e., economic security and political justice for all—which attract church bureaucrats in places like Ethiopia, then they are attracted to an idea whose time has never come despite any claims to the contrary. Karl Marx envisioned working Marxism as a system not only linked to democracy, but one which would eventually make all government obsolete: the state, he said, would (and should) "wither" away. Instead of a withered state, however, Marxism has become the almighty state. Instead of political justice for all, there is little justice for anyone.[53]

Marx wanted a "society in which the full and free development of every individual forms the ruling principle," a society in which "the full and free development of each is the condition for the free development of all," a society that seeks for its members "the completely unrestricted development and exercise of their physical and mental faculties." These things were more important than the material standard of living.[54]

Friedrich Engels, in his introduction to Marx's *The Civil War in France*, explains that the Paris Commune, an early experiment in communism, was what Marx believed the "dictatorship of the proletariat" should emulate. According to Marx, the Commune practiced:[55]

• Universal suffrage—voting for its government;[56]

- An open society—a government which was open for inspection;[57]

- Freedom of speech and religion and separation of church and state.

Contrary to popular perception, Marx did not believe in forcibly abolishing religion. He merely thought that religion would also wither away in the new society. He did loathe religion in general and Christianity in particular, but he did not advocate its suppression.[58]

- The Commune also practiced a nonmilitaristic viewpoint.[59]

Marx said the social legislation of the Commune "could but betoken the tendency of a government of the people, by the people."[60] (Since Abraham Lincoln's famous "Gettysburg Address" preceded Marx's writing on this subject, we must assume Marx was paraphrasing.)

To be sure, Marx the man was tyrannical in all his dealings and never renounced violence in service of the revolution. However, the revolution's ultimate goals were made perfectly clear. In contrast, not one allegedly Marxist country has instituted Marx's vision of ideal communism—which includes joint ownership of the means of production and a classless society.

THE USE OF ERSATZ MARXISM

Most governments which allegedly practice Marxist theory have instead based their economic life on the feudal system. Instead of joint ownership of the means of production, the state owns the means of production: a large part of the population works for very little of anything and a small part, government officials, who control the property and the profits, benefit. Marxism has become the ideological facade for imperialistic ambition (Marxism-Leninism) and for practicing totalitarianism.

The original and best example of this vicious hypocrisy, and its inevitable result, is the Soviet Union. The Menshevik and Bolshevik parties (the former deposed the Czar and were governing Russia before the latter seized power) undoubtedly had many members who genuinely wanted to change Imperial Russia for the benefit of its oppressed people. However, Bolshevik Vladimir Lenin, the first leader of the revolutionary Soviet Union, not only twisted Marxism into a force which insists on instigating violent revolutionary change throughout the world; he also created the present Soviet ruling class: the Nomenklatura.

NOMENKLATURA

This small class of people, numbering about three million including family members, is about 1.5 percent of the Soviet population. It consists of select members of the Soviet bureaucracy, who not only rule the country but are privileged to shop in special stores (which actually have good and plentiful products), own nice apartments and country homes, and travel abroad—things not dreamed of by the remainder of the Soviet population. Becoming a member of the Nomenklatura entitles a Soviet citizen in live in luxury the rest of his or her life and, most importantly, to share the power.[61]

Noted Russian historian Michael Voslensky, who was banished from the Soviet Union in 1977, argues that the Nomenklatura is extremely dangerous because of its extraordinary paranoia concerning the West. The very fact that the West enjoys a high standard of living while the Soviet government cannot even provide a decent standard of living for its people is a constant threat. The Nomenklatura is also "terrified" of what will happen when its citizens, whom it contains only by constant intimidation, "tire of living in fear." The new Soviet rulers, Voslensky believes, will only be able to rest easy when they control the world or have destroyed the telling contrast.[62]

If Voslensky is correct, there is almost no hope that the Soviet government will ever evolve into a less threatening entity because there is almost no hope that the gasping Soviet economy will improve. The Soviets, as well as every Marxist-Leninist society which apes them, have trapped themselves. The very process that grants the Nomenklatura its power strangles the Soviet economy. In order that this new class be able to spread the power among themselves, every head-of-household in the Nomenklatura has a position with the state. In that position the bureaucrat makes decisions. It is his (in the U.S.S.R., the great majority of bureaucrats are men) function and his power base. Even the smallest economic decision—the price of products, the number to be produced, where they are to be sent—has to go through many offices. Economic decisions are subsequently glacially slow and unable to respond to changes in need or demand.

For example, if the deputy commissar in the Ukraine needs to switch a trainload of fertilizer from one place to another he must obtain permission from Moscow, and it is possible (and common in the Soviet Union) to wait indefinitely for permission . . . until the harvest is ruined.[63] Efficiency also falls by the wayside with this system. Workers do not care what they produce, or how much they produce, because they are not benefiting from their production.

THE ECONOMIC FAILURE OF ERSATZ MARXISM

The figures speak for themselves. Gross national product for the Soviet Union was only $1.2 billion in 1978, as compared to $2.1 billion for the United States. The per capita income for Soviet citizens was only $4,800. At the end of the 1970s, the living standard for the average Soviet was estimated at approximately the same as the American worker at the beginning of the 1920s. Because urban housing did not keep pace with the movement to the cities, the Soviets had "the poorest living accommodations of any industrialized nation, with per capita floor space only about 72 square feet (1,200 in America)." Only one Soviet in forty-six owned a car.[64]

Although the Soviet Union once had twice as much land under cultivation as any other nation, "including some of the best on earth in the Ukraine, and a relatively low population density, her import demands, sometimes 15 million tons of grain a year, sometimes 30 million tons, placed an increasing burden on the world's available food surpluses."[65]

Eastern-bloc countries patterned their economic and social systems after the Soviet system and have consequently had the same results. It is regrettable that most who are tempted to experiment with Marxism-Leninism will miss the chance to discuss it with its victims. When people behind the Iron Curtain are asked what they think about their system, and they are able to answer freely, they express deep dislike. This attitude was exemplified by the Pole who said, "When I graduated from university in 1954 I really believed in Communism. They said, 'Work hard and every year things will get better and better.' And we worked hard, but every year things got worse and worse. They always lied to us and now I don't believe a word they say."[66]

The Eastern Bloc is not the only area economically ruined by Marxism-Leninism. Africa is a prime example of the devastation caused by governments which believe the "dictatorship of the proletariat" and the dictatorship of the state are the same thing. In 1962 the African continent fed itself. During the next twenty years, however, in countries in which "people's revolutions" were victorious, per-capita food production declined. Although today Africa holds only 15 percent of the undeveloped world's population, it receives 60 percent of world food aid.[67]

During the reign of Emperor Haile Selassie, Ethiopian food production grew at an annual rate of about 3 percent, keeping pace with population growth. After Selassie was deposed in 1974 (he died mysteriously eleven months later) Ethiopia's new government nationalized most land and turned commercial farms into state farms. As soon as they did, food production began to drop. The farms—run by students—comprise about 6 percent of Ethiopian farmland, produce less than 5 percent of all farm produce, but consume 90 percent of all agricultural spending. The government aggravated the problem by keeping food prices as much as 70 percent below world standards to keep its urban population and army—which takes up nearly half the national budget—well fed. At the same time it raised the price of fertilizers and seed above the amount small farmers could afford.[68]

As a result of these collective blows, farmers were forced off the land into the cities or into desperate straits.[69] Then the drought hit. Despite everything, the rural population might have escaped famine if the stored food reserves had not been seized "in the name of collectivization."

Tragically, Western society has probably not heard the last of famine in Ethiopia. The government planned—as of 1985—to collectivize half of all its country's farmland by the next decade.[70] Most of these facts have not been acknowledged publicly by Church World Service or other mainline church bureaucracies.

The best testimony concerning the failure of pseudo-Marxist economics is China's turn toward less centralized economic control. That turn has had some successes, the most important of which is the enormous increase in crop production. China is now a net exporter of grain, allowing average peasants—which are the most numerous class in China—to more than double their cash income.[71]

SUPPORT FOR LIBERATION

Not content to merely lend moral support to Marxist-Leninist governments and verbally attack the United States, the National and World Council of Churches and denominational agencies also back "liberation" groups. Moreover, they keep on supporting them even after their true natures are revealed, then go still further and denounce the authentic freedom-fighters that inevitably organize to fight the oppressive regime.

One example is Southern Africa. The church supported the Marxist-Leninists who were attempting to seize power in Angola. When they won, the United Methodist Board of Church and Society passed a resolution which, among other things, urged the United States government to extend full and immediate recognition—as if the Angolan people had won a victory. But of course they had not. In fact, Angola was probably less free than any time in its history. Portugal abdicated its power in Angola in 1975 and left it to three groups which had fought for independence. Those groups were the Soviet-backed Popular Movement for the Independence of Angola (MPLA), the anticolonial National Front for the Liberation of Angola (FNLA) and the democratically inclined Union for the Independence of Angola (UNITA).

The Popular Movement expelled the other two groups and emerged victorious. They had received help from massive Soviet financial aid, arms, and an army of about thirty-five thousand Cuban military "advisors." The United States did nothing to stop the process, but voted against giving any aid to the National Front and UNITA. Now Angola suffers under a totalitarian government which, sustained by a Cuban army, East German-operated secret police, and Soviet arms, keeps its people in an iron grip. They suffer all the usual abuses including disappearances, torture, and a disastrous economy. Meanwhile, UNITA, which is widely supported among the Angolan people, is doing its best to overthrow the regime.

The United Methodist Global Ministries magazine, however, did not blame the Angolan government for hunger. It blamed South Africa and UNITA. "Compounding the problem are actions taken by UNITA . . ." it said.[72]

AN INSTRUCTIVE EXPERIENCE

Koestler's explanation of his turn to, and away from, communism is instructive and sheds some light on why American Christians manage to close their eyes to so much in Angola and elsewhere. He writes that he was ripe for conversion because he lived in a "disintegrating society [Europe] thirsting for faith," and his conversion was one of the more pleasant experiences of his life. Nothing can disturb a convert's inner peace and serenity, he wrote, because the new faith answers every question and settles all doubts and conflicts. As the "only righteous men in a crooked world, we were happy."[73]

The only thing Koestler feared thereafter, he wrote, was losing the faith that had become so comforting—an experience which he attributes to all converted Marxists and his explanation for why only a few have recanted. Koestler believed so deeply that he even propagandized (twisted the facts) for communism at a European newspaper, the explanation being that he had learned to distrust facts and regarded the world around him through the light of dialectic interpretation. He believed that the Party was infallible.

Although he did not immediately renounce the Party after his visit to the Soviet Union in 1933, Koestler attributes his awakening to what he saw on that tour. He was assigned to write a book titled *The Soviet Land Through Bourgeois Eyes*, a supposed account of a skeptic who is convinced of the goodness of communism after a tour of the U.S.S.R.

during its "five year plan." Research for the book (which was eventually published under another title) allowed him to travel throughout the U.S.S.R. without guides or restrictions and to receive enough pay to take care of all expenses.

The trip backfired for the Soviets because Koestler witnessed the famine in the Ukraine (which was deliberately induced by the Soviet government) and the millions who died as a result. He saw the extreme poverty, the uniform oppression, the lies that the Soviet government told about the countries of the West, the wholesale liquidation of opposition.

After being imprisoned in Spain during the Spanish Civil War, Koestler, already unconsciously ready to learn from experience, renounced the faith that had meant so much to him. He saw, he said, that "man is a reality, mankind an abstraction." He saw that men cannot be treated as "units in operations of political arithmetic . . . that the end justifies the means only within very narrow limits; that ethics is not a function of social utility, and charity not a petty bourgeois sentiment but the gravitational force which keeps civilization in its orbit.[74]

". . . every one of these trivial statements was incompatible with the Communist faith which I held . . . they deal in slogans as bootleggers deal in faked spirits; and the more innocent the customer, the more easily he becomes a victim of the ideological hooch sold under the trademark of Peace, Democracy, Progress or what you will."[75]

Author Susan Sontag made a similar about-face in 1982 when she declared that American leftists have deliberately overlooked the murderousness of Marxist-Leninist regimes. Communism is "fascism with a human face," she said.[76]

Marxism. Fascism. Democracy. What does it all mean? It means—as numerous philosophers through the ages have pointed out—that ideas are the germ of action. Societies are founded on ideas; people base their conduct on ideas and ideals; the whole of Western civilization is based on the Judeo-Christian ethic and the democratic political ideas of ancient Greece. The Western belief in human rights is a direct descendant of the Biblical assertion that men and women were fashioned in the image of God. The Gulag was invented by people who believe the idea that there is no God but themselves. Systems do not invent themselves. People invent systems which are based on their values.

When Christians propagandize for Marxist-Leninist regimes and attack democracy, things happen. It influences some to believe those regimes are beneficial. It undermines resistance to Christianity's worst enemy. It undermines America's determination to promote freedom at home and abroad. It destroys the credibility of the church as Christ's shepherd on earth.

Most of all, it stains the soul of Christians who overlook the murderousness of Marxist-Leninist regimes to justify their politics.

The next church bureaucrat who travels to Cuba, or Albania, or the U.S.S.R., should be required to read what Marx actually said. He wrote a poem while at the University of Berlin which eerily predicted the use totalitarians would make of his theories:

"Then I will wander godlike and victorious,
Through the ruins of the world . . ."[77]

The National Council of Churches and the Soviet Union

The photographs, taken June 18, 1984, tell the story better than an article, more poignantly than an essay. The religious dissidents are unfolding their banners over the balcony rails of an Evangelical Christian Baptist church in Moscow, carefully watching to see that their signs are visible to the congregation below. But many of the National Council of Church delegates are ignoring the demonstration.

Some of the Americans are looking up, expressionless; most are looking at nothing at all. Their faces seem to be saying this is odd, or this is boring, or this isn't happening. A few seem intent and questioning. The banner reads, "Number of Prisoners for the Work of the Gospel Is Constantly Increasing and Reaches 200 Persons Now."[1]

Immediately after the photographs were taken, KGB agents consulted with church deacons who rushed to the balcony and threw the Evangelical Christian Baptists to the floor, then hustled many of them out of the church. After a second banner was unfurled, men once again rushed to the balcony and violently dragged the demonstrators away.[2]

Although NCC tour leader Bruce Rigdon was at the lecture when the first banner was unfurled, he ignored the message. Other American delegates took turns speaking from the pulpit, but not one delegate mentioned the banner, offered a prayer for their fellow Christians, or mentioned a second sign which read, "Pray for Persecuted Church in Our Country."[3]

After the service, as a handful of independent delegates were questioning one lone stubborn dissident who had remained outside—despite frantic efforts by Soviet Intourist guides to end the conversation—tour coordinator John Lindner ordered the delegates away from the woman. According to some delegates, he complained that they were being impolite to their Soviet hosts.[4]

Lindner, on loan to the NCC from the Presbyterian Church, later told a news conference that he found it "disturbing to have worship

interrupted by any kind of group. . . . Just because people do something to grab media attention doesn't mean that's the best way to settle
things."[5]

Rigdon later commented that he believed that the dissidents "are
free. . . . I understand that in the United States a situation like this
would have been handled by the police."[6]

If you have seen the photographs, remember the man immediately
behind and to the right of the woman unfurling the banner? He is
Veniamin Naprienko, and he was sent to a Soviet labor camp because
he had the courage to tell the truth to the National Council of
Churches. Obviously, the situation was handled by the police.[7]

Naprienko and his wife, Natasha, members of a Moscow Baptist
congregation which is persecuted because it refuses to register with the
government, soon smuggled an explanation out of Russia concerning
their actions. It was subsequently quoted in a newsletter published by
emigré Georgi Vins. "We believed," the Naprienkos wrote, "that if we
did not speak out, we would be guilty before the Lord. We could not
remain silent. . . ."[8]

Evidently the National Council has no such compunction. The
NCC has not protested Naprienko's plight or the persecution of the
"Church of Silence" in the U.S.S.R. When asked about Naprienko's
arrest (occurring three weeks after the NCC delegation left the Soviet
Union) spokesmen for the Council said they thought Naprienko had
been arrested for another incident—therefore, it was not the National
Council's concern.

As sad as it is, it is not surprising that the National Council has not
commented on Naprienko's imprisonment. From the first round of
exchanges between the Russian Orthodox Church and the NCC in
1956, until the mid-1980s, there has been little from Council officials
but admiration for the state of religion in Soviet Russia. It has sent
dozens of delegations (many of whom have been NCC officials), who
have returned either extolling the Soviets or declaring that there is
little or no abuse of religious dissidents. Those statements have not
been, and are not, true. Not content to merely send delegations, the
NCC has also brought delegations from the U.S.S.R. to the United
States, and a majority of them have been used by their government for
propaganda purposes.

It is difficult to understand why the National Council behaves in
this manner, but it has certainly been damaging. At worst, it has
managed to convince some people that the Soviet government is
peace-loving and fairly tolerant of Christianity; at best it has caused
doubt that the persecution of Christians is as bad as religious dissidents
have said it is.

Further, because some delegates have claimed it is the United

States who forces the Soviets to behave badly, the real difference in Soviet and American behavior, and its implications, has been clouded. This is not a minor matter. Geopolitical ignorance is dangerous. Another way in which this clouding has been achieved is through the NCC's concealment of the true position of the Russian Orthodox Church. The National Council made a 1984 television documentary, in conjunction with NBC, which, in effect, denied the Russian church is captive to its government. This is an important point, as the Russian Orthodox Church makes many statements regarding arms control and Soviet foreign policy.

Perhaps most damaging, however, has been the NCC's lack of concern for Soviet Christians. By ignoring their persecution, they have helped isolate them. By isolating them, those Christians, many of whom are courageous people, have been denied the sympathy of the outside world and the help that would have come as a result. The Soviet government may not have stopped the persecution, but had the NCC been loudly outraged through the years, the Soviets might have lessened the degree of persecution. There is a lot of difference, for a dissident, between lack of freedom to worship and a labor camp in the Ural mountains.

Typical of the false or misleading statements made by NCC delegates (over the decades) were comments made by Lindner and Rigdon in 1984. "We discovered vital religious communities wherever we went, from Tallin to Taskent. We have heard of a couple of instances of new churches being built," Lindner said.[9]

Izvestia, the Soviets' official government newspaper, quoted Rigdon as saying the delegates had been "completely satisfied in their interest regarding the position of the churches." *Izvestia* continued, "During the press conference and in conversations, members of the delegation repeatedly stated that in their view the church in the USSR is not persecuted."[10]

SOVIET PERSECUTION OF CHRISTIANS

These statements are disgraceful. Besides the everyday persecution of Christians, who are denied good jobs and admittance to universities, besides even the labor camps—which many do survive—there have also been numerous instances of priests and church activists being "accidentally" killed. Moreover, Soviet soldiers have been sent to "psychiatric hospitals" merely for believing in God, an offense that is considered evidence of mental disturbance. Psychiatrists have told these "patients" that they will not be released until they renounce their faith, and stubborn believers are treated with drugs that turn them into vegetables.[11]

The very laws governing any kind of religious activity in the Soviet Union are of a persecutory nature. Churchmen and believers are forbidden to organize schools, teach classes, use the media, establish youth groups, or hold any meetings apart from worship. Churches may not have libraries or reading rooms, may not keep any kind of literature except prayer books and hymnals (literature directly needed for worship), may not conduct trips or pilgrimages, may not hold prayer or Bible study, and may not give charitable aid for sick or aged church members. Priests or clergymen may not perform any religious function outside the church except last rites, and must have permission from authorities to do so and may not act as clergymen in any church but their own. Clerical appointments to churches must also be approved by the state.

It is true that the official structure of the Russian Orthodox Church is still in existence, but it is tolerated only because the Soviets have found a way to use it as a tool of the state. The Soviet government finds it convenient to have "godly" spokesmen mouth the Soviet line; somewhat like a puppet and a puppet-master. It also finds the American religious pilgrimages, and unending "peace" meetings which they inevitably arrange for the delegates, extremely useful. The meetings are extensively covered by the Soviet press, and the propaganda value, for the Soviets, is substantial. Nevertheless, the National Council continues to maintain the church is not only thriving, but independent, and gives its predictable positions on "peace" and disarmament great weight.

This is true to such an extent that NCC officials and Orthodox churchmen now hold joint arms control meetings in Geneva. The meetings are held, according to NCC, to seal a common position on the moral imperatives of arms reductions. That ordinary Soviets, or those used as tools of Soviet propaganda, do not influence the Politburo is something that seems to escape notice.

NCC spokesmen not only deny the real state of religion in the U.S.S.R., but often choose sides between the two governments—and it is not the United States whom they support. NCC delegate Alan Geyer was asked at a Moscow press conference if Russian Orthodox churchmen could bring pressure on their government to return to arms negotiations. Geyer (a member of CAREE and a participant in the National Council's visit to the U.S.S.R. in 1984) said, "I think they'd (the U.S.S.R.) be happy if the talks resumed but there is a widespread feeling in the United States, which I share, that it is not the Soviet Union's fault."[12] Geyer, you will remember, was the principal consultant to the United Methodist bishops as they prepared their pastoral letter on nuclear arms.

(CAREE, Christians Associated for Relationships in Eastern Europe, is a sponsor-related organization to the National Council of Churches. It is also a child and partner of the Christian Peace Conference, an organization which the U.S. government believes is a Soviet front. This does not mean CAREE members are Soviet agents. They are generally well-meaning Christians who sincerely believe—contrary to all evidence—that they can make a difference in world geopolitics through displaying their sincere desire for peace to the average Russian citizen. However, the organization has been used by the Peace Conference to sponsor Marxist-Christian encounters[13] and for originating delegations to the Soviet Union, trips which are used by the Soviets to further their image as peacemaker.)

The sympathy for the Soviet perspective is so strong among NCC delegates that even when aware of tactics most people would consider persecution, they often find reasons to justify their hosts. After Soviet officials told a vice-president of the United Presbyterian Women (an NCC delegate) that Christians are not imprisoned in the Soviet Union because they were Christians, but because they had committed other offenses, she commented she was uncertain what the truth was but ". . . wondered what percentage of our prison population are members of Christian Churches and why it never occurred to me that Soviet Christians may break the law."[14]

BAPTISTS FIGHT—ORTHODOX PROTEST

If the 1984 NCC delegation had conducted a real investigation—or had been allowed to do so—they would have found that thousands of Baptist congregations (about one hundred thousand people) such as the one represented at the demonstration in the Moscow church, break the law by refusing to register with the government because to do so would invite the same sort of treatment accorded the Russian Orthodox: surveillance, inability to proselytize (it is against the law), the inability to teach religion to children under eighteen years of age and denial of the right to appoint their own clergy or for clergy to decide the content of their own sermons. Sometimes it means destruction.

Russian Orthodox Archbishop Feodosy, in a letter to the late Leonid Brezhnev, complained that government officials, among other things, refuse to allow registered Christian churches to make repairs on their buildings and refuse to allow some churches to meet at all. He also said officials persecute Christians who choose to be baptized, steal church inventory, refuse to allow the bishop to ordain priests (a tactic which the Archbishop referred to as "smothering diligence [which] dooms the Russian Orthodox Church to a slow death"), and persecute priests.[15]

The bishop cited a registered church in the Ukrainian Hlobyne

District of Poltava, which had one very small registered house of prayer. Because the mud walls were decaying, members decided to brick-face the building. After spending months begging for a permit, the faithful began the work. However, at midnight on July 31, 1971, when they were almost through with the building, the chairman of the village council appeared in the company of militiamen and twenty Komsomol members with crowbars and the house started to "shake from the strong blows. . . ."[16]

He recalled, the archbishop told Brezhnev, that the following morning, members of the Hlobyne religious congregation—older men, former front-line soldiers—sat in his office sobbing. "From the above, it is obvious that even the smallest, so to say, insignificant work—renovation of a rather ordinary peasant cottage in which the house of prayer is situated—requires of the faithful an enormous effort to overcome all the opposition and obstacles . . ." he wrote.[17]

CATHOLICS, UNIATES, PROTESTANTS

Brezhnev did not reply to the bishop's letter, and the bishop was probably not surprised. After all, the Soviets also persecute the Lithuanian Roman Catholics, Ukrainian Greek (Uniate) Catholics, Adventists-Reformists, Pentecostals, Jehovah's Witnesses, Mennonites, and the remnants of the True Orthodox Christians. Some of these religious bodies refuse to register, and some are simply forbidden to exist.

Outlawed since Russia formally absorbed the Ukraine after the Second World War, and forced to merge with the Russian Orthodox, the Uniate Catholic Church is a hotbed of defiant and unregistered religious activity—so much so that dozens of priests and believers have been sent to labor camps.[18]

The Soviets claim the church "voluntarily" liquidated itself in the late 1940s, an absurd allegation—the Uniates had a one thousand-year tradition and four million members in 1946. In 1974, Father Volodymyr Prokopiv led a delegation of Ukrainian Catholics to Moscow, where they presented to the government a petition calling for legalization of the church: the petition was ignored. But Ukrainians are stubborn. In 1982 five of them formed a regional Committee for the Rights of Believers and the Church, branches of an organization which has since sprung up all over the Soviet Union. Most of the founders are in labor camps.

The Lithuanian Catholic Church, to which 70 percent of all Lithuanians belong (about three million) is still legal, but is nevertheless persecuted. Its priests have also organized Committees for the Defense of Believers' Rights and are, predictably, in labor camps. A typical example is Father Sigitas Tamkevicus, who, besides organizing the committee, was accused of giving children religious instruction and organizing Christmas celebrations for children. The Lithuanians have responded to the persecution by sending dozens of petitions to Moscow, signed by thousands of believers, calling for more religious freedom.

LITHUANIANS PROTEST FOR PRIEST

A typical petition drive, launched in 1979, was signed by one hundred and forty-eight thousand people or 5 percent of the population. It called for the restoration of the Church of Mary, Queen of Peace in Klaipeda. The church has been used as a concert hall since 1960. Other petitions complain about the subordination of priests to the Soviet Council for Religious Affairs, about the shortage of priests due to the closing of seminaries, the shortage of religious literature, the official disruption of religious processions, the desecration of shrines, and the taunting of their children in school.

Another recent petition expresses support for Father Alfonsas Svarinskas, sentenced in 1983 to seven years' imprisonment and three years in internal exile for his part in organizing a believer's rights committee. Svarinskas was also accused of preaching anti-Soviet sermons, sermons in which he reportedly denounced the murder of priests, the burglarizing of churches, and the desecration of the sacraments by government agents.

In a 1983 letter to the investigator of Svarinskas' case, Soviet citizen (and exprisoner of conscience) Liudvikas Simutis offered an appeal for Svarinskas and, indirectly, a cry from the heart for all the persecuted. "Having been summoned to a hearing in connection with the case," he wrote, ". . . I hereby declare: I have known Father Alfonsas Svarinskas very well for a long time and associated with him in places of incarceration where inhumanly difficult conditions of life offer especially good opportunity to get to know a person. People who have suffered for long from hunger and exhaustion cannot hide even the least of their vices or virtues.[19]

". . . Love is the sole source of Father Svarinskas' energy and the driving force of his activity. . . . Father Svarinskas did only what most Lithuanian priests wanted to do but did not dare. In his sermons he spoke out loud and clear on those issues about which the priests and faithful in Lithuania spoke in whispers, about which most priests and believers would not speak from lack of courage or ability but about which they repeatedly asked him to speak up.[20]

". . . Strong in his faith, he almost never succumbed to elemental fear, but often worried that to keep quiet and do nothing would mean to acquiesce in criminal actions. He was afraid that silence would offend

God in those things where conscience demands not only that one speak out, but that one cry out at the top of his voice."[21]

The Chronicle of the Catholic Church in Lithuania, a *samizdat* (underground) publication, accuses the Soviets of worse than mere persecution: one of its issues charged them with the murder of Father Bronius Laurinavicius, a member of the Lithuanian Helsinki Watch Group. Laurinavicius had been attacked in the state press a few days before his death, the publication said, for "luring youth to church." The *Chronicle* claimed that on November 24, 1981 three or four witnesses saw men (who were believed to be KGB agents) seize Laurinavicius and push him under a passing truck. The testimony of doctors on the scene was included in the article.

Father Laurinavicius was the third Lithuanian priest to die under suspicious circumstances since 1980.

The Soviet attitude toward religion is mirrored in the policies of its satellite states throughout Eastern Europe. Father Jaroslav Duka, a member of a banned Dominican Order in Czechoslovakia, is a typical victim. He was sent to prison for saying Mass without state approval, copying religious texts, and attempting to revive the Dominican order.

TYPEWRITERS AND MUSIC BANNED

In Romania, typewriters must be registered because Romanians have used them to copy Christian literature and Bible passages. The U.S. Congress granted Romania most favored nation status in 1975 because, among other things, it had agreed to allow twenty thousand Bibles, supplied by Western churches, to be given to the Hungarian Reformed Church—only to later find that the Bibles had been immediately recycled into toilet tissue.[22]

Music is, apparently, also a threat to the Soviets. Two members of an underground Christian band (the only kind able to exist) were caught in 1984 and sentenced to two and a half years at hard labor. "The Trumpet Call" band members, Valeri Barinov and Sergei Timokhin, were sentenced only after spending eight months in psychiatric hospitals and prisons. Barinov and Timokhin may have had the last word, however. Their Christian rock opera, which they secretly recorded, was smuggled out of the U.S.S.R. and was performed in Europe in the summer of 1985.[23]

Although the persecution of apolitical Christians like Barinov and Timokhin seems unreasonable, it is not: it is an absolute necessity for the Soviet government. Marxists-Leninists work at eradicating religion because any belief in a higher authority is dangerous for them. They rightly believe that if totalitarianism is to succeed, there can be no higher authority than the state.

Psychiatrist Carl Jung understood this principle. Religions, he said, give mankind a "point of reference" outside itself, allowing humans to exercise judgment and the power of decision. Religion builds up a spiritual reserve and a different kind of reality. "If statistical reality is the only reality, then it is the sole authority . . . then the individual is bound to be a fraction of statistics and hence a function of the state.."[24]

Marx believed that religion would fade away when confronted with "scientific communism." Since it has not, other means have been employed to assist destiny.

HISTORICAL PERSECUTION

Lenin obviously understood the need to eradicate religious belief. Just a few days after he seized power, in 1917, widespread arrests of bishops and clergy began. Between 1918 and 1930 at least three hundred Orthodox bishops, forty thousand priests, tens of thousands of monks, and millions of lay Orthodox were either shot or sent to their deaths in prison camps.[25] Lenin also confiscated all church property and ruled that no person under eighteen could be instructed in the faith.

Additional legislation was passed in 1929 which restricted the number of churches to those the state was willing to register and banned any religious activity outside the building.

In the U.S.S.R., religious persecution tends to come in waves. In the 1920s thousands more church leaders, priests, nuns, and bishops were imprisoned, tortured, and shot. Patriarch Tikhon was interrogated by the Cheka-GPU (the forerunners of the modern KGB), then died under "suspicious circumstances."[26] In order to weaken the Russian Orthodox Church, the Communist government also encouraged a schismatic pro-Bolshevik group of clergy who called their group the "Living Church." It was probably the original version of Nicaragua's "people's church."

Under Stalin, thousands more churches were closed because the state refused them registration. When his famous purges began in the 1940s, many of the remaining priests and pastors disappeared to Siberia or were executed—to the point that there was scarcely a church left open. Stalin also took the opportunity to destroy religion in the Baltic "republics" by literally stuffing the labor camps with Lutherans from Latvia and Estonia. Never one to do things halfway, he also took the opportunity to liquidate the Eastern Rite Catholic Church in the Ukraine.[27]

During the Second World War, however, the fortunes of the Russian Orthodox Church took a dramatic upswing. Stalin was unprepared for hostilities and needed the church to develop patriotism. Some of the subsequent improvements, such as the installation of the Moscow Patriarchate and the central church administration, became permanent when Stalin realized that the church could be used for propaganda purposes—a realization which has served the Soviets to this day.

During this period an attempt was even made to woo back Russian emigrants. The patriarch assured the strayed that "the Russian Orthodox church, like a Mother, opens her loving arms and calls you, her children, back into her fold."[28]

A recent Russian *samizdat* sneered at this phase of Soviet history, revealing that those who returned "found that apart from the Mother Church they also had a Father Stalin, who thought a stay in concentration camp in Siberia or exile in Central Asia would do them a lot of good."[29]

When Nikita Khrushchev took power, the picture once again changed for the worse. Khrushchev led one of the most vicious antireligion campaigns since the 1930s, while denying it completely to the outside world. Hundreds of priests were sent to prison camps while the archbishops were mouthing Moscow's latest "peace line."

NCC CAMPAIGNS FOR SOVIETS

Nevertheless, despite the venomous treatment accorded Christians by the Soviets from the revolution on, most NCC delegates obviously did not understand the true state of religion in the U.S.S.R. before they left home—and the NCC made sure they did not and could not understand once they arrived. The NCC Committee on U.S.-U.S.S.R. Church Relations—of which Rigdon is chairman—distributed a booklet to delegates titled *Together on the Way,* a booklet filled with pro-Soviet apologia. It was also made clear to delegates that their main function was not to change the Soviets, but to change American attitudes toward the Soviet Union.

In one of the briefing books given to delegates, written by Alan Geyer, the trip's purpose was made explicit. "There is . . . no escaping the political, or 'pre-political,' role of our educational and religious institutions in equipping the American public with a sounder and more balanced understanding of the Soviet Union" in order to overcome "the extraordinary strength and resilience of anti-Soviet sentiment in this country."[30] Once the delegates arrived, the Soviet government's Intourist travel agency controlled the itinerary. Hot spots, of course, were excluded from the tour. There were no scheduled meetings with representatives of the unregistered churches, and the delegates were kept constantly busy with banquets, receptions, "peace meetings," and summit conferences with government spokesman Georgy Arbatov. Those who were interested in meetings with dissidents were discouraged.[31]

Unfortunately the tour, which was cosponsored by the Joint Peacemaking Program of the United Presbyterian Church, the Presbyterian Church of the United States, and the Presbyterian Bi-National Service Program, was just one of many planned for the coming years and only one of five planned for 1984-1985. Those included three delegations of Soviet churchmen visiting this country and several more NCC delegations visiting the U.S.S.R.

The Presbyterians (who were the most represented group on the June 1984 trip and the denomination which has been the largest contributor to the U.S.-U.S.S.R. committee) also sponsored a 1985 youth delegation to the Soviet Union. According to Presbyterian material, applicants had to "be able to show a commitment to peacemaking."

NCC BROADCASTS PROPAGANDA

Tours are not the only method used by the NCC to convince church members and the public at large that the Soviets are benign. In 1984 the NCC sponsored a television documentary which shamelessly distorted the religious situation in the Soviet Union. "The Church of the Russians" was first aired during the summer of 1984, just in time to enhance the publicity of the returning NCC delegation. It had nothing but praise for freedom of religion in Russia, mentioned no dissidents, and barely mentioned nonorthodox groups such as the independent Baptists.

The award-winning program featured a scenic travelogue, shots of beautiful churches and elaborate Orthodox services, infant baptisms, and interviews with church and government officials who insist the U.S.S.R. has an officially sanctioned growing church. It did not discuss the hundreds of Christians now in prisons for breaking the antireligious laws or the myriad ways in which the government suppresses belief and believers.

Typical comments from the film's host and commentator, Bruce Rigdon, and others, are as follows:

- "Without any announcements or declarations of policy from the Kremlin, the position of the Orthodox Church has improved dramatically, over the past several decades." (Rigdon)

- "You see the church minds her own business. The state does not interfere into church affairs and the church does not interfere into state affairs." (Peter Makartsev, vice-chairman of the (Soviet) Council on Religious Affairs)

- "Our discussions are absolutely free. There is absolutely no control over us . . . not in the preparation of our work, nor in our work, nor in our conversation. Such control cannot exist because the sphere of our work is clearly religious. It is quite apart from government concerns." (Alexei Buevsky, executive secretary, External Relations Department, Moscow Patriarchate)

- "I would tell you frankly that at the moment the peacemaking cause of the church just coincides with the foreign policy of our government. And we're glad. But all our peace activity is based on our Christian views." (Metropolitan Filaret, chairman, External Church Relations, Moscow Patriarchate)

- "We've discovered that it's impossible to talk for very long with leaders of the Russian Orthodox Church or with faithful members of the church without recognizing that one of their most fundamental and passionate concerns is that of peacemaking. How many times in the last few weeks have we heard bishops and metropolitans as well as crowds of the faithful who surrounded us wherever we went, quote to us that familiar phrase from the Gospels: 'Blessed are the peacemakers, for they shall be called the children of God.'" (Rigdon)

FACTS

Fact: as a result of official anger over the refusal of many Baptists to register, Soviet authorities in 1979 began a fresh campaign of religious persecution. The persecution gained such fresh impetus in 1984 that it was mentioned in the U.S. State Department's annual report on worldwide human rights. There are now an estimated four hundred-plus Christians in Soviet labor camps, two hundred of which are unregistered Baptists. This is up from the one hundred and forty-seven Christians who were in Soviet camps prior to 1979.[32]

There is a strong possibility these Christians will stay in prison twice as long as they were originally sentenced. During Yuri Andropov's short tenure, he initiated legislation which made it possible to resentence prisoners for performance of religious acts or even recitation of private prayers.

Further, the Soviet Union has rarely had as few active churches as it has today. Before the revolution there were 54,174 Orthodox churches and hundreds of monasteries, most of which were closed after the revolution. During the late forties there were still about twenty thousand open, but as many as ten thousand more were closed during the reign of Nikita Khrushchev. Very few have been opened since, elimination through attrition being a policy which was resumed during the tenure of Brezhnev and Andropov.[33]

According to statistics gathered by Keston College, a research institute which gathers data on religious liberty in the Eastern Bloc, there are now approximately six thousand and five hundred Orthodox churches open for worship in the Soviet Union. There are an estimated thirty-five to forty million Orthodox believers. Moscow itself, which once had one thousand and five hundred churches, now has less than fifty. Russia's second largest city, Leningrad, has ten. Further, there are only 5,994 registered priests in all the Soviet Union. There are approximately fourteen thousand and four hundred churches total for all denominations for a total Christian population of fifty-eight million: one church for every 3,973 believers.[34]

There are now only six monasteries and ten convents remaining open, down from sixty-nine before Khrushchev's purge of the churches—only two of which, Soviet expert Michael Bourdeaux points out, are actually on Russian soil. The other fourteen are in the non-Russian republics. There were several hundred before 1917.[35]

THE FUROV REPORT

Almost everything else stated in "The Church of the Russians" is equally false and can be proved so by a Soviet secret report on the Orthodox Church. The report, officially labeled "From the Records of the Council for Religious Affairs to the Members of the Central Committee of the Communist Party of the Soviet Union," was written by Vasily Furov, the deputy head of the Council on Religious Affairs, and was smuggled out of the Soviet Union in 1980. The council oversees all religious activities in the U.S.S.R.

The 1975 report was first published in Paris and then in the New York-based Religion in Communist Dominated Areas (RCDA) publication and Monastery Press, publishers of the Free Russian Orthodox Church Outside of Russia. It was predictably blasted by the Soviet press, but its authenticity had been confirmed by numerous experts on the Soviet Union and the Orthodox Church.

The Furov report proves that the price the Russian Orthodox Church pays for its survival is its use by the Soviet government as a propagandizing tool. Ergo, any negotiations conducted between the NCC and spokesmen for the Orthodox Church is, in truth, an exercise in manipulation. "The council controls the synod (the body that supposedly governs the Orthodox Church)," the report asserts. "The question of selection and appointment of its permanent members used to be, and still is, completely in the hands of the council; candidacy of special members is also determined upon previous agreement by appropriate officials of the council.

"All topics to be presented for discussion at the Synod are first submitted by Patriarch Pimen and the permanent members of the Synod to the executive committee of the council and its departments. . . . Furthermore, the Council approves the final 'Decision of the Holy Synod.'

"In exercising its constant and unrelenting control over the activities of the Synod appropriate officials of the council conduct systematic work to educate and enlighten the members of the Synod, maintain confidential contacts with them, shape their patriotic views and attitudes, and exert necessary influence on the entire episcopate through the members of the Synod and with their help."

THE THREE GROUPS

Furov divided the church's top clergymen into three groups. Group A, which included Russian Orthodox Patriarch Pimen, "strictly observe laws . . . realistically acknowledge that our government is not interested in expanding the role of religion and who, realizing this fact, are not personally involved in the spreading of orthodoxy among our populations." Group B, Furov said, follow the law and have correct attitudes, but "try to activate the clergy and the church body . . . and recruit young zealots for the priesthood."

Condemnation was reserved for Group C, a dangerous group of men who "evade the law on cults," "bribe and slander" council officials, and "stimulate religious feeling, provoke unwholesome interest among non-believers and persons indifferent to religion." This is undoubtedly the group to which Archbishop Feodosy—the man who dared to complain to Brezhnev—belongs.

Furov noted that Orthodox priests are "ideal" for handling foreigners because they "are loyal, operate within the law, are well informed and can influence many people; therefore we are interested in working with them individually . . . particularly when they meet and accompany foreign tourists, religious and governmental organizations."

KGB CONTROL

The news about council control is particularly ominous because, according to Soviet expert John Barron, the Council on Religious Affairs is under the control of the KGB. In John Barron's book *KGB: The Secret Work of Soviet Secret Agents*, he quoted ex-KGB officer Vladimir Sakharov recalling his friend Anatoli Kaznovetsky—the

Russian Orthodox Archbishop of Africa—who was "the most colorful KGB agent in the Middle East."[36]

Archbishop Kaznovetsky, Sakharov said, was "perfectly capable of administering religious sacraments one hour and writing reports for the KGB the next." The archbishop's main mission was "to persuade clergymen of other faiths to adopt and propound the Soviet view on international issues such as Vietnam, the world peace movement and the Arab-Israeli conflict."[37]

The duty of the KGB's Fifth Directorate, Barron maintains, is to clandestinely control religion in the Soviet Union. It works to identify all believers in the Soviet Union and ensure that the Russian Orthodox Church and all other churches serve as instruments of Soviet policy.

Barron believes that the Directorate places KGB officers within the church hierarchy and recruits bona fide clergymen as agents. Much of its work is accomplished through the Council on Religious Affairs, which is heavily staffed with retired and disabled KGB officers.

If any more confirmation is needed, it can be supplied by ex-Polish official Zdzislaw Rurarz. Rurarz, who resigned as Polish Ambassador to Japan after martial law was imposed in his country in 1981, was visiting Zagorsk in 1967. Zagorsk, a monastery, is in a sense the Russian Orthodox holy city. It is about forty-four miles from Moscow. While there, Rurarz was surprised to see the large number of priests and religious pilgrims. When he mentioned his surprise to his hosts one of the men, an official high in the Soviet hierarchy, laughed and said of the priests, "All of them are ours."[38]

The purpose of the Soviet Council on Religious Affairs was made even more abundantly clear when Furov wrote, "Thus, the plethora of measures . . . enables us to influence future clergymen in a specific way beneficial to us and to expand their theoretical and practical knowledge in the spirit of materialism. In our opinion, this will undercut the religious and mystical ideals of the future clergy and in conjunction with other objective and subjective factors, it may bring them to understand their own uselessness as clergymen."

Soviet officials were so pleased with Bruce Rigdon's performance on the "The Church of the Russians" broadcast that they awarded him the Order of the Holy Prince Vladimir, Third Class.

NCC HOSTS SOVIET SPOKESMEN

In addition to the propaganda spouted by NCC delegates after visiting the Soviet Union, the National Council inflicts more by bringing Soviet delegates to this country. These guests, many of them Russian Orthodox "churchmen," use every possible opportunity to act as agents of influence for the Soviet government. A typical delegation visited for three weeks in May 1984. Those nineteen "churchmen" consistently touted religious freedom in the U.S.S.R., blamed the U.S. for the arms race, and encouraged peace groups to fight their government's defense policies.

Their cynical attitude was revealed, however, when they were asked hard questions. Would the church intercede on behalf of Andrei Sakharov, Metropolitan Juvenaly was asked. Juvenaly replied, "I don't think he belongs to the Russian Orthodox Church."[39]

The Orthodox Church did send a priest to the Reverend Gleb Yakunin, Juvenaly claimed, to give him Communion and a Bible. That was decent of them, since Yakunin, as has been stated, is an Orthodox priest who has been imprisoned since 1980 in a Urals labor camp (sentenced to a five-year "strict regime"), to be followed by five years of internal exile. The Soviets may not let Yakunin out of the camp the rest of his life, however, because he committed a serious crime. He was one of the founders of the Christian Committee for the Defense of Believers' Rights. Aleksandr Solzhenitsyn said in 1983 that Yakunin has been punished by being held in a "freezing stone cubicle without bed, clothes or food."[40]

It is also interesting to note that Yakunin's futile appeals for help to the World Council of Churches (mentioned in Chapter One) were used against him at his trial.

During the same 1984 tour of Soviet churchmen, a Ukrainian who now lives in the U.S. asked the Soviets why Christians in the Soviet Union are being held in jail for their faith. Archbishop Job of Sareisk answered that they were in prison not because of their religion, but because they had broken the law. When the question was raised again at a news conference, Archpriest Vladimir Kucheryavy said that "religious persecution simply isn't an issue in our country."[41]

Perhaps the most tragic aspect of the Soviets' use of the Orthodox church is that its clergy apparently feel that refusal to cooperate with their government would be useless. One bishop told a Western friend, "Of course I could stand up and proclaim the truth in a loud voice. But what would that achieve? Would the West rise to the defense of our church? Hardly, for all the information about our difficulties is available to the Western public.[42]

"For a few days they might write about me in secular Western newspapers: the church ones would probably remain silent so as not to jeopardize relations and trips to Moscow. And then what? Even if I were allowed to return home, I would be imprisoned immediately, which would be good for my conscience, but could be disastrous to my diocese. . . ."[43]

Part of the explanation for the willingness of the Orthodox clergy to cooperate with the Soviet government can be attributed to Orthodox belief that the church is incorruptible and its sacredness does not depend on its members and priests. Michael Bourdeaux has delineated this attitude in his writing and speeches. Bourdeaux points out that there is even a popular saying to the effect that if the celebrant is unworthy, then the angels, who are mystically present at the Eucharist, perform the sacrament instead.[44]

This belief must offer some comfort to their conscience, as they are forced to spend so much of their time spouting mendacious nonsense. In 1982 Russian Orthodox leadership sponsored a "peace" conference entitled "Saving the Sacred Gift of Life from Nuclear Catastrophe." The conference was attended by hundreds of religious leaders from six continents, including evangelist Billy Graham. The conference produced an abundance of pro-Soviet propaganda, including repeated endorsements of a nuclear freeze and a halt to the American neutron bomb, plus proposed steps which would have, if taken, stopped the modernization of NATO defenses.

The Soviets propagandized so successfully at the conference that Graham defended Soviet attitudes toward religion, declaring that "It would seem to me that in the churches I visited—and there are thousands of them—services are allowed to go on freely."[45]

Graham was almost universally castigated for his naive comment; and Russian Baptists felt, according to an American student who studied in Leningrad during that period, that "He sold them out." In a story for the *Houston Chronicle*, Marcus Sloan, who was in Moscow at the time Graham visited, wrote, "But then I doubt he realized what he was doing. He never got to meet Baptists there. People participating in services at that church told me that he never met one person at that church who was not a KGB agent."[46]

THE AMERICAN PEACENIKI

Even if the true believers have not been replaced with KGB agents when Americans visit, it is doubtful that most Russians would speak frankly. *Los Angeles Times* reporter Robert Gillette quoted a Moscow scientist—who is bitterly opposed to his country's invasion of Afghanistan—about the naiveté of Americans concerning Soviet statements on their system. "Don't your people know anything about our system?" he asked an American friend. "Believe me, if you came to my institute with a foreign delegation and you asked me what I thought of Afghanistan, I would tell you we were helping a fraternal socialist country at the invitation of the legitimate government there. You could talk to me for a week and you still wouldn't know what I really thought."[47]

According to Soviet intellectuals, Americans who swallow their line are fools, commonly called "peaceniki."[48]

One of the problems of American delegations results from a kind of native American naiveté. Americans find it very difficult to accept evil as a reality and deception as a way of life. They reject with horror the notion that the nice people who guide them and see to their every comfort are Soviet-controlled, or Soviet agents trained to do their best to brainwash visitors. Soviets, however, are past masters at the art of concocting "not merely a favorable impression of this complex and contradictory land, but often a false and entirely imaginary one."[49] For more information on this subject see Appendix, Document III.

POKAZUKHA

The most famous deception of this sort (which the Soviets call *"pokazukha"*) occurred when Vice-President Henry Wallace visited forced labor camps in the U.S.S.R. during World War II. The Soviets dismantled the wooden watchtowers, hid the prisoners, and made the camp guards play the role of hardy miners. The Soviets cleaned up the surrounding area, and the city of Magadan had its stores stuffed with food and clothing—most of the inventory coming from the American lend-lease program. Wallace came home with glowing reports; thirty years later it was revealed that from 1937 to 1953, over three million people died in those very camps.[50]

Now the targets of *"pokazukha"* are American and European visitors, especially religious and "peace" activists. These people, who often come in groups, are pushed into a heavily crowded (and strictly guided) schedule of tours of Orthodox churches, banquets, and speeches. There is no time or opportunity to go out alone and no way for most Americans to communicate with average Russians. It helps the Soviets that there is no obvious repression on the streets, no heavily armed security police or a palpable aura of fear. When these things are absent (on the surface) and the crowds move freely, when visitors conduct friendly conversations with normal people (who rarely discuss their real thoughts and feelings), they conclude they have been the victims of propaganda about the "evil empire."

Barron has quoted KGB defector Yuri Nosenko—who once directed operations against Americans visiting Moscow—as saying the KGB can invisibly restrict the lodgings, travel, and contacts of foreign visitors by simply insuring that the foreigner talks to the right officials and by determining what the visitor may or may not see. ". . . the KGB can shape impressions without mounting a complicated operation."[51]

It helps that emotions of pity and "understanding" are often stirred by the Soviets' unrelenting propaganda concerning their casualties during the Second World War. These civilian losses, which resulted from the German invasion, have been used by the Soviets to justify the greatest arms buildup in world history. Look, we are just afraid of our neighbors, they say. The Soviets, Gillette points out, did not put unrelenting emphasis on World War II until the early 1960s, when their massive arms buildup began.

Soviets who come into contact with Americans are also trained to speak constantly of *"mir,"* or peace. "I feel like I've been tortured for peace,"[52] one NCC delegate commented regarding the many "peace" meetings which he was required to attend. That visitors are feted and flattered often has an impact. Visiting Americans are impressed both by what seems a sincere desire for peace and by the elevated status the visitor seemingly has in the U.S.S.R. It leads the foreigner to conclude that he/she is helping to bring the two governments together.

As difficult as the propaganda is to resist, however, there is no excuse for Americans, especially American Christians, to allow themselves to be manipulated. It seems a particularly American folly to believe a short trip to another country, especially those which specialize in Potemkin villages, will make the observer a specialist.

GIDE'S TOUR

André Gide, the noted French author and former Marxist sympathizer, was given such a conducted tour of the Soviet Union during the 1930s. As long as his trip was "conducted," everything "seemed to me wonderful," he said. Gide was taken to model villages where there was plentiful food, where there were recreation centers and kindergartens, model factories, clubs, pleasure grounds. "I asked for nothing better than to be carried away with admiration," he said. Gide was provided luxurious train compartments and the best hotel rooms. He was feted everywhere he went and was treated to magnificent banquets. "Nothing was too good for me."[53]

However, when Gide began to travel alone he saw a completely different picture. He saw that most Russians lived in the "direst poverty." He saw the conformity, the ban of foreign publications, the lies and propaganda told the people concerning the West and almost everything else, the exploitation of the people by the Communist Party in order that Party officials could live luxuriously, the government's promotion of informing as a way of life, and total repression of opposition.[54]

Gide finally concluded that in no country in the world, "not even in Hitler's Germany—have the mind and heart been less free, more bent, more terrorized over—and indeed vassalized—than in the Soviet Union."[55]

Soviet tours, however, still work to the Soviet government's advantage. Gillette, who came into contact with the NCC delegation while he was assigned to Moscow, quoted a "dismayed" Western ambassador who said, "These people are going to go back to I don't know how many hundred communities in the United States saying these are peace-loving people, there's freedom of religion in the Soviet Union, and they've got just wonderful arms control policy. It's extraordinary."[56]

WILLING BLINDNESS

Ironically, some of the Soviet religious leaders who preach peace to Americans have nothing but contempt for the "peace activists" with whom they mingle. Bourdeaux tells a story about a Soviet churchman who, after listening to an impassioned speech by a Western clergyman who declared that he "would rather the whole world became Communist than even one bomb be dropped," turned to a Western friend and murmured, "And you expect me to tell the likes of him that my church is being persecuted!"[57]

Worse, however, are some American delegates and clergy who apparently know the truth about the church in the U.S.S.R., but make excuses for the Soviets to protect their coveted trips to the U.S.S.R.—during which their hosts treat them to elaborate feasts and pander to their egos.

Others refuse to see what is evident in order to protect some ideological commitment of their own. Bourdeaux tells of a meeting between an Orthodox and an American clergyman in which the Orthodox told the American that the Soviet government always had to be considered in their meetings: "What you are talking about is ecumenism with our persecutors, for a close union between Russian bishops and bishops of the Western Church inevitably includes a third party, the big brother," he said.[58]

The American then condescendingly rebuked him for his warning: "A friend may have weaknesses. . . . In the final analysis, Communist victories always lead to a religious upsurge. For example, the number of baptisms has sharply increased since the Communists came to power in Vietnam. Similarly, in your country the Holy Spirit is more active."[59]

"MORAL EQUIVALENCY"

Finally, not content with inundating the church with propaganda sympathetic to the Soviet Union, the NCC has also produced literature which gives equal weight to Soviet and American morality. *Must Walls Divide*, by the Reverend James Will, published by the NCC's Friendship Press, has received wide distribution among the United Methodists, Presbyterians, and United Church of Christ. The study book treats the human rights record of the U.S. and the U.S.S.R. as morally equal by stating, among other things, that Stalin's reign of terror "though compressed into a shorter period and thus, more terrible, . . . was not unlike the oppression of men, women, and children in mine and factory—to say nothing of outright slavery—which accompanied early industrialization in Europe and North America."

Consider this fallacy—Will states that Communist regimes have been roughly as successful as the European democracies in meeting the economic needs of their people. And this claim for the efficacy of communism was said of countries in which chronic shortages, black markets, and low income are endemic; about a place where life expectancy is actually falling.

Will's attitude cannot be separated, in the long run, from the fact that he is a CAREE director.

The end result of NCC naiveté, however, adds up to more than ridiculous statements and useless meetings in the U.S.S.R. and Geneva. It achieves Soviet propaganda coups accomplished through an organization which represents American Christians. It influences the world when the NCC vouches for the religious tolerance of the Soviets. It makes a difference to Soviet Christians that their persecution has not only been ignored, but covered up by fellow-Christians. It makes a difference to Gleb Yakunin that as he freezes in his cell, punished for his faithfulness to God, fellow-Christians ignore his suffering.

How much NCC statements matter was demonstrated when the NCC delegation that visited the Soviet Union in June 1984 was officially defended by the National Council of American-Soviet Friendship. Employee Alan Thomson claimed the bad publicity resulting from the delegation's remarks at various press conferences was a result of "the anti-Soviet public relations establishment." He also went to some effort to defend NCC statements, claiming, among other things, that the Orthodox Church has freedom it did not have under the Tsars.[60]

The Friendship Council was created by the American Communist Party in 1943 and, according to American intelligence, is a tool of the Soviets. Obviously the credibility of NCC statements matters to those who have the most to gain from them.

Despite all opposition, however, despite its isolation, despite the cooperation of the NCC and the Soviet inquisition, many believers in the Soviet Union remain faithful. Documents captured in Afghanistan, often letters taken from dead Soviet soldiers, exhibit a degree of startling religious devotion.

CHRISTIANITY SURVIVES

In the Soviet Union itself, youth are attending religious seminars that have grown so in popularity that the state has begun active persecution of anyone caught attending. *Startsy*, or elders, have reappeared in public consciousness. The *startsy* are monks or hermits who are known for their godly lives and deep wisdom and are consulted by the people for spiritual guidance. There is also a significant upsurge in religious ceremonies to sanctify state weddings and funerals.

The trial of Father Svarinskas was a compelling example of the endurance of belief and of believers, despite all difficulties, despite all persecution. Christians from all Lithuania flocked to the trial, so many that to keep them from attending, the KGB brought buses to Vilnius, forced the people on, and hauled them to the forest.[61]

The underground journals reported that "Those arrested prayed the rosary out loud the whole way, finishing it on their knees in the woods." During the trial, which Father Svarinskas referred to as his "Golgatha," he gave a speech accusing the state of persecuting the faithful. When the judge tried to stop his speech, Svarinskas requested that before death he be able to have his say. "You won't have to try me again," he said, "I shall remain a debtor. I don't expect to finish my sentence. Are you afraid of me? Surely, I'm not going to destroy your tanks with my bare hands (you even took away my rosary). . . ."[62]

Nothing the state did, however, not the threats and not the arrests, extinguished the witness of God's faithful priest. "Even on the trolley buses one could hear people saying, 'What a powerful priest. Against him are assembled the greatest forces. . . .'"[63]

Liberation Theology: What It Is and What It Does

Father Uriel Molina, the head of Nicaragua's "popular church," Nicaragua's premier liberation theologian, conducted a rather strange commemorative Mass in November 1985. He draped an M-19 banner across the altar and called the M-19 guerrillas "martyrs." Then he allowed a representative of M-19 to speak from the pulpit.[1]

M-19 are Colombian Marxist-Leninist guerrillas, and they were being commemorated because forty-one of them had died six days before. The Colombian army attacked them after they had invaded Colombia's Ministry of Justice in Bogatá. Before the guerrillas were routed, ninety-five people were dead.

It is ironic that "liberation theology" should present itself as a legitimate interpretation of Christian faith. It might be a theology, but it is not a Christian theology. It claims to be a new aspect of Christian social teaching. It is not. It is an activist humanism based on Marxist theory which seeks to completely change the focus and the meaning of traditional Christianity: it replaces faith in Christ and hope of resurrection with the justification and sanctification of political revolution. Father Molina is not the exception, but the rule in action.

As such, liberation theology has been, and is, extremely dangerous. This is neither a prediction nor a supposition. Liberation theology serves as an excuse for much of the radical politics of the American mainline church; it has seduced some of its missionaries and has infected whole orders of Roman Catholicism. Liberation theologians greatly assisted the Sandinista triumph in Nicaragua, which as we shall see in the next chapter has had terrible results for the Nicaraguan people. Those same theologians are now busy in other parts of Latin America.

Worse, liberation theology has had such a profound effect on Philippine priests and nuns that hundreds have joined the New People's Army (NPA), a ruthless Marxist-Leninist organization. In fact, the NPA is so bloodthirsty that it has been compared to the Khmer Rouge, the Cambodian guerrillas who attempted genocide against their own people.

MARXISM AND LIBERATION

When the nature of liberation theology is studied, it is not difficult to understand why these events have occurred. Although there are some variations of liberation theology, most liberation theologians either use Marxist analysis, or Marxist concepts, in their thesis. They justify the use of Marxism as a new way of understanding the Scriptures, or have adopted the Marxist goal of social transformation, or both. The salvation of this world is Christianity's proper role, they believe, not the search for God's grace, a practice which is considered "otherworldly."[2]

Leonardo Boff, the liberation theologian who was disciplined by the Roman Catholic Church as a result of his writing, thus describes the Kingdom of God as the "realization of a fundamental Utopia of the human heart, the total transformation of this world."[3] Father Molina describes Nicaragua as a country which now has "the option to create the Kingdom of God on earth."[4] There should be a "preferential option for the poor" in real Christianity, liberation theologians believe. Many go so far as to proclaim that the struggle to liberate the poor and oppressed becomes "the true sacrament of God's historic saving activity."[5]

Most liberation theologians subsequently accept the concept that all history is a narrative of class struggle, which will continue until the underclasses triumph. Much of their teaching flows from this premise. Liberation theologians, for the most part, do not believe that Christ's return is the aim of history: it is, they think, the triumph of class over class. They place the emphasis on the poor to such an extent that they infer others cannot be redeemed. "The Gospel has not the same message for all," Father Joseph Comblin has said. "To the poor it announces Liberation and to the rich deprivation."[6]

Jesus the redeemer is replaced, in liberation thought, with Jesus the symbol, one which sums up the struggle of the oppressed. His death is given an "exclusively political interpretation . . . in this way its value for salvation and . . . redemption is denied." The Eucharist is then viewed as the celebration of the "people in their struggles," not as the symbol of the sacrificial gift of Christ.[7]

THE REALM OF THE NATURAL

These ideas place both Marxism and liberation theology in the realm of the natural. Supernatural metaphysics places importance on the spiritual. Belief in an all-powerful God assumes that God can, and does, intervene in this world. What is not subject to God's direct intervention is left to humanity's free will. The realm of the natural, however, is the opposite. Liberation theologians and Marxists are both humanists. They believe that humanity is both the beginning and end of study.[8] History then becomes all-important to both. Liberation theologians pay lip-service to the idea of God, but deny Him any place in this world; Marxists deny His presence altogether. They accept history as the "independent driving force behind human actions. . . . The Marxists and liberation theologians use history where the Catholic uses the Supreme Being."[9]

Their attitude also declares that humanity is perfectible, and will be perfected by the cleansing action of history. Christians, however, believe that moral authority comes from God and have traditionally viewed humanity as fallen into sin, redeemable only by God's grace.

VIOLENT LIBERATION

The idea of violence is inextricably woven into liberation theology because class struggle implies that society is founded on violence. This is often explained as a type of self-defense, economic repression being the original aggressive action. Justifying this violence is the foremost priority of liberation theologians because believers claim the revolution and "subsequent establishment of the Kingdom of God on earth" is inevitable. When they claim that the revolution is the only way to this perfect society, they are then forced to justify the violence inherent in it.[10]

Justification is usually presented in an argument citing the necessity of total revolution to change entrenched economic systems. Having already discarded the Biblical injunctions against the anger which causes violence,[11] justifying violence itself is easy. "The revolution is the criterion of everything; of truth, of culture, etc.," one prominent liberation theologian explained.[12] The prized revolution which they justify is almost always a Socialist revolution, one which transforms (abolishes) the "private property system."[13]

One of the greatest dangers in liberation theology is that because it shares Marxist goals, its adherents often identify fidelity to their beliefs with fidelity to a Marxist-Leninist political organization. This is a form of madness, but it is logical madness. The Marxists-Leninists have been sanctified, in the minds of liberation theologians, because they are also allegedly working for social reformation. What Christians can expect from the Sandinistas, a Nicaraguan theologian explained, ". . . and not as a literary expression . . . is that they make us Christians."[14]

Those theologians have been working toward that goal for some time. Nicaragua's liberation theologians were allied with the Sandinistas in the fight against Anastasio Somoza. Once he was defeated in 1979, and the Sandinistas revealed they had no intention of establishing democracy, the revolutionary Christians did not denounce them. Instead, they stated they believed that "preference for and solidarity with the poor" meant that they had to work with the regime. Father Juan Hernandez Pico, one of Nicaragua's prominent liberation theologians, declared that there was "no other way for a Christian to show his faith in the Kingdom than by committing himself absolutely to a contingent project (the Sandinista regime)." Thus their logic brought them to conclude that one's identity as a Christian depended on a partisan political commitment.[15]

That liberation theology produces partisan political commitment is proven in action as well as words. One short example of this is the five Salvadoran priests who now travel with their country's Marxist-Leninist guerrillas. They have declared that the guerrillas will bring the "new society," and that liberation theology was the "revelation" that led them to this conclusion.[16]

"There is no great contradiction between Marxism and Christianity. . . . Marxists try to fight for justice. They try to resolve the situation of exploitation and inequality. The new society they desire and the kingdom of God are the same," one of the priests said.[17]

DEPENDENCY THEORY

Another dangerous viewpoint shared by both Marxists and liberation theologians is the "dependency theory." It asserts that the developed world, especially the United States, is responsible for the poverty of the Third World. America has exploited its natural resources, drained its capital, and imposed its consumer culture on Latin America, they claim. This is an interesting way to absolve Latin America as the originator of its own problems, but it does not explain why the southern half of the continent has been poor for over four hundred years. Poverty existed in Latin America "long before capitalism was a gleam in Adam Smith's eye."[18] It also fails to explain why other Third-World countries, such as Taiwan, have managed to become prosperous despite having many of the same problems as Latin America. When the evidence is examined in depth, the dependency theory becomes irrational.

Dependency theorists rarely note that only about one-fourth of

U.S. foreign investment is committed to less developed countries. The same thing is true of other developed nations. The majority of their capital is invested in First-World projects. It is unfortunate that the United States and other developed nations do not invest more in developing countries because studies have proven that where foreign investment is lowest, income and output remains very small. Africa, a continent where foreign investment remains minuscule, has twenty of the world's thirty-one least developed countries. As for exploitation, only 11 percent of U.S. investment in the Third World is in petroleum and only about 6 percent more in "extractive" industries. Thirty-five percent of the investment is in manufacturing, 10 percent in trade, and 27 percent in finance and insurance.[19]

Even if the United States concentrated on extractive industries, reasonable people would have a hard time believing it was unfair to the Third World. Most nations extract minerals and sell them to other countries—or they hire someone to do it for them. Minerals and oil are useless in the ground. John Kenneth Galbraith has pointed out that the greatest suppliers of wheat, feed grains, coal, wood, wood pulp, and cotton fibers are the United States and Canada, countries no one claims are exploited.[20] When dependency theorists charge that exhaustion of resources causes poverty, they ignore Japan—a country with very, very few natural resources, but one that is very, very prosperous.

However, these facts are ignored by both Marxists and liberation theologians, an attitude which turns the dependency theory into nothing but a convenient party line.

TERMINOLOGY AND MEANING

One of the more puzzling aspects of liberation theology is that although its belief system is different from Christianity, it freely uses Christian terminology. Since its method of interpretation (called hermeneutics) of the terminology is completely different, it perverts traditional Christian meaning. There is a clear difference between what is traditionally meant by "the poor" and what liberation theologians mean. The poor are now the proletariat in a Marxist sense. It is also quite possible for a priest who favors liberation theology to proclaim that he believes in personal salvation—and not be discussing Christ.[21]

There are now many liberation theologians, and they offer variations of their faith. This makes it difficult to cover all aspects. The man on whom most liberation theologians rely for their main thesis, however, is Gustavo Gutierrez. In his seminal *A Theology of Liberation*, published in 1973, Gutierrez prefaced his work by presenting prior assumptions which have been accepted by most of his colleagues. These assumptions must be accepted before the theology as a whole is viable.

Gutierrez first argues that theology is a science, which he states was a traditional viewpoint until the fourteenth century. It is an intellectual discipline born of the meeting of faith and reason, he said, which produces rational knowledge. That is standard Catholic thinking. However, he goes a great deal further and asserts that reason is found (and implies only found) in the social sciences—that is, in the study of man, not in the study of God or Scriptures. Therefore, he concludes, any theology not characterized by this rationality is invalid.[22]

THEOLOGY AS SCIENCE

Taking this line of thought to its logical conclusion, Gutierrez suggests that since reason is found in social science, theology should start with "real questions" derived from this world, not revelation (Scriptures). He quotes Henri Bouillard's assertion, "A theology which is not up to date is a false theology." A theology is only prophetic insofar as it interprets historic events for our day, with the purpose of making Christian commitment more "radical and clear." A person only discovers the meaning of the Kingdom of God, he concludes, by making this world a better place.[23]

This is specious reasoning, however, and it totally contradicts traditional Christian thought. Cardinal Joseph Ratzinger, the prefect of the Congregation for the Doctrine of the Faith at the Vatican, has pointed out that it is "the light of faith" which provides theology with its principles. "It is only in the light of faith and what faith teaches us about the truth of man and the ultimate meaning of his destiny that one can judge the validity or degree of validity of what other disciplines propose."[24]

WORLD TRANSFORMATION AS SALVATION

Marxist thought has influenced him, Gutierrez admits, because it is geared to the "transformation of the world," which he, throughout his work, claims is Christianity's proper goal. He dismisses orthodox Christianity as "an obsolete tradition or a debatable interpretation" and proffers "orthopraxis," which he believes will balance or cause orthodoxy's primacy to be rejected. It is a term which he explains recognizes the work and importance of action which is taken to change society.[25]

Gutierrez really reveals his deviance from traditional Christianity when he states that it teaches universalism—the idea that all people will be saved. That is nonsense. Nothing of the sort has been accepted by traditional Christianity, Protestant or Catholic. Individual theologians may proffer such theories and some clerics may believe them, but Roman Catholics and most Protestant churches still believe in the atonement of Christ for the sins of humanity and His subsequent resurrection.[26]

Protestant and Catholic doctrine is based on the Apostle's Creed, the Nicene Creed, and the Athanasian Creed, and all these creeds affirm the resurrection and the atonement.

CHRISTIAN PREREQUISITES

When Gutierrez asserts that universal salvation has been accepted as a fact, he is then able to claim that real salvation is in this life; and one is not truly a Christian until one works for social and political revolution. He openly declares his commitment to socialism and "appears to believe that greed began with capitalism and will end with its demise."[27]

His theology, then, is internally valid because he has dismissed the need to search for the will of God and the need to believe in the sacrifice of Christ, and replaced them with the deification of humanity.

Gutierrez obviously believes that humanity "can make heaven on earth. He traces sin and evil to systems, not to human nature."[28] Scriptural Christianity, of course, is based on the premise that unredeemed human nature is the cause of evil. Hearts, it suggests, must be changed or evil systems will persist.

SALVATION BY WORKS

Cardinal Ratzinger points out that liberation theology explains Christianity as a "praxis of liberation" and claims that it is the guide to that praxis. Praxis is generally interpreted as practical application of a branch of learning. Gutierrez, Ratzinger points out, said, "Nothing remains outside political commitment. All exists with a political coloration." This means, the Cardinal pointed out, that any theology that is not political is considered "'idealistic' and condemned as unreal or as a vehicle to maintain the oppressors in power."[29]

Ratzinger, who is known as the principal foe of liberation theology within the Catholic Church, attributes the rise of political religion to events within Roman Catholicism. After Vatican II, many in the church began to believe that the existing theological tradition was "no longer acceptable," and that new theological and spiritual directions must be developed. The idea of openness to the world and of commitment to the world was "often transformed into a naive faith in science, a faith which accepted human sciences as a new gospel without trying to recognize their limits and their own particular problems. Psychology, sociology and the Marxist interpretations of history were considered as scientifically certain and as instances of Christian thought that are no longer debatable."[30]

Christian scholars then began to attack the traditional interpretations of Scriptures, Ratzinger added, which shook the historic credibility of the Gospels. Instead of the traditional Jesus which the church taught, the revisionists substituted the idea that Jesus is only important for what He can say to our age and new terms were needed to explain what that is. In order to use these new terms, Ratzinger explained, the revisionists included certain preliminary decisions.[31]

Theologian J. Sobrino gave a good example of such decisions when he stated the experience Jesus had of God is radically historical. "His faith is converted into fidelity," Sobrino writes. "Fidelity" means "fidelity to history," which replaces faith altogether. He then asserts that God was "revealed historically and scandalously in Jesus and in the poor who continue his presence. Only one who maintains these two affirmations together is orthodox."[32]

TRUTH THROUGH PRACTICE

Sobrino, Gutierrez, and most other liberation theologians believe that truth cannot be understood in a spiritual way, because it is "idealism." Truth, they say, must be realized in history and in practice (praxis). Action, to them, is truth. Ratzinger points out that even the ideas that are used for action are "interchangeable. The only decisive thing is praxis. Orthopraxis becomes the only true orthodoxy."[33]

According to liberation theologians, the hierarchy (Magisterium) of the church is no longer the interpreter of the Scripture. Liberation theologians believe that the community should interpret, and this allows a new interpretation when anyone feels the urge. Because the experience of the people explains the Scriptures, Ratzinger points out, the "people" become opposed to the hierarchy of the church and, theoretically, participate in a class struggle against it.[34] This premise is the basis for the establishment of the "popular church" (by liberation theologians) in Nicaragua.

HISTORY AS REVELATION

Liberation theologians also believe that the Bible "reasons exclusively in terms of history of salvation," and therefore in a nonspiritual way is compatible with the Marxist idea of history as the "authentic revelation." They then take this idea one step further and say that Marxism is the real interpreter of the Bible. Liberation theologians then progress to the viewpoint that since the hierarchy of the church insists on permanent spiritual truths, it is hostile to progress because it contradicts history.[35]

Cardinal Ratzinger made some pertinent points against liberation theology in his official *Instructions on Certain Aspects of the 'Theology of Liberation.'* Orthodox Roman Catholicism maintains, he said, that liberation is liberation from sin, which is the "gift of grace." That deliverance is offered to all, Ratzinger pointed out, be they politically free or slaves—the New Testament does not require a change in the political or social condition as a prerequisite.[36]

The heart of evil, Ratzinger further pointed out, does not lie in systems, but in "free and responsible" persons who have to be converted by the grace of Jesus Christ "in order to live and act as new creatures . . . to demand first of all a radical revolution in social relations and then to criticize the search for personal perfection is to set out on a road which leads to the denial of the meaning of the person and his transcendence, and to destroy ethics and its foundation, which is the absolute character of the distinction between good and evil."[37]

It is "illusionary and dangerous" to accept Marxist analysis, Ratzinger maintained, while failing to see the sort of "totalitarian society to which this process leads." The core of Marxist praxis is atheism and the denial of liberty and human rights. To integrate into Christian theology an analysis which depends on an atheistic premise "is to involve oneself in a terrible contradiction," he said.[38,39]

NICARAGUA AND LIBERATION THEOLOGY

This contradiction has proven both true and fatal in Nicaragua. Influenced by liberation theology, the Catholic bishops criticized the Anastasio Somoza regime and "explicitly condoned the use of violence."[40] In 1979, immediately proceeding Somoza's overthrow, the bishops wrote a pastoral letter which "proclaimed the right of the Nicaraguan people to engage in revolutionary insurrection."[41] Nicaragua is a devoutly Catholic country, and it can be safely assumed that the bishops' blessing of violence had an impact on political affairs.

These were not simply blessings on a justified revolution. In 1972 the bishops of two of Nicaragua's largest dioceses declared their support for "a completely new order."[42] The new order should include the "preferential option for the poor" and a "planned economy for the benefit of humankind."[43]

Another translation of liberation theology into politics occurred when a "progressive" faction of the moderate, democratic Social Christian Party broke away and formed the Popular Social Christians. That faction was heavily influenced by liberation theology and rejected gradual change. They adopted a "revolutionary Christian attitude."[44]

The Popular Social Christians aligned themselves with the Sandinistas, a move which weakened the anti-Somoza democratic movement. The Sandinistas obviously appreciated these developments and made Social Christian leader Reinaldo Tefel a member of the revolutionary junta.[49]

Further, many of the Sandinistas were educated at Managua's Jesuit-run Central American University, and the Jesuits were, and are, enthusiastic advocates of liberation theology. Some of them are now Sandinista advisors.[46] All four of the priests who were given positions in the Sandinista government were advocates of liberation theology.

CHRISTIANS TURN TO POLITICS

Perhaps most important for the revolution, liberation theologians (many of whom were foreigners) established Christian Base Communities all over Nicaragua during the decades of the sixties and seventies. The community members—who were usually from the very poor neighborhoods—were taught the Bible as a story of liberation. The effect was "profound."[47] In Matagalpa, in 1972, the Base Communities soon "produced enough political organizations to lead to conflict between parishioners and the government."[48] They subsequently began to collaborate with the Sandinistas and were soon considered subversive themselves. The government eventually used the National Guard against some of them. Another organization which was important to the Sandinista effort was the Association of Rural Workers. It used homes of peasant members as places of refuge, storehouses for arms, and supply depots for the guerrillas.[49]

The Rural Workers were an outgrowth of the Committees of Agricultural Workers, which were, in turn, outgrowths of the Evangelical Committee for Agrarian Advancement. The latter was created in 1969 by the Jesuit order with the expressed purpose of training peasant leaders to "politically organize their communities."[50]

Not only did radical Christians work behind the scenes before the revolution; many of the clergy gave the Sandinista guerrillas active support. Some churches provided food and medicine and at least one church was used as a drop-off and pick-up point for messages. Churches were used as places of refuge and as sources of fresh drinking water (which was stored in baptismal fonts) and "even as centers for the making of bombs and the storage of arms."[51]

THE CHURCH LEGITIMATES THE SANDINISTAS

Some priests and nuns who were, undoubtedly, practitioners of liberation theology fought with the Sandinistas.[52] Edward Lynch, who wrote about liberation theology and the Nicaraguan revolution in an insightful, well-documented Master's thesis, points out that these developments were highly beneficial to the guerrillas. It "legitimized" the Sandinistas "to an extent unthinkable without their participation," and created "enormous difficulties" for Somoza. When Somoza tried to fight the Sandinistas, it often looked as though he was persecuting the church.

As Daniel Ortega, the current president of Nicaragua, said, "The best arguments the Sandinistas had urging the people to take up revolutionary struggle were Christian arguments."[53]

This is not to say that Somoza was a good man, or that he should have been tolerated, or that the bishops should have been silent about his abuses. It does mean, however, that clergy should not practice violence and the church should work for nonviolent change. Violent revolutions rarely bring about the positive change they seek. It is also true that while violence may be necessary for a people in order to rid themselves of an abusive government, it is not the church's place to encourage it. Most of all, it means that collaboration with Marxists-Leninists leads to Marxist-Leninist governments.

LIBERATION IN THE PHILIPPINES

The same pattern is now repeating itself in the Philippines. First, the liberation theologians created the "theology of struggle," a liberation theology that baldly states the church should be actively involved in a "struggle for justice."[54] They subsequently established Christian Base Communities, which teach "liberation" and "themes which have sounded similar to the propaganda of the Communist-led New People's Army insurgency."[55] Many of the base communities now form the "basic infrastructure for the NPA (New People's Army)."[56]

The New People's Army of the Philippines is the "fastest growing, most threatening, and arguably the most brutal Communist insurgency in the world today." The NPA has over twenty thousand guerrillas who are "waging a largely unreported campaign of terror, assassination, and torture in the Philippine countryside." An independent Philippine leftist told *Time* correspondent Ross Munro that he was afraid that if the New People's Army were victorious, "We might be staring at a Pol Pot future." Pol Pot was the leader of the Khmer Rouge, the Cambodian Marxists-Leninists who murdered millions of their own countrymen.[57]

CLERGY JOINS THE NEW PEOPLE'S ARMY

Yet, "Nowhere else in the world, it seems, have so many priests and nuns been so committed to the Communist cause. As a Philippine leftist puts it, 'Liberation theology has gone much farther in the Philippines than in Latin America. In Latin America it justifies collaboration with the Communists. Here it means joining the Communists.'"[58]

Approximately twelve hundred priests and nuns have joined the "highly secretive" Christians for National Liberation[59] and have formed "secret cells" in the church. The organization's constitution requires members to promise support for a "protracted people's war" and the "armed struggle and the underground movement." Another section of the constitution states that one of the group's aims is to fight for "self-reliant and self-determining Filipino churches against the intervention of foreign Church bodies and institutions." Munro believes this includes the Pope.[60]

True to their promise, Liberation members provide shelter for wounded guerrillas, serve as message drops, and help guerrillas move safely through their towns.[61]

Munro believes that one of the particularly "insidious" aspects of the Christians for National Liberation is that it is so secret. Leftists Munro interviewed told him that priests live and work with other priests for years and never reveal they are Liberation members. Therefore, there is no debate about the merits of the organization or its aims. Because little is known about the group in the Philippines, Munro points out, Filipinos still believe that the presence of Catholic clergy in the Marxist-Leninist movement is a "force for moderation and mercy. . . . Yet the evidence suggests that the Liberation members are more radical and rigid than other Communists." When the Filipino Communist Party in 1983 called for protest against the government, both violent and nonviolent, Christians for National Liberation only called for "armed struggle."[62]

Priests have progressed to the point that they organize sugar workers for the Communist Party. One man told Munro that "When priests come to organize the workers under the banner of religion, better yet when the priests are Australian or Irish, it's easy. The landlords will never think that this is a Communist organization. But that is what happened; the Basic Christian Communities (organized by the priests) in Negros became the infrastructure of the NPA (New People's Army)."[63]

During an interview with writer John Whitehall, four New People's Party commanders said they had known a total of over twenty priests and nuns who had actually fought with their army, as well as a Protestant pastor of the Philippine United Church of Christ. When asked how the clergy were recruited, the commanders said they were not told, at first, that Communists do not believe in God. Only when the clergy "progress in the education" is the topic approached. "Some accept the ideology of communism and lose their belief in God; the longer they stay, the fewer believe."[64]

In order to gain more clerical support, the NPA may have changed its tactics. The nonmilitary front of the Philippine Communist Party has decided, one leftist priest said, that the "religious" are no longer "pushed to repudiate religion. . . . Even the word 'Communism' is no longer encouraged—they just say 'nationalism.'"[65]

The commanders admitted that the New People's Army is "riding on the programs of the church." Hundreds of thousands of dollars are also going to Communist-controlled organizations and projects in the Philippines through church-related organizations.

One such turn of events, which proves the commanders' veracity, occurred in 1982. The bishops of twenty dioceses in the southern region of Mindanao-Sulu were forced to withdraw their support from the secretariat of their own Mindanao-Sulu Pastoral Conference. They explained that the secretariat (the conference executive committee) had become sympathetic "to those who view armed rebellion as necessary for liberation and that it claimed to speak for the entire conference."[66] The "Farmers consultation program" is a current example. The commanders said it was organized by the church, but is largely attended (therefore controlled) by NPA underground supporters.

In fairness to the Catholic Church in the Philippines, less than 10 percent of the Philippines' fourteen thousand priests and nuns are Liberation members. However, Munro claims that even the "most conservative bishops" try to ignore pro-Communist activism among their priests and do not themselves make anti-Communist statements. The bishops and official organs of the Catholic Church constantly lament government abuses, but rarely say anything regarding the horrible atrocities committed by the New People's Army.

Since the ascension of Corazon Aquino to the presidency of the Philippines, it is possible that the New People's Army will lose its appeal for Catholic clergy. There is no way to ascertain that, however, until Aquino has been in office for a reasonable length of time.

HISTORICAL DEVIANCE

In the Philippines as well as the rest of the Third World, the development of liberation theology has been so threatening to the integrity of the church and so dangerous politically that it takes on a dramatic cast. It is not, however, the first variation from the faith, merely the latest. The history of Christianity is marked by beliefs which were based more on wishful thinking than on Scripture. A prime example is Arianism, the belief that Jesus was not of the same essence as God, but merely the highest created being. The Gnostics, an early Christian sect, believed that Jesus never had a human body and that the created universe is evil. Salvation was attainable, they believed, only by the few who were able to transcend matter.

In the Middle Ages, the doctrine of Cathari was widely accepted. Its basic assertion was that the principle of good and evil equally reign in the universe, neither taking precedence. Both were considered timeless. The reward of choosing good, the Cathari believed, was in having a superior life.

Some of these deviations from traditional faith flourished in Catholic orders. The Jesuits, for instance, practiced accommodation with other cultures in their missionary activities. One famous example of this was Father Ricci, who concentrated on the resurrection in his teaching to the Chinese because he could not get them to accept the crucifixion. He also made changes in the Catholic Mass, so it would appear similar to Confucian rites.[67] Jesuits also created Probabilism, which was the practice of searching for several church authorities who would agree with a desired moral judgment. The purpose seems to have been to make moral judgments more flexible, thus keeping people in the church.[68]

There have also been historical precedents for some aspects of liberation theology. The clergy, especially those in Catholic orders, have many times placed themselves in opposition to the state. The Jesuits were widely known for this practice, so much so that it was believed they advocated regicide. They believed that if temporal rulers forced their subjects to commit a sin in order to obey them, they would lose their right to rule and it would revert to the people. In earlier centuries it was assumed the people would then search for another ruler.

To the Jesuits' eternal credit, they were stridently opposed to slavery in the new world. In their effort to protect the Indians from the slave-owning classes in Latin America, they earned the violent and "everlasting hatred" of those classes. In the sixteenth century the Jesuits gathered Peruvian, Bolivian, and Brazilian Indians in villages (which they ruled themselves) modeled on utopian thought. After losing approximately thirty thousand of the villagers to abduction and death, the Jesuits armed them against the incursions of slave hunters. This use of armed force by the Jesuits, to protect themselves, is often used as a modern justification for the use of violence by liberation theologians.[69]

Although there are some precursors to liberation theology in Catholic thought and practice, the church has always affirmed the right of people to own property. Pope Leo XIII said in the encyclical *Rerum Novarum* that land, earned through the renumeration of labor, was "inviolate as the renumeration itself."[70] On the other hand, the Catholic hierarchy has always rejected pure capitalism and pure socialism. The encyclical *Quadragessimo Anno* of Pope Pius XI put forward the notion that economic life cannot be left solely to free competition.[71]

MEDELLIN AND ITS EFFECT

Therefore, when the (Catholic) Conference of Latin American Bishops met in 1968 for their fateful conference in Medellin, Colombia—which ignited the liberation theology movement—they had the precedent of past doctrinal differences within the church, a history of conflict with the state, and disapproval of pure capitalism. Medellin produced the atmosphere for liberation theology, but it was not an extraordinary event. It was the meeting of frustration with apparent answers built on past deviance.

It is understandable that the bishops, as well as priests and nuns, are frustrated when faced with Latin America's poverty and oppression. It is a system highly resistant to change. Latin America's upper classes often fight any change in the status quo which they feel will threaten their privileges, and these people generally control the military. Anyone touring Latin America feels queasy observing the shacks no better than bare boards thrown together, the lack of sanitation, running water, electricity, the children running half naked and hungry through the streets. A theology which preaches social revolution can seem attractive in these circumstances.

At Medellin the bishops produced rhetoric which advocated this social revolution. That rhetoric and the documents which followed created an electric atmosphere in Latin America, one which encouraged the most revolutionary of social visions. Unfortunately, it was also stained with Marxist concepts and hostility to free enterprise. That is not surprising since many of Latin America's bishops "look upon Marxism with favor." The bishop of Cuernavaca and the archbishop of Recife have been "unambiguous in their preference for Marxism."[72] Their political preference, however, was not the correct way to approach Latin poverty (as the failure of Marxist praxis in Nicaragua proves). It would have been much more useful to confront the real reasons for Latin poverty and create solutions to those problems.

WHY LATIN AMERICA IS POOR

Venezuelan journalist Carlos Rangel believes that Latin American history has been the product of Hispanic culture, which has a long record of failure. He cites the inability of Hispanic cultures to evolve into "harmonious and cohesive nations" capable of improving the lot of their people; Latin America's "impotence" in its relations with the world, militarily, economically, politically—hence its vulnerability to outside action; the lack of stable governments except dictatorship; the absence of "noteworthy" contributions to the sciences and arts; its population growth, which is one of the highest in the world; its own feelings of inferiority.[73]

In 1700, Rangel observed, the Spanish Americas "still gave the impression of being incomparably richer (which it was), much more powerful, and more likely to succeed than the British colonies of North America."[74]

By 1830, however, Simon Bolivar's final judgment on Latin America was shattering. The hero who freed Bolivia, Colombia, Ecuador, Peru, and Venezuela from the Spanish, the man who is called *"El Libertador"* (The Liberator), said Latin America is "ungovernable and whosoever works for revolution is plowing the sea." With bitterness in every word, he advised the sensible to emigrate, correctly predicted that the countries he had governed would end as mobs or as the fiefs of tyrants, and that Latin America was destined for poverty and chaos.[75]

It is very difficult, however, to persuade Latin America to be objective about itself as it has a long intellectual history of blaming everything but its own nature. America has been a convenient scapegoat. However, the major problems of Latin America spring from its Spanish traditions. They have left a legacy of mysticism which created a general disdain for material well-being, a tradition of centralized authority and social hierarchy. The centralized authority, seen both in traditional Roman Catholicism and in Latin government, has produced a mentality which feels comfortable in taking orders instead of thinking for oneself. The social hierarchy, perhaps the most destructive of all the Spanish legacy, has made it very difficult for anyone from the lower ranks to rise in life.[76]

Those in the hierarchy have also found it difficult to understand that private privilege is not the same as public. Traditionally, public servants have felt they could do anything they chose, a belief which helped create and perpetuate oppression of classes. The marriage of centralized authority and social hierarchy also produced a "patron" system, both on a public and private basis. The patron system establishes one man, or a social oligarchy, as the source of material privilege. These combined systems have discouraged private enterprise.

Nonetheless, from 1945 to 1975 (until the OPEC-induced depression) Latin America averaged an annual growth of 5.2 percent, one of the strongest in the world. Since World War II, manufacturing has grown at the rate of 6.5 percent each year and agricultural output per worker grew 2 percent a year. Total agricultural output grew by 3.5 percent annually. Wages and salaries have also grown more than 2 percent a year since World War II. The figures are even better when compared with population growth. From 1945 to 1975 Latin America's population grew from one hundred and forty million to three hundred and twenty-four million. Despite this, the per capita income grew at rates "seldom equaled" anywhere.[77]

At the same time, infant mortality was almost cut in half, life expectancy extended by twenty years, illiteracy reduced by 25 percent, and school attendance increased to 90 percent. Obviously, something had been working in Latin America.[78]

Instead of facing these problems and these truths, instead of opting for real solutions and gradual change based on proven methods, the bishops chose to blame capitalism and encourage revolution. There was bitter fruit in that choice. Two years later, after the bishops had put their stamp of approval on "progressive" thought, the first liberation theologians began to publish their work.

So accepted has been its legitimacy that the basic tenets of liberation theology are rarely questioned in many orders of the Catholic church. The Dominican Interprovincial Conference of Latin America held its first seminar in Costa Rica in 1983. Its final document asserts that Latin America's troubles are "the consequences of world-wide imperialism," instigated by the United States. They advocate socialism and condone any violence needed to institute this system. Just to make sure that all Dominicans agree with them, the conference recommended that future Dominicans be screened as to their political beliefs.[79]

AMERICAN CLERGY ACCEPT LIBERATION THEOLOGY

Although the first liberation theologians were Latin (and Catholic), liberation theology soon jumped to the United States and began to make an impact on Catholic orders. The Maryknolls, based in New York state, are the principal distribution point of both liberation theology literature and activism in the United States.

Orbis Books, the Maryknoll publishing house established in 1970, publishes a very large volume of liberation theology literature and authors every year. *A Theology of Liberation* by Gustavo Gutierrez was first published in the United States by Orbis Books. Father Miguel D'Escoto, a Maryknoll priest who is now foreign minister in the Sandinista regime in Nicaragua, worked for years as the editor of *Maryknoll* magazine. He then founded Orbis Books. Shortly thereafter he went home to Nicaragua and began fighting with the Sandinistas.

Approximately half of the books in the Orbis catalog each year are devoted to liberation theology and radical political thought. *Maryknoll* has almost deserted the traditional missionary emphasis and now devotes its issues to leftist political themes. The editors and writers seem to particularly appreciate Cuba as a role model for the Third World. The Maryknoll priests and nuns have been so politically active in Latin "liberation movements" that their presence is unwelcome in Honduras and many other Latin countries.

Never far behind the latest leftist movement, the Protestant mainline church is also now imbued with the rhetoric of liberation theology. United Methodist Roy Sano, the president of the United Methodist Board of Global Ministries, declared in 1984 that it is "profanity" in theological thinking when God's salvation is seen only in acts of "reconciliation," the forgiveness of sins, and rebirth in Christ. People have to understand the importance of liberation in salvation. "That is why I have supported liberation theology and the liberation movements that are under attack," he said. Sano had strong words for a mission board which published a pamphlet criticizing the Board of Global Ministries for embracing liberation theology. He called it "an act of blasphemy" against the Holy Spirit.[80]

UNITED METHODISTS SPREAD THE WORD

Considering that viewpoint, it is not surprising that Peggy Billings, head of the World Division of the United Methodist Board of Global Ministries, wrote *Fire Beneath the Frost* in 1984. It was written for denominations who are members of the National Council of Churches. It sings the praises of "Minjung," a liberation theology slanted for Korean consumption. The book portrays the United States as the oppressor of South Korea (instead of its liberator) and presents the South Korean government as an unmitigated oppressor.

"Today, in the ancient nation of Korea, lives a generation of people battling foreign occupation, war, human rights violations and restricted freedom," Billings wrote. The book did not mention that the American presence is required to keep North Korea from invading or how the North Koreans (who are some of the most oppressed people on earth) are treated by their government.

Indignant South Korean Christians immediately charged that the book is distorted and pushes a theology of which most Koreans have never heard. At the time Billings wrote the book, Korea's ten million Christians were reporting a church which was rapidly growing, were building hundreds of new churches, and were reporting a climate of eased political repression. *Fire Beneath the Frost* focused on a small percentage of Korean Christians who are political activists, they charged, but ignored "the vast majority of Christians who are moving toward a more humane society in a slower and more indirect way."[81]

Billings admitted to the *United Methodist Reporter* that the book "has a bias." Spokesmen for the editor and publisher said that the material was not meant to provide a balanced overview but to introduce the "cutting edge" of theological thought in Korea.

It appears that liberation theology has infiltrated the ranks of Methodist missionaries. After the newspaper articles appeared, several missionaries contacted the *Reporter*. Their ranks were divided over which route to take in serving Korean Christians. Some, characterized as "old-style," identified with the "pietistic," church-growth-oriented majority of Korean United Methodists. Another faction identified with Christians who are working against oppression in their country. The latter, obviously influenced by liberation theology, seemed to disapprove of the "pietistic" missionaries and noted that many of them are near retirement.[82]

It is true that the South Korean government is oppressive and it is true that it needs to change. It does not follow, however, that the American church should attempt to lure Korean Christians away from traditional teaching for political purposes.

To sum up, liberation theology is not only a serious deviation from traditional Christianity, it justifies violent revolution and is often aligned with destructive political movements. And like all ideas which blur the distinctions between the moral and immoral, it has rapidly gained followers.

Rejecting liberation theology as unacceptable does not mean the Christian church should hold itself aloof from social issues. The church should lead the drive for social justice. But that drive should be based on Christ's admonition that we love our neighbors as ourselves, not a call for armed revolution. The church should condone revolution only when it is the last resort to cruel tyranny—not as a means to overthrow unjust (or allegedly unjust) economic systems. Most importantly, the church itself should not participate in violence for any reason. The Christian church is the bride of Christ, and to stain that church with blood is to destroy its sanctity.

Those who believe that the ends justify the means should do two things. They should read what ends the means of liberation theology has brought Nicaragua, in the next chapter, and they should remember what Pope John Paul said to Peruvians sympathetic to Communist guerrillas: "Evil is never a road to good . . . violence inexorably engenders new forms of oppression and slavery, ordinarily more grave than those which it pretends to liberate. . . . I ask you, then, in the name of God: Change your course!"[83]

The Sandinista Persecution of Christians

In the poor Nicaraguan village of Cuapa, located almost in the center of the country, lived, not so long ago, a sacristan named Bernardo. Bernardo, like all Roman Catholic sacristans, was in charge of the sacred vessels and vestments of his church. One night in 1981, Bernardo went into the sanctuary and saw a light radiating from the statue of the Virgin. But when Bernardo turned on the electric light it disappeared.[1]

Three weeks later, in the morning, as Bernardo was fishing in the river, the landscape changed. The sun was in eclipse, he heard birdsong, leaves rustling, and he saw flashes of lightning. A cloud on which a beautiful, barefoot young woman was standing descended to earth. She had chestnut hair, honey-colored eyes, Bernardo said, and was wrapped in a cape embroidered with jewels. She had a crown of stars on her head.[2]

"My name is Mary," the young woman said, the Mother of God. The vision appeared to Bernardo many times. The young woman told him that the Sandinistas were "atheists, Communists" and they were the reason she had chosen to appear in Nicaragua. She also said, Bernardo reported, that if his country did not change, it would continue to suffer and would hasten the coming of the Third World War.[3]

Monsignor Vega, the Bishop of Juigalpa, authorized Bernardo to reveal the miracle, and the Virgin's visits became well-known throughout the country.[4]

One day Bernardo had visitors; three government officials. They offered him a farm with good land and cows—absolutely free—if only he would say the Virgin was a Sandinista. When Bernardo said he could only tell the truth, the officials offered a sensible compromise. "All he had to do was to stop saying she was anti-Sandinista." Bernardo refused.[5]

Campaigns were then conducted against him in the government's newspapers, *Barricada* and *Nuevo Diario*, and on state-owned television. "He was called insane, hysterical, delusional. One morning at dawn, the police broke into his house and tried to kidnap him." The church, fearing for his safety, took him to a seminary in Managua, where he takes care of the garden.[6]

This, then, is the ultimate outcome of liberation theology in Nicaragua. When Nicaragua's Sandinista government is able to use religion for its own ends—as it did before it successfully overthrew former dictator Anastasio Somoza—it does so. When the Sandinistas can use Christians and the Christian church for propaganda purposes, they do so. When they can do neither, they attack.

The nine-member junta has been so successful with the first two tactics since former dictator Anastasio Somoza was deposed in 1979 that Nicaragua has become "the magnet for liberation theologians, socialist Catholics, radical theologians, apocalyptic prophets and Marxist-Leninist priests from all over the world."[7] It is also the sacred pilgrimage for thousands of American Christians—most of whom return reporting that Nicaragua's government is dedicated to nothing but the good of its people; that it is demonstratively Christianity in action.

Meanwhile, bureaucracies and leadership of the mainline church and the National Council of Churches have worked steadily to convince Congress to end funding for the anti-Sandinista guerrillas.

They have achieved partial success, as of 1986, in that funding for the anti-Sandinistas is extremely controversial among Christians (as well as other Americans). Many also believe American foreign policy—at least regarding Central America—is as evil as the Soviets'. In helping shape these opinions, the church has harmed its country's interests and has helped to perpetuate a regime that is actively persecuting Christians in Central America.

Should the Sandinistas be replaced by a government of another ideological stripe—by the anti-Sandinista guerrillas or some sort of democratic coalition—it would make no difference to this or the following chapter. The point is not whether the Sandinistas are destined to rule forever. This chapter examines the FSLN's (Sandinista Front for National Liberation) hostility to Christianity and attempts to prove that the American mainline church has once again indulged itself in illusions about a Marxist-Leninist regime.

Due to limited space, only Sandinista aggression against Christianity will be examined. However, the Sandinista war on the Indians of Nicaragua provides an excellent forum to examine both the Sandinistas' real character and their hostility to Christianity. It is a story covering eight years of murder, racial prejudice, and religious persecution. Most Americans are unaware of the story because the Sandinistas have diligently worked to camouflage their actions, and because the Miskitos are one of the world's little-known peoples. The Miskitos do, however, have a long history and share a common heritage with American Christians.

About one hundred and sixty thousand Miskito, Sumo, and Rama Indians have lived for centuries on the Caribbean coast of Nicaragua in two hundred and fifty-six villages. About 55 percent are Moravian Christians and the rest Roman Catholic. Many of them have adopted European surnames as a result of missionary work done among their tribe.

The Miskitos were discovered by Christopher Columbus on his fourth voyage. It was once a powerful, rich tribe until ravaged by sixteenth-century slave traders. It was not destroyed, however, and Europeans were welcomed to the Atlantic Coast because they brought mutually profitable trade. The Indians speak English (as well as their native language) because Great Britain was highly visible as a trading presence for two hundred years. The Indians have been historically isolated from Spanish-speaking Nicaragua, although Spain and later Nicaraguan governments tried many times to colonize the area.[8]

Miskitos have always lived communally, feeding themselves by farming, hunting, and fishing. They elect elders, through local councils, to govern. Traditionally, they have enjoyed the right to self-government, to use tax money through their political structure, to speak their own language and practice their own religion, to own their own lands, and have possessed total exemption from military service. Nicaraguan governments tried to change these rules occasionally, but always retreated in the face of Indian defiance.[9]

OPPRESSION OF INDIANS

The Sandinistas were apparently determined to do what no Nicaraguan government had succeeded in doing before: controlling the Indians. Immediately after the revolution the Sandinistas ordered that Sandinista Defense Committees be established in the villages and attempted to replace the council of elders with Sandinista organizations.[10] They seized control of the economic infrastructure of the Caribbean coast in 1980 and 1981, including the Indians' food cooperatives, fishing fleets and the transportation systems to remote areas.

The defense committees (already established elsewhere in Nicaragua) are officially charged with spying on their neighbors and in organizing—and enforcing—Sandinista activities and policies. Weapons used in this enforcement are ration cards needed to buy food and official documents needed for internal travel. Resentment was intensified when the Sandinistas expropriated all Indian land and resources in 1980 and 1981, including lucrative lumbering areas.[11] When food became scarce the Indian organization which was the traditional authority for the tribes (The Alliance for the Development of the Miskitos and Sumo people) called a strike. The government violently suppressed the demonstrators.[12]

Indian leaders were then arrested, including Lester Athers, an Alliance leader whom the Sandinista government subsequently murdered in October 1979.[13] Education was next. The Sandinistas distributed atheist tracts to the population and forced Marxist indoctrination on the school system. Most of the instructors were Cuban. They also forced the other teachers to teach in Spanish.[14]

After months of demonstrations against the government and active resistance by sixty-five Indian warriors who were called the *"Tropa Cruce"* (Crucifix Troop), the regime in 1982 began a massive "resettlement program," beginning with ten thousand Miskitos and Sumos who lived on the Rio Coco.[15]

INDIAN UPRISING AND CONCENTRATION CAMPS

By 1985 the regime had herded approximately eighteen thousand Indians into thirteen concentration camps, only six of which they acknowledged. They now use their prisoners as slave labor on coffee plantations in Jinotega and Matagalpa.[16] Refugees to Honduras have confirmed this report. They have also charged that the camps are holding-pens for Indians forced to work as slave laborers on the state's sugar and palm oil plantations.[17]

Thousands more have fled to Honduras and Costa Rica as refugees, and another three thousand to six thousand Indian warriors are fighting the Sandinista government. They call their war "Indian *aiklabanka*," or Indian war. The Indian resistance has coalesced in the MISURASATA and MISURA organizations. The former, an acronym which stands for the first syllables of Miskito, Sumo, Rama, and Sandinista, was a member of the anti-Sandinista organization of the Democratic Revolutionary Alliance. MISURA is partially coordinated with the Nicaraguan Democratic Force, the largest anti-Sandinista guerrilla army.[18]

Indian warriors have had hand-to-hand battles with Sandinista forces, many of which they have won. The government has retaliated by bombing and strafing villages in an attempt to destroy the warrior's access to tribal food and help. Little information on this war has reached the outside world because Nicaragua's Caribbean Coast has been closed to most civilians since 1982.[19]

In November 1982, the MISURASATA Council of Ancients (elders) produced a document which charges that the FSLN, as a part of the "relocations," had destroyed forty-nine communities, burned more than four thousand homes, cut down the fruit trees, shot all the live-stock, and sent the people on a forced march to the camps which lasted from eleven to fifteen days.[20]

MURDERS AND ATROCITIES

"During the forced march . . . the invalids, lame, blind and paralyzed persons were gathered together in the village of Tulinbila, they were put inside the church and they were burned—13 persons thus died," the ancients charged.[21]

According to the testimony, villages continued to be burned there-after and in April Rev. Abel Flores and thirteen deacons were arrested and taken away by helicopter. Women and girls as young as twelve were raped (some in churches), whole groups of people were machine-gunned to death, men were tortured, people were buried alive, people were prevented from attending church, and services were forbidden.[22]

The testimony of the elders regarding the people who were buried alive was inadvertently confirmed by a leader of the Indian resistance. He mentioned the incident in an American publication in 1982. The event happened in Leimus, he said, in December 1981. About thirty-five people were buried alive, some of whom were rescued by their relatives after the Sandinistas left the village.[23]

In publications from the council, the elders charged that men had even been murdered on the "patios" of their churches; that people mysteriously disappeared; that people were dragged from church and shot immediately outside; that it was forbidden to fish; that children starved to death and died of dehydration on the forced marches; and that Moravian pastors were ordered to submit their sermons before they were delivered.[24]

"I DENOUNCE"

Personal testimonies to these atrocities are mind-numbing. Always beginning "I denounce," the witnesses explain in calm language atroc-ities most humans can barely comprehend. Typical is Emilia Smith's testimony. He says the Sandinistas gathered about one thousand and thirty people from his village, Asang, on December 27, 1981 and forced them to leave. They were marched to San Carlos, thirty kilome-ters downriver. When they reached their destination eight soldiers took Smith, his brother Ernesto Smith, and friend Benigno Valle to "Ispail" beach.[25]

". . . then we realized that they had taken us there to assassinate us," Smith wrote. "There, while four guarded us, four others went down to the beach with my brother Ernesto Smith, they tied his hands and feet with black nylon rope, then made a bonfire and began to burn his feet, hands, chest and penis, asking that he tell them if (he) had contact with the counter-revolutionaries. When my brother denied this, they said: 'Son of a bitch, you are a counter-revolutionary and today we are going to kill you, your brother and the other man also.' On seeing him tortured, I wished to help him and they hit me with their rifle butts.[26]

"Later they cut off both his feet with a new machete, my brother cried and asked them not to torture him, that he was innocent but that they should know that God exists and that one day He would make justice for all.[27]

"Later they cut his neck as if he were a pig, and once dead, they shoveled a grave in the sand, put his body in it with the machete on top of my brother's chest. . . . This occurred January, 1982.[28]

"They took Benigno Valle and myself to Asan, and made us sleep in·the village school, and on January 21, 1982 at 4 a.m. when our guards were careless, we got out of the school and crossed the river swimming. Thus we suffered and thus they killed my brother Ernesto Smith, 50 years old, married, with 10 children that today are left forsaken."[29]

OAS TESTIMONY

Bernard Nietschmann, professor of geography at the University of California at Berkeley and author of books on the Miskitos (which he has researched for eighteen years), corroborated the Indian's testimony before the Organization of American States in October 1983.

Nietschmann traveled to Costa Rica, Honduras, and Nicaragua in 1983 to interview Miskito, Sumo, and Rama Indians about their difficulties. He told the OAS that he had used the standard systematic techniques of formal interviews, informal discussions, crosschecking, corroboration, and obtaining multiple confirmations to establish validity and reliability of the information. A tape recording, film, and photographic record was made.

Nietschmann found, to his horror, that the Sandinistas had done everything that the Council of Ancients claimed they had. Plus, Indians were forbidden to travel and were denied access to basic food stores. There was also a complete absence of any medicine, health care, or educational service in the camps; most of their goods had been stolen, and last, but not least, they were denied their right to worship God.

"For example, it was reported to me," Nietschmann testified, "by several firsthand sources that one man was nailed through his hands and ankles to a wall and told he would remain there until he either confessed to being a 'contra' or died. He died. . . . I was shown scars from what they said were bayonet wounds (a man of 60 years), fingernails pulled out (a man of 48 years), deep scars under fingernails from nails driven in (a man of 52 years). Several men reported that they had been held under water for long periods to extract confessions. Another man had been tied by his feet and hung upside down and beaten repeatedly with sticks. His body still showed evidence of bruises and his shoulders were deformed."[30]

RAPE AND RELIGIOUS PERSECUTION

"Rape by Sandinista soldiers of Miskito girls and women has been common. In one village, for example, six women between the ages of 15 and 42 were raped by the occupying Sandinista soldiers. Two were gang-raped. . . . Only in those villages now under the protection of Miskito warriors are religious services being held. . . . And even in this large zone many villages cannot hold church services because their religious leaders are in jail or are in exile in Honduras or Costa Rica.[31]

"During the Sandinista military occupation villages or churches have commonly been used as jails, to detain men and women accused or suspected of counterrevolutionary activities. Churches have been used to house Sandinista soldiers. Bibles and hymn books have been destroyed. Villagers accuse the Sandinista soldiers of defecating and urinating in the churches. . . . I heard reports of churches that had been burned elsewhere in Indian communities. . . . [32]

"The Miskitos are a very religious people, and they have suffered greatly from the denial of their freedom of religion. In almost all of my discussions with hundreds of Miskito men and women, this was a principal grievance they reported to me."[33]

Accusing the Moravian church of being the center of Indian resistance,[34] the regime closed over fifty Moravian churches, and jailed and killed pastors. The Moravian Social Action Committee was closed, and Moravian pastors have been jailed in an attempt to force them to become informers on fellow clerics.[35] The Moravian Biblical Institute (which trained lay pastors) was forcibly closed.[36]

The Sandinistas claim they released the Indians whom they had held captive and allowed them to return to their villages. This is untrue. The Sandinistas released approximately nine thousand Indians in mid-1985, in return for a ceasefire with some Indian warriors. There are still approximately nine thousand to fifteen thousand Indians left in concentration camps. Worse, the Sandinistas soon violated the ceasefire. Indian fighters who had not seen their families for more than three years crossed the river from Honduras to visit. Knowing that the Indian resistance was low on ammunition, the Sandinistas attacked the villages with mortar fire and armor-backed troop invasions. This happened March 25, 1986. About nine thousand Indians subsequently fled to Honduras. These were the same Indians which had been released from the camps. The Sandinistas have also made it a practice to bomb villages in general (the few which still have inhabitants), a practice which has been reported by *The New York Times*.[37]

SANDINISTAS PERSECUTE THE CATHOLIC CHURCH

Obviously not satisfied in just attempting to destroy the Indians' worship of God, the Sandinistas have made serious attempts to destroy traditional Christianity in the rest of Nicaragua as well. The beginning salvo in this campaign was the 1980 announcement that Christians were not permitted to evangelize within the Sandinista organization.[38]

About a year later the regime announced that the weekly televised Masses would be rotated among Catholic priests. Customarily Cardinal Obando y Bravo (then archbishop) or his designated stand-in celebrated this Mass. The Cardinal, believing that pro-Sandinista priests would be chosen, refused to cooperate. The televised masses were cancelled. Catholic Radio then fell under heavy daily censorship and has now been taken off the air; issues of *Iglesia*, the church newspaper, have been confiscated and its press and printing equipment have been seized as well. Open air Masses have also been forbidden, the Catholic social welfare office has been closed, and the Sandinistas have prevented the church from establishing a human rights office. They have also begun taking seminarians out of school and forcing them to join the army.[39]

THE "POPULAR CHURCH"

Not content to merely silence the church, the Sandinistas have made a concerted effort to separate the Catholic grass-roots from the influence of the Catholic hierarchy by creating an *"Iglesia Popular,"* or Popular Church. It is composed of about twenty priests out of approximately three hundred and sixty now in Nicaragua.[40] Priests from the Popular Church base their beliefs on liberation theology. Some lead the basic Christian communities which are centered around liberation theology, and some work for the liberation theology research and propaganda centers (the Centro Antonio Valdivieso, CEPAD, and the Instituto Historico Centroamericano). (More on these organizations in the next chapter.)[41]

The basic Christian communities are neighborhood groups of Catholics which meet for prayer and study. The groups were originally organized by practitioners of liberation theology—the goal of most of the communities, therefore, is social and political reform based on

Marx's concept of class conflict. The radical groups (there are conservative basic communities which do not follow liberation theology) are greatly outnumbered in Nicaragua by the more traditional Catholics.

THE RESEARCH CENTERS

The research and propaganda centers traditionally claimed that Marxism and Christianity are "compatible" because they both provide an option for the poor. After they gained access to Sandinista state media, however, they began to claim only Marxists could be good Christians. They now declare that to be a Christian means giving "unconditional support" to the revolution.[42]

Abundant international aid supports this apostasy. Most of these centers, however, are financially supported by the American church; through the years, the United Methodists had given (as of Summer 1985) about $100,000, the National Council of Churches had contributed $365,329, the Presbyterians $100,000, and the World Council of Churches had donated approximately $176,000.[43]

The centers have full-time employees, both theologians and laity, and recording and printing facilities. It is evident that they have full government backing because they have exclusive access to the state's communications network.[44]

Having access to the state network is important because it runs 100 percent of the television channels, 90 percent of the radio stations, and two of the three newspapers.[45] (The third newspaper, *La Prensa*, is opposed to the regime. It is so heavily censored, however, that it has sometimes been unable to publish at all for lack of material.) Unlike the centers based on liberation theology, the Catholic Church is forbidden from receiving funds or contributions from abroad.[46]

MOLINA HOSTS THE LIBERATION THEOLOGY SHOW

Santa Maria de Los Angeles, a "Popular Church" staffed by Franciscan Uriel Molina (who presided over the Mass which memorialized Colombia's M-19 guerrillas), has few traditional Catholic statues. It is festooned instead with "huge revolutionary murals in which Christ is dressed as a Nicaraguan peasant and villainous Yankee imperialists and well-fed soldiers shoot young people carrying Sandinista flags. The Peasant Mass, (used at the church) by composer Carlos Mejia Godoy, is punctuated by revolutionary songs. . . ."[47]

Mario Vargas Llosa, a Peruvian novelist, attended a service at Santa Maria. At least half those attending, Llosa reported, were North American visitors. Molina's sermon dealt with the "process of revolutionary social change which Christians should experience through their faith." When it was time for the embrace of peace, a feature of most Catholic services, the North Americans rushed to Interior Minister (and head of State Security) Tomas Borgé—who was attending with Llosa—and asked for his autograph.[48]

At most services, other visitors have revealed, Molina ran quickly through his homily and Bible lesson. Then he took off his robe to "reveal a polyester-blend leisure suit" and came down from the altar with a small microphone (like a "talk-show host") and encouraged the audience to expound on political issues. The chosen participants, of course, always spoke on themes dear to the hearts of the Sandinista government.[49]

Molina has a history of close cooperation with the Sandinistas, including one instance in which his students (before Somoza's fall) left their studies to join the guerrillas. Some of the students now hold important positions in the government. One is now a member of the National Directorate and one is chief of staff in the army.[50]

"DIVINE MOBS"

The *Iglesia Popular* has so little support from Nicaraguans that the services, as Llosa saw, are filled mostly with foreign Sandinista sympathizers. The lack of support for the Popular Church in Nicaragua also forces the regime to recruit people involved in the defense committees for use as "*las turbas divinas*," or divine mobs. These mobs are ostensibly indignant members of the Popular Church, and they are used to attack traditional Catholic churches and the Catholic hierarchy. This is done at the direction of Nicaraguan State Security (secret police).[51] The attacks are useful for propaganda against the hierarchy (it proves how allegedly unpopular the Catholic hierarchy is among the people) and for purposes of intimidation.

Despite the name, members of these mobs are less than divine. Some mob members have fought with the Marxist guerrillas in El Salvador,[52] and most of them appear at demonstrations carrying clubs.

Father Mario Madrid, a Catholic priest expelled from the country in 1984, told *Policy Forum* that people in his Managua parish had been forced to join the *turbas*. Many of the people who had no houses were allowed to build "shanties" in empty lots. After building the houses, however, they were forced to participate in "every single political demonstration of the Sandinista front." When the Pope arrived, Madrid said, the coerced parishioners were forced to go to his Mass with their Sandinista Defense Committees and demonstrate against John Paul.[53]

Exiled Sandinista dissident Humberto Belli attended Mass at a small church at the university three times a week before he left the country and consequently knew all the parishioners. After one service, he remembers, about eight "revolutionary Christians" entered the chapel to stage a one-week sit-in as a protest against Cardinal Obando. No one belonging to the church knew them.[54]

Miguel Bolaños-Hunter, a former Sandinista field commander and member of Nicaraguan State Security, subsequently confirmed Belli's comments in an interview with the Washington-based Institute on Religion and Democracy. Bolaños said when the Cardinal tried to transfer a "progressive" priest to another position the Sandinistas placed *turbas* around the church. In that particular parish there were not enough Sandinista sympathizers to create a mob, so the regime brought in Defense Committee members from other neighborhoods who then pretended to be from the parish they were invading.[55]

"I knew a couple of the officers involved who were in charge of another area on the other side of the city," Bolaños said. "I told them, 'I saw you on T.V. What were you doing over there? It's not your sector.' They said, 'Well, you know, I had to bring some people from my sector to make this demonstration bigger.'"[56]

"When Monsignor Obando refused to talk to the mob, they bolted and shut the doors of the church, and occupied the church. They slept in the church and did various things that profaned the building. When Monsignor Obando found out, he sent Bishop Bosco Vivas to recover the tabernacle from the altar. When Bosco Vivas arrived, the mob beat him and knocked him to the ground."[57]

THREE DAYS IN OCTOBER

The regime's real feelings about the Roman Catholic Church became most apparent when its actions, during three days in October 1983, are examined:

- October 29—mobs began to demonstrate at twenty-two churches in Managua and some outside the city. They interrupted Masses, chanted at churchgoers, and threatened priests;[58]

- October 30—a mob gathered at Saint Jude church in Managua. The mob was acting against a church-planned demonstration against the new draft law, according to the progovernment press. The mob interrupted Mass and struck Father Silvio Fionseca. The mob refused to allow Monsignor Bosco Vivas to enter the area. A second mob, acting on the same day, refused to allow the church to hold a bazaar;[59]

- October 30—Catholic leadership decided to cancel Masses for the day, but were not able to contact all priests. A mob armed with clubs subsequently interrupted Mass at San Francisco church in the Bolonia area, broke windows, and vandalized cars. That night a mob gathered in front of the Santa Maria church in the San Juan neighborhood and another burned a tire on the front steps of Santa Carmen church;[60]

- October 31—Two foreign priests, Luis Corral Prieto and Jose Maria Pacheco, had their residencies revoked. They were, respectively, the director and assistant director of Salesian School in Managua. The government then announced the arrest of one Father Antonio for preaching against the draft and allegedly advocating counter-revolutionary activities.[61]

FATHER PEÑA ARRESTED

Accusing priests of various crimes is a favorite Sandinista activity. Father Luis Amado Peña was arrested by the Sandinistas in 1983 and accused of transporting explosives. Peña denied the whole accusation. He claimed he had merely been taking a package to a car when he was arrested. He said he had delivered the package as a favor for an acquaintance. The government never explained how State Security nabbed Peña at the exact moment he was in possession of the alleged explosives or why they were accompanied by state television crews.

Church authorities then hired international lawyer Roger Guevara Meña for Pena's defense, only to have the Sandinistas arrest him. Cubans interrogated Meña and then placed him in total solitary confinement. He was placed in his cell without most of his clothes. The cell had no toilet, and he was fed only rice, moldy cheese, and stale bread for ten days. He was finally taken from his cell, given a shave, and put into the sun for two hours to make him presentable to the world. State Security told him they hoped he had "learned something" from his lesson.[62]

Father Peña later said he pardoned "those who participated in this trap."[63] Presumably he also forgives approximately one thousand members of the mob who broke up Mass at his church (Church of the Holy Ghost) on June 21, 1984, shouting "*Paredon!*"—Spanish for "to the firing squad."[64]

EXPULSIONS

Soon after the Peña incident, in July of 1984, the government exiled ten priests.* The regime claimed they were involved in subversive political action because they had participated in an antigovernment demonstration led by Cardinal Obando y Bravo. That demonstration had been called to support Peña. The priests were also accused of using their pastoral ministry to preach against the revolution and promote opposition.

The Rev. Santiago Anitua was the only ordained priest for a flock of about fifty thousand when he was expelled. He later said he did not participate in the demonstration. The reason he was expelled, he said, was because he was "faithful to the bishops."[65]

Other reasons, he said, had to do with the nature of his work. He and all of the other expelled priests were working on areas the Sandinistas considered "key and sensitive," primarily youth work and work with urban workers and peasants. The regime has made a concerted effort to win Nicaragua's children, using youth organizations and indoctrination in the schools.[66]

Several of the expelled priests had been stationed in barrios which were famous because they had been some of the first to rise against Somoza—the barrios Orientales and the Indian Monimbo. Other priests were organizers of strong grass-roots Catholic organizations such as the Cursillos and the charismatic renewal movement. Expulsion of the priests undermined the Catholic presence in Nicaragua, as it was meant to, Anitua said.[67]

Sandinista State Security went on another rampage in the fall of 1985. They "detained" more than fifty priests, who were subsequently treated as prisoners. They took the priests' fingerprints and photographs. At least one was beaten. About one hundred Catholic laymen were treated in the same manner, including eight men who had organized a welcoming procession for Cardinal Obando in Chinandega on November 10. Obando y Bravo is not allowed to hold open-air Masses or processionals.

SANDINISTAS ATTACK POPE JOHN PAUL II

The most blatant action by the Sandinistas against the church, however, occurred during the 1983 visit of Pope John Paul II. The Pope was forced to say Mass in Managua's main plaza before an altar without a cross while thousands of hecklers planted by State Security shouted Sandinista slogans and verbally attacked him.

The goal of State Security was to force the Pope to bless the Sandinista "martyrs" who had died in combat against the anti-Sandinista guerrillas and to punish him if he refused to do so. They arranged where Sandinista Defense Committee members (the neighborhood organizations which are responsible for party fidelity on every block in Nicaragua) would stand, what they would chant, and what they would say to the Pope.[68] In order to insure that these activities went well, highly trusted defense members and about one hundred and fifty security officers went to the plaza well before the Mass. They placed themselves in front of the stage directly below where the Pope would stand.

Buses from the neighborhoods were also subordinated to the committees, and real Catholics were forced to travel to the Mass with Defense Committee escorts. Many Catholics tried to go to the plaza early in order to circumvent the Sandinistas, but many of them first went to church to pray. That was a mistake. Members of the divine mobs surrounded the churches and would not allow them to leave until the Mass had begun. The real Catholics were still in the majority at the plaza, Bolaños-Hunter (who was there) said, but they found it impossible to interfere with Sandinista activities without being beaten, killed, or reported to State Security.[69]

All the planning was rewarded. Pope John Paul was subjected to extreme verbal abuse from the hecklers when he refused to bless the Sandinista dead. Further, during the Mass women from the Heroes' Mothers organization—whose sons were said to have been killed in combat—and some men from the *turbas* went on stage. They grabbed the microphone from the Pope's hands and demanded he pray for their "heroes." These activities were directed by Commander Manuel Calderon of State Security.[70]

When a group of five or six Catholics tried to go to the stage to help the Pope, Lenin Cerna, the head of State Security, took a machine-gun from one of his body guards, pulled the bolt, and told them if they went any further he would shoot them.[71]

There was so much shouting and chanting from the crowd that the Pope could not continue. The mob leaders had taken the microphone which was connected to an enormous sound system the government had bought especially for the event. There is no question that this unforgivable demonstration was blessed by the *junta*. Daniel Ortega and the other eight *commandantes* stood on a platform near the Pope, urging the mob on, shouting slogans themselves and raising their fists in the air.[72]

Sandinista attitudes toward the Pope (and of religion in general) are now well understood by the people of Nicaragua. When they wish to protest against the regime they put a picture of John Paul on the front of their houses and stores.[73]

CARBALLO AND HIS "PARISHIONER"

Another ugly attack against a religious figure occurred in 1982 when the Cardinal's assistant, the Rev. Bismark Carballo (who is also head of Catholic Radio), was having lunch with a woman parishioner. Carballo said the woman had come to him for counseling and later begged him to come to her home for lunch. As they were eating, however, an armed man burst into the house, pistol-whipped the priest, and forced him to take off all his clothes. The woman also undressed. At that time a photographer strolled in and took a picture of Carballo.

In the meantime, a demonstration just happened to be marching down the woman's street, ostensibly on its way to the Argentine Embassy. They had to take a detour to pass the woman's home, however, a detail which was not overlooked by the foreign press. The street outside the woman's house was also filled with television cameras and reporters from government newspapers. They were supposedly covering the march.

When Carballo was dragged out of the house (the armed man had to have help from members of State Security), he was photographed again by television cameras and jeered by the crowd. The woman claimed she was having an afternoon frolic with Carballo when her husband unexpectedly returned home. The government press had a field day with the story. *Barricada*, however, did not bother to explain why the mob just happened to take a detour, why they disbanded after the incident (instead of continuing to the Argentine Embassy), or why State Security officers just happened to be at the house in time to rush in and help the "husband" pull Carballo out of the house. The woman and her supposed husband were never named.

The entire incident soon took on the characteristics of a vaudeville act. It was discovered at the beginning of the "*juicio*," or preliminary hearing, that the alleged husband was not the same man whose picture appeared in the paper as the husband. When the anti-Sandinista newspaper *La Prensa* tried to publish this fact, it was censored.[74] The government eventually dropped plans for a trial (the woman had brought suit against Carballo) but continued to attack Carballo by printing lewd cartoons of him in officially backed publications.[75]

The incident caused such anger in Nicaragua that Catholic high school students occupied numerous school buildings to show their support for Carballo. Subsequently the pro-Carballo students and pro-government youth clashed, leaving two young people dead and seven injured.[76] The Monimboseno Indians (who rose first against Somoza) rioted and attacked police stations, leaving three dead.[77]

"THE INVASION OF THE SECTS"

Moravians are not the only Protestants that have been attacked in Nicaragua. The official government newspaper *Barricada* in 1982 published two front-page, eight-column reports on Nicaragua's Protestants titled "The Invasion of the Sects." Seventh-Day Adventists, Mormons, and the Jehovah's Witnesses were portrayed as superstitious, manipulative fanatics who are part of a world strategy of cultural penetration directed by the United States government.[78]

Tomás Borgé subsequently went on the radio and announced that the churches under investigation were "enemies" funded by the CIA. He said that the State Council would require religious sects to register with authorities before they could open their doors.[79]

He then encouraged the *turbas* to act against the Protestant churches. By August 1982, more than twenty Managuan Protestant churches had been seized by the mobs. Some of the confiscated properties were eventually returned, but only on condition that the pastors not criticize the government.[80] The Salvation Army left Nicaragua permanently in 1980 after "ominous verbal threats from authorities, and, finally, instructions to close up the program and leave the country."[81]

Threats against Protestants materialized in 1985 when the Sandinistas begun to arrest Protestant Christians. Many of the Protestants were arrested in the middle of the night, stripped naked, and interrogated in "refrigerator" rooms. State Security attempted to force them to confess they were involved with the anti-Sandinista guerrillas. The interrogators also made attempts to entrap church workers in what would appear to be "sexual improprieties."[82] Several had their lives threatened and were ordered to cease all evangelical activity.

Turbas, once the favorite weapon used against Catholics, became ecumenical when they were sent to disrupt services in the Managua neighborhood of San Judas. Members of the Protestant church were attacked, and the pastor was forced to stop his crusade.[83]

Nicaragua's Jewish community has been treated almost as badly as the Christian community. After receiving death threats, having had their businesses and property confiscated, and the synagogue torched and later confiscated, almost the entire Jewish population in Nicaragua fled.[84]

There were approximately two hundred Jews in Nicaragua in the early 1970s and there are now approximately fifty. Typical harassment tactics have been incidents such as the jailing of Abraham Gorn, the president of the Jewish community. Gorn was forced to sweep the streets, his factory was expropriated, his bank account seized, and he was evicted from his home. The government-controlled newspaper *Nuevo Diario* has called Jewish places of worship "Synagogues of Satan."[85]

BALTODANO'S STORY

Protestant pastors have also been assaulted with the intent to kill, and Christian workers have been murdered. Pentecostal Prudencio Baltodano, speaking at a White House briefing in 1984, related his torture at the hands of the Sandinistas. After witnessing a battle between the contras and Sandinistas Baltodano said he, his family, and about forty neighbors—only one of whom was a grown man—fled to the mountains. The next day the Sandinista forces found them and tied up both men. The Sandinistas let the women go, but marched the men to a nearby farm and beat them, accusing them of recruiting for the contras.[86]

"This was an accusation that was not based in fact, not true . . . the only kind of conquest that I was trying to make was to conquer people to convince them to come over to God and Christ," Baltodano said. "The soldiers said to me 'Pastors and preachers are our enemies. We do not believe in God. In case you're interested, and for your information, we are Communist.' Then he introduced me to one of his colleagues and said: 'This is God.'[87]

"Then he said to me: 'Start to pray and see if your God will save you.' Then he ordered another soldier to take me up to a hill. They took me into a wooden area about 10 meters (30 feet) away. One guy said to another: 'Tie him up.' . . . The soldier tried to put the bayonet on the end of his rifle, but he was not able to get it in, so he threw the rifle down and took the bayonet, took me by the hair and cut one ear off. . . ." The soldiers tried to cut off a second ear, but only succeeded in maiming it.[88]

The soldiers believed they cut Baltodano's jugular vein and left him for what they thought was certain death. Fortunately, they were wrong and he was rescued before he bled to death. His ears have subsequently been restored through plastic surgery.

BALDIZON'S ACCUSATIONS

Baltodano told the group that his case was not an isolated instance, but one of many. That accusation was verified in 1985 when former Sandinista State Security officer Alvaro Baldizon-Aviles defected to the United States and accused his former government of murdering thousands of political dissidents.

Baldizon-Aviles told the American government and the Institute on Religion and Democracy that in 1983 he personally investigated the case of members of a Catholic organization, Delegates of the Word, who were tortured and murdered by officers of State Security. Baldizon said the couple (who had small children) were kidnapped from their home in San Miguelito (with a neighbor who had witnessed the kidnapping) and taken to the country. The woman was raped, and all the prisoners had their throats cut. The killers left to get a shovel, but when they returned they found the woman still alive. They then cut her throat again, then shot her with a AK-47 rifle.[89]

After the government was pressured by a Dutch commission on

human rights, the officers were tried for the murders and sentenced to thirty years in prison. However, when the commission left the country, the men were released from prison and returned to duty.[90]

Other instances which reveal the Sandinistas' real attitudes toward Christianity are as follows:

INSTRUCTIVE INCIDENTS

- Encarnacion Valdivia, a former Sandinista guerrilla fighter and now a contra with the nickname of *"El Tigrillo,"* said that after the FSLN came to power the army offered a six-day pass to anyone who renounced God. Soldiers who defended God, Valdivia said, got a red M in their record books and after the third M they would disappear. The letter M was short for *muerte* (death).[91]

- Geraldine de Macias—a former Maryknoll nun and now wife to exiled Sandinista cabinet member Edgard de Macias—has said the director of CEPAD, a "religious" organization now affiliated with the FSLN, told her that he had been approached by one of the organization's youth leaders. The young man, who had recently joined the FSLN, was troubled because he had been told that he could never have military status while he remained a Christian.[92]

- Miguel Bolaños-Hunter recalls a Mass given by Ernesto Cardenal, the erstwhile priest who now holds a post in the Sandinista government, while he was a guerrilla in the mountains. "It was the strangest Mass I ever experienced," he said. "Cardenal said that we were Christ, and the revolution was God. We were the saviors of Nicaragua. He said that it was a Christian duty to be a guerrilla.[93]

"He spoke of his own ideas about Marxism and the new society in the daily political training meetings in the mountains. I asked him privately how he combined God and Marxism. He explained that he really believed in history. He didn't believe in God anymore. He wasn't confused. He confused the people."[94]

Bolaños's testimony was upheld by Cardenal's statement to *Barricada*, made in 1985. Cardenal said, "For me, the Revolution is the Kingdom of God on earth."[95] According to Bolaños, State Security is considering sending young Sandinistas to seminary to become priests, in order to control the church. The party has already infiltrated the evangelical church, he said, because it is easier to become a pastor than a priest.

PRISONERS PERSECUTED

- According to a spokesman for Nicaragua's Discipleship Training Seminars there have been attempts to stop the practice of Christianity in the prison system.[96]

"In one instance," he said, "guards were ordered to separate all the Christian leaders from the general prison population. They then removed all the Christian literature they could find and burned it in front of the prisoners. Many of the most noted church leaders were removed from their usual cell blocks and reassigned to undisclosed locations."[97]

"Prisoners immediately staged a hunger strike protesting the drastic action against their leaders," the publication carrying the interview said, "and officials eventually relented by allowing the prisoners to have one Bible each. Many guards were removed because they appeared to sympathize with the Christians. It is known that several guards accepted Christ while guarding the 'notorious' Christian prisoners.[98]

"Today the trend has shifted once again. In April 1984, families visiting Christian prisoners reported that it appears that all Christian literature has been removed from prison cells, and the organized churches have been prohibited from holding worship services."[99]

CAMPUS CRUSADE FOR CHRIST

- Jimmy Hassan, a member of Nicaragua's Campus Crusade for Christ, said in a prayer letter released to the general public in May 1984 that he had been summoned, for the seventh time, by the Ministry of Justice. The official interrogated Hassan about Crusade activities, then handed him a document which stated that Hassan would "discontinue developing all evangelistic efforts; further, our coordinators were to promise to desist from going to the National University campus or any other secondary school.

"When she asked me to sign this document," Hassan said, "I firmly protested and refused to do so, and after several explanations she presented me with another document. In this one I was notified that Campus Crusade for Christ was strictly prohibited to carry off any activities that results in the preaching of the gospel." Hassan signed the document but added a note that said he did not intend to carry out its directives.

Hassan left Nicaragua in 1985 after the Nicaraguan government unjustly charged that he, and other ministers, were guilty of breaking a law banning criticism of the military draft. Hassan said the campaign against Christians had been intensified in 1985; pastors are followed on the streets, phones are tapped, ministers are questioned nearly every day, and all organizations that are not related to the Sandinista government (such as CEPAD) have been closed.[100]

EVANGELISTS FRUSTRATED

- Evangelists have been deliberately frustrated in their attempts to hold crusades in Nicaragua. The Sandinistas forbade Alberto Mottesi, an Argentinian evangelist, to advertise his November 1984 crusade except for spot announcements on Ondas de Luz, a heavily censored Christian radio station. No commercial television, other radio stations, or newspapers were allowed to publicize the meeting. On the second crusade night an enormous Russian-made military truck appeared and dozens of heavily-armed *turbas*-members jumped off the back. When they saw thousands of people in the stands, however, they were ordered back into the truck and were driven away.[101] One night the power was cut off in the section of the city where the crusade was being held, and the bus routes were detoured so that those wishing to attend were forced to walk several kilometers to reach the stadium.[102]

Oklahoma evangelist Larry Jones had the same experience as Mottesi. He told the authors that he was invited to Nicaragua in 1985 by the National Council of Evangelical Pastors. He had prior approval to hold his crusade from government officials as important as Daniel Ortega. He had also been promised that he could use the National Stadium in Managua. However, when Jones and the shipment of food and Bibles he brought for the poor reached Nicaragua, it was a different story. The government announced he could not use the National Stadium after all and did not tell him, until forty-five minutes before the crusade was scheduled to begin, which stadium he could use.[103]

Luckily for Jones, he had already despaired of using a stadium and had arranged to use a local churchyard. Due to the confusion, however, he only had two thousand people at the crusade instead of the planned forty thousand. Government officials had promised he could broadcast the service, but the power just happened to go off at the station the night Jones was supposed to broadcast.[104]

Jones had brought $100,000 worth of rice, beans, and Bibles to Nicaragua to distribute to the poor, as his organization has done all over the world. The government refused to release the supplies from government warehouses for six months. When they finally did so, the recipients were only given half of the rice that had been brought into the country and suspected that it had been switched. It was extremely stale although most rice can be safely stored for six months. The Bibles were finally released, but the government refused to release the twelve thousand copies of a sermon Jones had planned to distribute.[105]

When Jones tried to enter the country again, in September of 1985, the Sandinistas first refused to let him enter because he lacked a six months validation on his passport. He spent that night in Managua with a guard at his door, then flew to El Salvador to get his passport brought up to date. When he returned the next day, the government refused to let him enter the country because, he was later told, they had passed a law that no foreign "gospel preachers" could address mass audiences.[106]

Jones said he had taken no political stance before going to Nicaragua and is willing to give any government the benefit of the doubt. His philosophy about politics, he said, is that "when the elephant walks, the grass gets trampled." He says, "I was literally lied to."[107]

If it is possible to pick an "absolutely worst" attack on religion by the Sandinistas, the following event would undoubtedly be the one. According to Alvaro Baldizon, Bernardo, the sacristan who had visions of the Virgin Mary, was kidnapped by State Security in 1982, drugged, taken to a motel, and raped by a homosexual. The rape, of course, was videotaped. For special effect, the Sandinistas placed a statue of the Virgin above the bed and had candles lit at the base. Baldizon said Bernardo was told to stop talking about his experiences with the Virgin Mary or face the consequences. He apparently decided to stop talking.

Bernardo's silence has not helped the Sandinistas. People still stream to Cuapa, and a new church is being built to commemorate Bernardo's visions.

It is ironic that the Catholic Church, under the leadership of Cardinal Obando, once supported the Sandinistas that are now trying to destroy it. The Sandinista claim that Obando has always opposed the revolution is a lie. Throughout the seventies, the church refused gifts from the dictator and Obando directed a campaign against Somoza's violations of human rights.[108] In 1979 Obando fearlessly announced that Somoza had become intolerable and that Christians could, in good conscience, rebel against him.[109]

An "infuriated" Somoza retaliated by conducting a defamation campaign against the archbishop, whom he once called "Commandante Obando."[110] The bishops of Nicaragua went so far as to issue a pastoral letter after the Sandinista triumph which supported the new regime. Obando gave a victory Mass. None of the church's support has made a difference. The Sandinistas are obviously determined to destroy Christianity.

That determination, however, has not made much difference to most Nicaraguans. They are still faithful. A 1981 poll proved the Cardinal the most popular man in Nicaragua. (Shortly after that poll was released, the Sandinistas banned polls altogether.) Crowds attend his Masses despite the Sandinista agents who take notes on the front pew, despite government forces which are often outside the church trying to drown out the homily.

The most telling incident concerning Nicaragua's real feelings about the Sandinistas and Christianity happened on Good Friday, 1984. According to ABC News, a crowd estimated at one hundred thousand gathered for a religious procession which turned into a "passionate demonstration of solidarity with the Catholic Church and opposition to the Sandinista regime.

"Marchers shouted, 'Free Nicaragua and Christ forever.'"[111]

---

*Since this book was completed, Bishop Vega and Monsignor Carballo have been exiled from Nicaragua. They were accused of seditious activities.

EIGHT

The Religious Left Fights for Sandinismo

"In the Name of God - Stop the Lies - Stop the Killing," the statement was headed. The Witness for Peace document alleged, among other things, that there is no religious persecution in Nicaragua. It alleged that there has been no "widespread" killing of Miskito Indians.

The document was signed, in March 1986, by over one hundred American religious leaders. They included five Catholic bishops, six United Methodist bishops, six Episcopal bishops, the president of the United Church of Christ, and both the president and general secretary of the National Council of Churches.[1] It also included numerous nuns, priests, and directors of Religious Left organizations.

As has been seen in the previous chapter, the Sandinistas are enemies of the church and persecute Christianity in numerous ways. Large segments of the American mainstream church, however, refuse to recognize the real nature of Sandinismo and defend it both verbally and politically.

That they do so is simply the logical result of their belief system. If one believes in liberation theology through a Marxist perspective, as many do; if one believes that the Soviets are more sinned against than sinning, as many do; if one believes that Marxist-Leninist societies are beneficial (or at least harmless) and capitalist societies are evil, as many obviously do; then the accumulation of such misconceptions will help persuade that person to believe the Sandinistas are doing God's work on earth.

The defense of Nicaragua's basic goodness by the Religious Left has taken several different forms. Church leadership, clergy, and bureaucracy have toured Nicaragua, then come back to reassure Americans that all accusations against the regime are false. The United States is an evil genie which takes delight in torturing a poor, helpless neighbor, they righteously exclaim. Then they send one more resolution to Congress asking that all American aid to the anti-Sandinista guerrillas be ended.

Those resolutions are often drafted by church agencies, such as the Presbyterian Board of Home Ministries or the United Methodist General Board of Global Ministries, and given to their respective church assemblies to approve. Those assemblies, influenced by leadership, dutifully do so.

Some mainline churches have organizations dedicated to forcing a cut-off of American aid to the anti-Sandinista guerrillas and to the government of El Salvador. The Presbyterian Advocates have a "hardcore of 2,600 people who agree to get in touch with local congressmen when the Washington office signals them." It was created by the Presbyterian Church U.S.A. at its 1983 convention. Another such network is run by the United Church of Christ, and they are said to be in touch with eight thousand local UCC churches.[2]

Quasi-church groups such as the Carolina Interfaith Task Force on Central America scorn mere letter-writing. They go personally to Congress to lobby for their cause. Rep. Tim Valentine's office (D-N.C.) was visited monthly for more than two years by church groups affiliated with the organization. Carolina Interfaith has fourteen chapters in North and South Carolina, and they have taken turns making weekly trips to Washington to visit Congressional offices.[3]

In January of 1985 a delegation composed of the Presbyterian state synod executive, a Duke University religion professor, a Baptist minister, and a state council of churches executive visited with Valentine. Early in April another group delivered a "letter of concern" signed by nine North Carolina United Methodists, Episcopal and Roman Catholic bishops.[4]

These visits were beneficial for the Left because Valentine voted against providing military aid for the anti-Sandinista guerrillas and once, in 1985, against providing humanitarian aid. Valentine's press secretary, Dean Brown, said he had been impressed with the visitors. They understood the legislation, they were prepared, they understood how Congress works, they were specific on the issues, and they knew the "jargon," he said.[5]

This same organization took out ads in *The Fayetteville Times* headed "An Open Letter to Soldiers at Fort Bragg," which urged soldiers interested in alternatives to combat duty in Central America to consider seeking conscientious objector status.

GOVERNMENT TARGETED

The American government is the constant target of well-orchestrated letter-writing campaigns by both these sorts of organizational and church bureaucracies. They are often bombarded by some sort of demonstration. The latest styles in demonstrations include sit-ins and candlelight vigils. Older tactics are also used. The more radical-than-thou sixties were recalled in 1983 when most major denominations and Catholic orders protested Central American policy (and the invasion of Grenada) in a march on Washington.

The United Methodist Women's Action Guide has been more imaginative than most in their lobbying efforts. They suggested, among other things, that Methodist women organize interfaith services to commemorate the "martyrs" of Central America.

Sojourners magazine has created the newest method of twisting government's arm; it has organized a plan to invade American public buildings (including, presumably, the Congress) in the event of American intervention in Nicaragua or escalation of military aid to El Salvador. That means anything from invasion or air strike on Nicaragua, to naval blockade, to invasion by American "Proxies," to "massive U.S.-backed bombings of El Salvador." The "pledge of resistance" has been signed by agencies of most American mainstream churches and by organizations like CISPES, the propaganda arm of the Salvadoran guerrillas.

Of all the methods employed to aid the Sandinistas, the visiting delegation has been both the most effective, the silliest, and the least educational. Most delegation members have made up their minds about the issues before they ever board the airplane and nothing that is said to them, nothing they see in Nicaragua, changes their minds.

THE WITNESS FOR PEACE TOUR

Alfredo Lanier, a senior editor at *Chicago* magazine, bolstered evidence for this point of view with his testimony on a 1984 Witness for Peace tour to Nicaragua. Lanier joined the delegation after he was invited to report on the trip.

Witness for Peace, which was partially created by *Sojourners*, is one of the most influential semireligious, pro-Sandinista organizations in the United States. It is heavily funded by American churches and boasts no less than four clergy on its steering committee.[6]

The most outstanding Witness specialty is in sending tours (the members of which are largely Christian) to Nicaragua which come home proclaiming Sandinista sainthood. As of December 1985 there have been approximately fifty-one delegations—a total of about twelve hundred participants. The organization has also been involved with such spurious (and media-directed) schemes as sending teams of Christians to the Nicaragua-Honduras border to form a "protective shield" between natives and anti-Sandinista guerrillas.

Lanier's delegation, as he described it, was typical of Witness for Peace tours. Approximately 90 percent of his delegation (half of which were Christian activists) "had already made their minds up" about Nicaragua and "were not in any frame of mind to question . . . there was very little questioning or openmindedness." Many of the Christians on the trip, he said, had been to Cuba and had returned "ecstatic," a condition Lanier, who is Cuban, could not understand.[7]

The inevitable process of affirmation for the regime was helped considerably by the tour leader's attitudes, Lanier said, which were not only clearly favorable to the regime, but manipulative of the tour as a whole.[8] The most outrageous action committed by Witness for Peace leadership was giving a press conference to attack the United States as soon as the delegation got off the airplane in Managua. When the one hundred and ninety-person delegation landed, they were escorted to the VIP Lounge. No one knew what to expect, Lanier said, but the delegation was served coffee while armed guards prevented them from leaving the room.[9]

Then, to the delegation's "complete astonishment," tape recorders, television lights, and cameras were turned on and the delegation became part of a press briefing for reporters of the Nicaraguan government's controlled television and radio stations and of *La Barricada*, the official government newspaper.[10]

Gail Phares, a former Maryknoll nun and one of the leaders of Witness for Peace, then read a statement condemning the "illegal war being waged against Nicaragua . . . designed, directed and funded by the (U.S.) government." Another spokesman, Lanier said, compared America's foreign policy to a "malignant tumor" that needed to be excised and "expressed our presumed wish that our visit would 'hurt' American policy in the region." The tour group had no idea they were going to be used in a press conference, Lanier said.[11]

Tour members who genuinely wanted to discover the real situation in Nicaragua were not likely to do so. Lanier described a journey in which the highlights were lectures from government officials, including Daniel Ortega, about the revolution. The only opposition voice heard by his tour, Lanier said, was from an uninvited visitor from *La Prensa*.

That *La Prensa* reporter subsequently wrote two stories about his visit to the delegates. One was based on his interview with Garnett Hennings, the president of Operation PUSH in St. Louis and one on Lanier's inquiries into censorship in Nicaragua. The story based on the interview with Hennings was printed, but the story about Lanier's inquiries was censored and never appeared in the newspaper.[12]

At one point the delegation discovered a camp of about eighty Cuban military advisors. When Lanier mentioned the camp, Witness for Peace tour leaders denied the men were Cuban. Lanier had talked to the men himself and insisted they were. The tour leaders then said the Cubans were medical advisors. Lanier, however, had seen the weaponry.[13]

WITNESS FOR PEACE PEP RALLIES

In order to influence the delegates emotionally, Witness for Peace provided political pep rallies (dubbed *Fogotas*) which supposedly displayed the pro-Sandinista attitudes of average Nicaraguans. A tire burned in the street, tour leaders said, is the method used to rally the gung-ho masses. At one point, after two tires were burned in one barrio the people still did not appear. The local Sandinista Defense Committees were forced to go door to door to recruit participants.[14]

When a few neighborhood residents finally gathered, the Americans and the Nicaraguans stared awkwardly at each other in the street. One "expressionless" woman, after a long pause, began to "mechanically" shout "*consignas*," or political slogans, which denounced American aggression and expressed support for the Sandinistas and the guerrillas of El Salvador. After a few minutes of shouting and a few more of hymn singing, the Nicaraguans and the bewildered delegates went back to their respective bases.[15]

Some rallies, Lanier said, featured *sufi* dances—a sort of conga line derived from Eastern religious rituals—wrapping bewildered Nicaraguan peasants in banners as symbolic shields against "American aggression," and emotional breast-beating about America's wrongs in Central America. At a high school rally at which Jesse Jackson was scheduled to appear, the students repeatedly cheered, "Here and there/We will kill Yankees everywhere." The delegates, who didn't understand Spanish, "cheered and danced along."[16]

The delegates were housed with "average" Nicaraguans which Lanier said were "clearly, clearly, clearly pressured to take us in."[17]

These blatantly manipulative activities are, unfortunately, par for the course for Witness for Peace. The organization was responsible for sending a boatload of people (twenty-nine activists and eighteen members of the media) down the San Juan river in 1985, ostensibly to protest American support for the anti-Sandinista rebels. The boat was allegedly captured by some armed men. Witness for Peace claims it was the rebels, despite the fact that that particular section of the river had been controlled by the Sandinistas for weeks and that a Sandinista helicopter, complete with television crew, conveniently hovered near the boat as it was being "captured."[18]

Sandinista officials had also organized "welcome home" demonstrations "before it was clear the activists would be returning."[19]

It should not surprise anyone that WFP involves itself in such activities; indeed, one of its steering committee members has acknowledged close cooperation with the Sandinista government. Joyce Hollyday, in an article for *Sojourners*, said the idea for WFP was first proposed to a member of the junta and later discussed with Tomás Borgé. "Borgé," Hollyday wrote, "agreed that such a presence on the border could have a strong impact on the situation in Nicaragua."[20]

THE UNITED METHODIST TOUR

Although Witness is usually more openly partisan, tours sponsored by denominations do not usually offer a much more balanced agenda. Kalmin Smith, a United Methodist from Michigan, took a tour to Nicaragua in 1984 which was initiated by the West Michigan Conference of his church. After being questioned about the one-sided schedule of interviews, the tour guide (who had been recommended by the General Board of Global Ministries) told the group that his goal was to spread the gospel of liberation theology and Sandinista social justice to the "exclusion of other points of view."[21] That same tour guide, it was later discovered, was persona non grata in Costa Rica as a result of his political activities.[22] (For more information on Smith's tour, see Appendix.)

Before the trip Smith requested that the tour include interviews with the hierarchy of the Catholic Church, *La Prensa*, leaders of opposition political parties, the U.S. Embassy, the Nicaraguan Human Rights Commission, and others critical of the government. Not even one of the requested interviews was scheduled. The tour was subjected, however, to lectures on Marxist economics and the virtues of liberation theology.[23]

At one point, the delegation visited a Moravian church which the tour guide addressed. Smith said that when the translator began to tell him what the tour guide was saying, he was astonished to find out that the man was telling the congregation that the delegation's mission in Nicaragua was to support the revolution and to work for a change in American policy when they returned home.[24]

When questioned about the delegation, Sharon Rader, trip organizer for the West Michigan Conference, said she felt there had been no need to schedule interviews with people in order to "hear Reagan's side. We can do that here." Rader, who is the conference liaison for the General Board of Global Ministries, said she did not believe that talking to pro-Sandinista spokesmen prevented the tour from asking, and getting answers to, hard questions.[25]

THE MASTER OF DECEIT

Most Americans, both Christian and non-Christian, seem to feel that a few weeks' visit will make them experts on Nicaragua and the Sandinista government. They have no idea, however, how deceiving appearances can be.

Merle Linda Wolin, a reporter for the *Los Angeles Herald Examiner*, interviewed Tomás Borgé—head of Nicaragua's secret police—for a series of articles on Sandinista leadership.[26] Wolin reported that Borgé took her to meet his wife and children in what he represented as his home, a small modest house in the suburbs. She was instantly suspicious, however, when she saw the house was furnished like a hotel room and that the toilet was filthy.

It was later confirmed by members of the FSLN, and from Borgé's bodyguards, that the house was a soldier's bungalow. Borgé actually lives in luxury elsewhere, they said.[27]

Borgé is a past master at such deception. Alvaro José Baldizon, the former Sandinista Minister of the Interior who fled to the United States in 1985, revealed many of Borgé's tactics. The great impersonator has two offices, Baldizon said, one for regular work and one for meeting with American religious groups. In the office he uses for the Christians he has "photographs of children, gilded, carved crucifixes, and a Bible or two." In the former office he has "Marxist literature and posters of Marx, Engels and Lenin."[28]

In early June 1985, Baldizon said, he was among five hundred people from the Interior Ministry whom Borgé ordered to dress as civilians and attend the closing session of an international assembly of Baptist youth. The government employees pretended they were evangelicals in order to make it appear Borgé had support among that community.[29]

Unfortunately for Americans who travel to Nicaragua free of bias, it is difficult to find average Nicaraguans who speak freely. The country has been so well-traveled by Americans who are blatantly pro-Sandinista that Nicaraguans assume all Americans are "*internationalistas*," their word for Marxist-Leninist sympathizers. It has not helped the situation that at least one Christian group took a tape recorder to an interview with anti-Sandinistas and then gave the tape to State Security.[30]

SANDINISTA INTIMIDATION

Baldizon revealed that the Sandinistas help this process along by having Sandinista security officers, dressed as civilians, follow the delegations. Baldizon claimed civilians know who the security officers are and "very few dare speak ill of the Sandinista regime."[31]

Also confusing is the Sandinista practice of setting up parallel organizations. For instance, there is a Nicaraguan Permanent Commission on Human Rights which has documented evidence of torture

in prisons and numerous mysterious disappearances. That same organization documented the abuse of human rights under Somoza. The
junta, however, soon after the revolution, established an organization
with almost the same name, the National Commission on the Promotion and Protection of Human Rights, which is simply a tool for
reassuring Americans about the human rights situation. That the organization was established to confuse, and that it is nothing but a front,
has been verified by its former director, José Esteban Gonzales, who
defected in 1985.

CATHOLIC SUPPORT FOR JUNTA

It is one signal of the ideological conflict that has marked the Catholic
Church in recent years that some of the strongest support for the junta
has come from Catholics—both American-based clergy and bureaucrats and missionaries living in Nicaragua. Some American Catholic
clergy, notably Archbishop John Roach and Cardinal John O'Connor,
have verbally supported Cardinal Obando. But many more Catholic
bishops, priests, nuns, and bureaucrats have relentlessly hammered at
American foreign policy regarding Nicaragua and ignored accusations
of persecution from the Nicaraguan Catholic hierarchy.

One such pro-Sandinista alliance was put on prominent display at
the Washington press conference at which Witness for Peace discussed
the "capture" of the boat on the San Juan. Catholic bishops Walter
Sullivan of Richmond, Thomas Gumbleton of Detroit, and Maurice
Dingman of Des Moines were all present on the organization's behalf.

Speaker of the House Tip O'Neil, it was revealed in 1984, has had
his view of the situation in Nicaragua shaped by the Maryknoll nuns in
general and Peggy Healy, the regional coordinator of the Maryknoll
nuns, in particular. O'Neil has been unrelentingly hostile to providing
American aid for the anti-Sandinista guerrillas.

O'Neil told *The New York Times* that "when the nuns and priests
come through, I ask them questions about their feelings, what they
see, who the enemy is, and I'm sure I get the truth. I haven't found any
of these missionaries who aren't absolutely opposed to this policy
(funding the contras)." Miss Healy corresponds "regularly" with Mr.
O'Neil, his aides said.[32]

Rep. Thomas Downey, Democrat from New York, told *The Wall
Street Journal* that in 1983 several Maryknoll nuns, just back from
Central America, came by his office to talk to him. When he suggest-
ed that they take their message to his constituents (most of whom are
Catholic), they did so with "astonishing" impact. For months, he said,
people would visit him at his district office and ask to discuss events in
Central America.[33]

"I'd ask them how they heard about it," Downey said, "and they'd say, 'Well, this nun came to talk.' "[34]

Monsignor Bismark Carballo—who you will remember is Cardinal Obando's assistant—wrote a letter to the general secretary of the U.S. Catholic Conference in 1984 to protest the activities of Thomas Quigley, the conference's Latin American specialist.[35] Quigley, the letter said, had hindered the Nicaraguan bishops' struggle against religious persecution. The Sandinista government had also used remarks made by Quigley to "fuel its propaganda effort against the Catholic Church."

The remarks—which Quigley said were merely a repetition of the U.S. Catholic Conference position on American covert operations in Nicaragua—appeared in the official Sandinista newspaper *Barricada* and on government radio broadcasts. They were attributed to, in some cases, "Bishop Quigley." Quigley is not a member of the clergy.

Carballo said that Quigley appeared to disagree with the Nicaraguan bishops' pastoral letters which urged national reconciliation. That reconciliation includes, in the cardinal's view, talks with the anti-Sandinista guerrillas.

Geraldine de Macias, a former Maryknoll nun and wife of Sandinista dissident Edgard de Macias, testified at a 1983 Senate hearing that Quigley, Washington Office on Latin America (WOLA) director Joe Eldridge (see Appendix), and Tony Ramos of the NCC's Church World Service advised her not to criticize the Sandinistas. It would, they said, give President Reagan ammunition to use against them. She repeated the same charge in a personal interview with the authors. Her husband, a former vice-minister of labor in the Sandinista government, was forced to leave the country when he found that the Sandinistas were planning to have him murdered.

Quigley said in a personal interview with one of the authors that the role of the U.S. Catholic Conference is not to support, or criticize, the Sandinistas, but to comment on American policy in the region. Officials from the conference have testified on this matter in Congress, arguing, of course, that the aid should be ended. However, the Sandinistas use the official position of the conference to aid them in their propaganda war against the Nicaraguan church, depicting "local church leaders as counterrevolutionaries and CIA operatives."[36]

It is not really surprising that Quigley has a seemingly pro-Sandinista viewpoint, as he is a member of the Religious Task Force on Central America steering committee, an organization blatantly dedicated to promoting the Sandinistas and ending American aid to anti-Sandinista guerrillas and the government of El Salvador (see Appendix).

Quigley is obviously not adverse to making his views known in public. Discussing the late Archbishop Oscar Romero, in an article for *The Witness*, a magazine published by the Episcopal Church and Society Network, Quigley said the archbishop had called to mind brilliant leaders like John XXIII and "maybe Mao, representatives of the people who knew that leadership has to do with evoking, calling forth the wisdom that is in the people."[37]

The Rev. Edward Killackey, director of Maryknoll's Washington-based Office of Justice and Peace, gave another example of extreme political bias in the Catholic Church when he told *The Washington Post* that the church-state conflict in Nicaragua is essentially a power struggle. "The church is still struggling to understand the role of the church in a revolutionary society," he explained.[38]

The National Council of Churches has not only denied religious persecution in Nicaragua many times over, it has said it "deplores the increasing deterioration of relations between the government of Nicaragua and a sector of the Roman Catholic Church in that nation."[39] In other words, the Council is saying that there are two Catholic Churches, the orthodox and the "Popular Church." Since the "Popular Church" is a creation of the Nicaraguan government, and the tool with which it seeks to destroy the Roman Catholic hierarchy, it can safely be concluded that the National Council is an accessory after the fact.

FLOOD OF SUPPORT

No less irresponsible have been the flood of articles published by religious publications which have, in a word, lied about events in Nicaragua. *The Churchwoman*, among others, declared that the Nicaraguan people had interrupted the Pope's Mass in Managua because he had failed them. "Those who had come joyously and lovingly to welcome the Pope—calling out, 'Papa, Papa, Papa'—left in weariness and disappointment. They had hoped for a few pastoral sentences and some recognition of their suffering."[40]

It is one thing for Protestant religious publications to criticize the Pope through blind ignorance, and another for a Catholic publication to do the same thing. But *The Catholic Times* quoted Sandinista sympathizers who accused the Pope of ignoring "the pleadings of the mothers" who only wanted the Pope to offer "a prayer for their martyred children" at his Mass in Managua. As we have seen, what John Paul did was to refuse to be used politically. And the "mothers" were hardly the innocents portrayed by the article.[41]

National Catholic Reporter, a Catholic publication which has been consistently sympathetic to the Sandinistas, has glorified and distorted the true position of the "Popular Church." In one article it lamented that the Catholic hierarchy in Nicaragua has "learned ways to reach the people at the emotional level." The article cites the support given weeping virgins and campaigns with "strong ideological overtones" which promote devotion to the Virgin Mary.[42]

The article also claimed that the hierarchy has wealth, influence, and access to powerful media. The truth, as we saw in the last chapter, is just the opposite. The church has no help from the outside and the organizations of the "Popular Church" are rich with international help and access to Sandinista mass media.[43]

PRINTED DISTORTIONS

Our Sunday Visitor, a Catholic publication, published a "White Paper" (on November 7, 1982) so blatantly pro-Sandinista and so hostile to the Nicaraguan Roman Catholic hierarchy that an anti-Sandinista organization—composed of exiled Nicaraguans—rebutted the article in a twenty-five page letter to Catholic Archbishop John Roach.[44] The White Paper was a result of a task force team visit to Nicaragua composed of Catholic clergy, including Father Vincent Giese, editor-in-chief of *Our Sunday Visitor*. Giese wrote the White Paper himself.

Alejandro Bolaños, head of the Nicaraguan Information Center, charged, among other things, that Giese whitewashed Sandinista efforts to censor information concerning their attacks on the Miskito Indians. Giese put the blame for the breakdown of relations between the government and the church hierarchy on Cardinal Obando y Bravo, Bolaños said. He also charged that Giese had misrepresented the position of the Nicaraguan people regarding priests in the "Popular Church" (to the point that Giese explained a *turba* as a group of simple parishioners), made Monsignor Carballo look guilty of having an affair with a woman, and misrepresented even letters to the Nicaraguan Church from Pope John Paul II.

Pope John Paul, Giese wrote, "pointed out some dangers in the popular church movement." What the Pope's letter really did, the Center said, was clearly condemn the Popular Church. The letter, not printed by Giese, bears out the Center's accusation. It reads in part: "A 'people's church' opposed to the church presided over by the lawful pastors is a grave deviation from the will and plan of salvation of Jesus Christ."[45]

Giese goes on to say that the Sandinistas first censored the letter, then allowed it to appear "in its entirety in the country's major newspapers." The Center pointed out, however, that the government censored the letter on three different occasions, then only allowed it to be printed with an official communique critical of the Pope's message. The government only relented about the communique when *La Prensa* refused to publish for three days rather than print it.

These are rather small matters, but taken all together misrepresent the situation in Nicaragua entirely. Giese, as of 1985, still believes the Nicaraguan government to be "worthwhile."[46]

WILLING BLINDNESS

One of the most difficult problems to overcome, when trying to inform Christians about the situation in Nicaragua, is their frequent refusal to accept facts. Christian advocates for the Sandinistas listen exclusively to pro-Sandinista priests in Nicaragua (of which there are approximately twenty, according to the Nicaraguan Roman Catholic hierarchy),[47] most of whom have supported the Marxists-Leninists for many years. It is almost unheard of that Christians who support the Sandinistas gather information from members of the anti-Sandinista opposition, or believe them when they do bother to ask their opinion.

Typical of this approach is that used by Phil Land, a Jesuit priest and a director of the Washington-based Center of Concern, a Catholic organization which is privately funded. Land explained in a personal interview that his pro-Sandinista stance results from his distrust for Cardinal Obando on one hand and his trust for the information given to him by his Jesuit colleagues in Nicaragua on the other.[48]

Land explained that he believes Obando "misreads" the situation, and adds that Obando perceives the Sandinistas as a threat to his social authority. Talk to Jesuit Cesar Juarez, he says, that's the man he trusts. He also said Commandante Daniel Ortega told him personally he was not a Marxist.

The Jesuits that Land believes in, however, are hardly dispassionate. They have been long-time supporters of the Sandinista National Liberation Front, to the extent that they openly criticized the Roman Catholic hierarchy for advocating that the government hold negotiations with the anti-Sandinista guerrillas. The Jesuit superior general, the Rev. Hans-Peter Kolvenbach, denounced them for that action and subsequently sent his assistant to Nicaragua to scold them in person.[49]

When Land was asked about Cardinal Obando's accusation that Father Amado Peña was framed by State Security (see the last chapter), Land answered that he did not believe State Security had done such a nasty thing. As far as the *turbas* are concerned, he believes them to be simple people of the barrio.

Typical of the revolutionary Christian's ability to ignore facts was one nun's explanation for the expulsion of ten priests from Nicaragua in 1983. Sister Mary Hartman, an American nun and an employee of the Sandinistas' National Commission for the Promotion and Protection of Human Rights, explained the expulsion as a response to the priests' "counterrevolutionary" behavior. "The priests would meet with young people and tell them they didn't have to register for the draft. They were counterrevolutionaries, that's all they were."[50]

THE LIBERATION THEOLOGY CENTERS

As explained in the previous chapter, some of the most influential agents for the Sandinistas are Nicaraguan research centers which specialize in books on liberation theology and news reports which advance the government's accusations against the Catholic hierarchy. It is the most telling feature of American Christian attitudes that these centers, listed below, are financed by American church money.

- *The Evangelical Committee for Aid to Development (CEPAD)*—this organization is the largest recipient of U.S. church support in Nicaragua. The Presbyterians (U.S.A.), for instance, gave CEPAD $20,000 in 1985. The United Methodists gave it $19,500 in 1983 and $6,000 in 1984. The National Council of Churches gave CEPAD $365,329 in 1981 and at least $8,500 in 1983. CEPAD claims to represent Nicaragua's Protestant churches and has been very persuasive in convincing American Christians that the Sandinistas are doing God's work on earth. It has proselyted for the Sandinistas among delegations visiting CEPAD headquarters in Managua and during American lecture tours.

CEPAD, however, not only works hand-in-hand with the Sandinista government; its director, Gustavo Parajon, has been accused of being a Sandinista agent who faithfully tape-records CEPAD meetings for State Security. The accusation was made by a highly placed defector from Sandinista State Security.[51] According to the same defector, CEPAD official Sixto Ulloa is obedient to the secret police and has direct access to Tomás Borgé. He also ran for office on the FSLN ticket in 1984.[52]

The National Council of Evangelical Pastors, which is one of the two evangelical organizations not recognized by the Sandinista government, does not trust CEPAD due to its governmental connections and questionable financial disbursements. Those disbursements may have included, as was charged by pastors in Mantagalpa province, the donation of eleven four-wheel drive vehicles for use by the Sandinista police. The Evangelical Council broke off all ties with CEPAD in 1983.[53]

CEPAD has also allegedly withheld financial aid to pastors who are insufficiently supportive of the Sandinistas and threatened, in 1984, to withhold benefits to organizations boycotting the elections.[54]

The Nicaraguan Conference of Catholic Bishops protested the

materials used in the literacy campaign of 1980, many of which were produced by CEPAD. The materials promoted a Marxist view of history and society, portraying the FSLN and its mass organizations as the only legitimate expressions of organized social actions in Nicaragua.

Not one to hide its ideological light under a bushel, CEPAD, in 1980, helped fund an educational booklet in the style of a comic book which was titled *Capitalism and Socialism for Beginners.* It is a beginner's guide to Marxism. CEPAD's leaders even admit their political orientation. In the March 1984 issue of *The Disciple*, CEPAD's executive director, Gilberto Aguirre, said, "We not only support the Sandinista government, but we are immersed in the revolution."

Geraldine de Macias worked for CEPAD while in Nicaragua. She told the authors that "after the revolution they were blatantly pro-Sandinista. Survival as an institution became more important than anything else. One of the National Council of Churches groups, foreign advisors, were the ones who got them to go to Cuba and come back with Cuban posters to give seminars on how to survive under the revolution.[55]

"They said if they were going to survive as an institution and as a church they had to be revolutionary, they had to be useful to the government. Translated, that means to be pro-FSLN and anti-American. That bothered me. I saw CEPAD's thrust as how to deepen faith. After 1979, that become less important to them and vast amounts of CEPAD funds began to go to government programs. Some of them in CEPAD had joined the FSLN and are Marxists."[56]

- *The Antonio Valdivieso Ecumenical Center* is directed by Father Molina, the head of Nicaragua's "Popular Church." Valdivieso has published, among many other things, a booklet which portrays evangelical and Pentecostal preachers as U.S. agents. The booklet features a cartoon of Uncle Sam winding up (like you do a toy) a man who is preaching to kneeling worshipers. The man is saying that there is a contradiction between faith and the revolution.

The Center received $19,500 from the The United Methodist General Board of Global Ministries in 1983 and $6,000 in 1984. The World Council of Churches' sharing book, which is a list of projects the WCC intends to fund if the budget passes its legislative test, has the Center down for $165,000. The WCC book states that the Center's main aim is "to accompany Christians committed to the revolutionary process in their reflections and actions." One of the activities planned to help this objective is "Bible courses in order to re-read the Bible in the light of the local situation." One-third of all Valdivieso's funds come from churches in the U.S.

- *The Central American Historical Institute* was initially created by Jesuits who support the Sandinistas. The cover of an Institute publication shows a soldier carrying a gun with Christ interposed on top. The words say, "Christian Faith and the Sandinista Revolution in Nicaragua." The picture is not so startling if you realize that the Institute also published a book called *Are You Afraid of Communism? I Am Not.* The Institute also maintains an office in Washington from which it propagandizes for the Sandinista government. The United Methodists gave the Institute $8,000 in 1983 and the 1983 World Council of Churches' resource sharing book proposed to give it $36,560.

- *The Latin American Evangelical Committee for Christian Education,* better known as CELADEC, produced material, much of it in comic-book format, called *What Is Liberation Theology.* One little lesson is titled "Knowing how to see reality with the eyes of God." The illustration is of three guerrillas toting machine-guns through the jungle. The text says that God does not present Himself solely through Christ, but through the liberation of men and women that are not considered Christians.

- *The Nicaraguan Institute for Economic and Social Research*—The Institute was created by the United Methodist Church and the government of Nicaragua. Its grant proposal said the Institute would establish "academic solidarity . . . with progressive social scientists of the west and the social research centers of the socialist countries." It continued by stating that "The work of INIES is therefore at the service of the organs of political decision-making which seek the social and political transformation of the region." Its spokesman, Father Xavier Gorostiaga, appears frequently in the American media. This Institute received $30,000 from the United Methodist Board of Global Ministries in 1983.

AMERICAN CHURCH FUNDING

The United Methodist Church, as well as most of the National Council of Churches' membership, contributes to the Council's Division of Overseas Ministries. That department distributed, for the Methodist Church, money for all the Nicaraguan organizations to which the United Methodists also contributed in their own name. For instance, the United Methodist Board of Global Ministries gave $30,000 to the Nicaraguan Institute for Economic and Social Research in 1983. But the United Methodist World Division of Global Ministries gave $30,000 to the National Council in 1982, which was, in turn, passed on to the Institute. In 1981 funds were given to both CELADEC and CEPAD through the National Council's Latin American division ($15,000 to CEDELAC) and CEPAD was given a grand total of $375,329 by the National Council through Church World Service. CEPAD has stated its annual budget is nine times larger than the amount it received from the National Council in 1981. No National Council budgets have been released since 1981.

The World Council of Churches has given considerable money to organizations in Nicaragua with funds it receives from American denominations. Presbyterians have contributed about three-fourths of the total U.S. money given to the Churches' Participation in Development. This money was used, in part, to fund the following grants to the Antonio Valdivieso Center and CELADEC: the Valdivieso Center was given $21,000 in 1981 and CELADEC was given $33,000. An additional $20,000 was given to CELADEC in 1983 and $50,000 to Valdivieso in 1983.

The World Council proposed to spend $36,000 for the Institute of Central American History in 1983 while openly admitting that the Center would act as an information outlet for the government. The 1983 sharing book (which lists funding proposals) states that ". . . cooperating agencies and solidarity committees have drawn attention to the lack of regular, speedy news, above all at the time when Nicaragua is being criticized by conservative circles throughout the world and news about the country is making the headlines in the world press."

Under "Aims," the sharing book explains, "The government of Nicaragua does not have the necessary resources to meet this challenge. The Institute of Central American History headquartered in Managua is therefore setting up an Information Center which will not only act as a news center but also as a channel of communication to and from Nicaragua.

"Many persons visiting Nicaragua for the first time find it very difficult to understand the dynamic revolutionary process as they are not familiar with the context or the background." The WCC also targeted $176,245 to the Antonio Valdivieso Center.

THE SANCTUARY MOVEMENT

Although promoting official Nicaragua is the trendy Christian's favorite method of bashing (or bending) the United States government, an alternative (or a correlative method for the energetic) is rapidly gaining popularity. This is the sanctuary movement, and it has enmeshed approximately two hundred and fifty churches in its activities.[57]

Movement spokesmen argue that the United States is deporting illegal aliens from El Salvador that will be murdered when they return. They usually point to the government of El Salvador as the likely culprit, citing horrible stories of torture and murder by death squads and government soldiers. Sanctuary workers argue that they are therefore doing their Christian duty by harboring and transporting aliens.

The real goal of the sanctuary movement, however, is not nurturing individuals or families, but in nurturing a political cause. Sanctuary workers believe that the United States should end military assistance to the government of El Salvador. Presumably they are aware that the Marxist guerrillas would then have a much better chance of overthrowing the duly-elected government of President Jose Napoleon Duarte.

ECONOMIC SANCTUARY

El Salvador has been the second largest source of illegal aliens in the U.S., after Mexico, for the last thirty years. Before the beginning of the guerrilla war the number of Salvadoran illegal aliens was approximately three hundred and fifty thousand. Today, it is about five hundred thousand. Terror did not begin the exodus, nor has it continued it. Salvadorans come to the U.S. for sound economic reasons.[58]

Confirming this viewpoint was an exit poll conducted by the Spanish International Network during El Salvador's recent presidential elections. It found that 70 percent of the people polled would like to emigrate to the United States—in order to work.[59]

Further, there has never been a case in which an illegal alien was returned to El Salvador and was then deliberately murdered. One case has been cited in which a man was killed, but it has never been determined if he was a deliberate victim or was simply caught in random violence.

The Chicago Religious Task Force, the key organizing agent in the sanctuary movement, claimed at one time that Amnesty International had documentation proving that 30 percent of all illegal aliens returned were tortured, maimed, or murdered. Amnesty International's area coordinator for Latin America, however, Rona Ellen Weitz, denied that Amnesty International had said any such thing.[60]

In 1983 the American Civil Liberties Union published a study on this matter. It was based on a comparison of the names of eighty-five hundred deportees with a list of the names of twenty-two thousand victims of human rights violations in El Salvador. After nine months it was found that only one hundred and thirteen possible matches among the names was found and only twenty-five cases where, by ACLU estimation, there was better than an average possibility of a match, about one-third of the one percent total. The ACLU could not establish one positive match.[61]

THE LACK OF VICTIMS

The American State Department investigated the same question. They took a random sample of four hundred and eighty-two deportees, interviewing the deportee or a close family connection and found only one case in which a deportee became a human rights victim. In that one case, the deportee was shot in 1981 by a guerrilla as an apparent result of mistaken identity.[62]

Further, no human rights organization in El Salvador has reported a case of a deportee being killed since two deaths in 1981. The Geneva-based Inter-government Committee for Migration, which provides resettlement services to returning Salvadorans, has not reported one case of deliberate violence being inflicted on a Salvadoran deported from the United States.[63]

Further, political violence in El Salvador has steadily dropped since 1981. There were only two thousand political murders in 1984 compared to sixteen thousand and two hundred in 1981.[64] Indeed, more Salvadorans fleeing violence go to regions held by the army. According to the U.S. government figures, in 1984 there were about four hundred thousand Salvadoran refugees who did so. Another twenty thousand fled to Honduras (which provides refugee camps open to all Salvadorans looking for safety), eighteen thousand to Costa Rica, seventeen thousand and five hundred to Nicaragua, thirty-five hundred to Mexico and two thousand to Belize. Only a small portion of these refugees claimed they were fleeing from Salvadoran authorities.[65]

Most of those who flee are in terror of the guerrillas, who kidnap, kill and terrorize local officials,[66] murder government sympathizers, and forcibly induct young men into their movement.

Moreover, the army has severed its ties with the extreme right and reorganized the three police security forces, largely ending officially sanctioned death squads. Human rights violations by government forces are at a five-year low.[67] Social and land reform programs are also being implemented. Salvadoran Archbishop Rivera y Damas, who has been a long-time advocate of Salvadoran reform, explained the guerrillas' lack of support as a result of the people realizing the guerrillas "were more interested in obtaining power than in fulfilling . . . hope for the people."[68]

None of these facts have been acknowledged by spokesmen for the sanctuary movement, neither the progress on the right or murderousness on the left. The same statement can be made about the mainline church, which has uniformly supported the guerrillas.

IMMIGRATION LAW

Sanctuary workers also act as though the U.S. government has no interest in providing asylum for people threatened with torture or death by political agents or agencies. Such is not the case. Under the Refugee Act of 1980 an alien may qualify for asylum if he or she has "a well-founded fear of persecution" in his/her homeland "on account of race, religion, nationality, membership in a particular social group or political opinion." It is not enough, however, to flee from generally violent conditions. The alien must prove it likely that he/she will be singled out for violence.

If an alien has a well-founded fear of persecution he/she is not automatically entitled to asylum, but the alien may not be forcibly returned to the country from whence he/she fled. Out of the five hundred thousand Salvadorans in the United States today, only twenty thousand to thirty thousand have applied for political asylum.[69] Still, the boards, assemblies, and agencies of the mainstream churches pass resolutions by the handful which are piously affirmative of sanctuary. The United Methodists, through the General Board of Global Ministries, even provided $25,000 for the legal defense of sanctuary workers and the World Council has done the same thing. The general secretary of the U.S. Catholic Conference, in what has to be the most clever rationalization of recent years, lamented the fact that government policies regarding Central America "entangle people of good will in criminal prosecutions."

DOUBLE STANDARDS

Worse than any resolution, at least to those who are subjected to the spectacle, are the publicity stunts created by sanctuary workers. Typical was the motorcade from Chicago to Weston, Vermont. It featured Felipe and Elena Excot and their five children in a brown Ford van, marimba music which played on a portable tape recorder, and a caravan of cars with signs proclaiming "U.S. Out of Central America" and "This Is a Freedom Train." The stunt was sponsored by the Chicago Task Force. At each stop the illegal aliens (these from Guatemala) stopped for the night at a church.

What was so heartbreaking about the caravan was not the silliness, nor the manipulative bid for publicity—it was all the help given the Excots while others had none. According to John O'Leary, director of New Exodus, a Washington organization which aids refugees, numerous Nicaraguans fleeing from Sandinista tyranny claim sanctuary workers have refused to help them . . . they are on the wrong side of the political fence.[70]

The World Council of Churches and African Terrorism

W hen you sit down for the offertory on Sundays, grateful to have nothing more to do than dig into your pocket or purse for money and listen to the choir, it is the first step in funding organizations whose existence you are probably unaware of. More damaging, most of the organizations your dollars are funding have a viewpoint with which you probably disagree. Most are simply the verbal arm of the church's viewpoint on disarmament, economics, Marxism, and democratic capitalism. Most of them, and their financing, are discussed in the Appendix.

At least two of the organizations your dollars are supporting, however, are also gathering support for bloody revolutionaries in Africa. These organizations are TransAfrica and the Washington Office on Africa. The African revolutionaries are the Southwest Africa People's Organization (SWAPO) and the African National Congress. SWAPO and the African National Congress specialize in killing people and they are controlled by the Soviet Union, a country not known to have genuine people's liberation in mind when they support armed insurrection. Further, some money has been directly granted to both SWAPO and the African Congress by American denominations, as well as the National and World Council of Churches.

SWAPO is an army ostensibly dedicated to driving out the South Africans who occupy and govern Namibia. Its bases are located in Angola and Zambia, which border Namibia. Namibia also borders South Africa on the south and southeast and the Atlantic Ocean on the west. Namibia itself is a country slightly smaller than Texas and Oklahoma combined, and has a population of a little over a million, 85 percent of which are black. Almost all of the population are Christians; nearly half are Lutherans and another 10 percent are Anglicans. The rest are divided between Catholicism and other Protestant denominations.

The African National Congress is a terrorist organization ostensibly dedicated to overthrowing South Africa's apartheid policies. After the organization was outlawed in South Africa, it created bases in Zambia and other bordering countries.

In the next few years these two groups may emerge victorious (and thoroughly bloody); if so, it will be, in part, because they were aided and abetted by the World Council of Churches and the United Methodist Church. The World Council gave the Congress $150,000 in 1980, $65,000 in 1982, $70,000 in 1983 and 1984 and $77,000 in 1985. SWAPO was granted $200,000 in 1980, $125,000 in 1981, $100,000 in 1982, $105,000 in 1983, $100,000 in 1984, and $110,000 in 1985. Both were granted money through the Special Program to Combat Racism.

Besides World Council funding, the Congress received $5,000 from the World Division of the United Methodist Board of Global Ministries in 1978. In 1981 Global Ministries gave $25,000 to the Congress, Women's Division, and in 1983 the Board gave a further $17,000 for a Congress day-care center. The Women's Division of Global Ministries gave $8,890 to SWAPO in 1982 for a "literacy program organized by women of SWAPO in refugee camps in Southern Angola."

Most of the special program funds do not come from the U.S., but from the governments of the Netherlands, Sweden, Norway, and from designated contributions from individuals from every country. However, the World Council used $200,000 from its general fund to start the special program and asked member churches for $300,000 more. Further, the grants are distributed in the name of the World Council as a whole.

SWAPO and the Congress have sought funding at various times, the World Council claims, for their administrative and legal defense costs, broadcasting programs, maintenance of their various offices, and humanitarian needs. It denies that the organizations are Communist or terrorist, and claims that their goal is free elections.

However, the Council admits that the grants are made without control of the manner in which they are spent. It proclaims that the antiracist contributions allow the World Council to "intervene in the redistribution of power beyond compassion."[1]

There is no question that South Africa apartheid policies are wrong or that South Africa has no legal right in Namibia. There is no question that apartheid is destructive to blacks in every way and morally destructive to whites who support the system. But both the African National Congress and SWAPO are controlled by the Soviets, and neither organization is interested in establishing democracy for anybody in South Africa or Namibia, black or white. It is likely that the lot of all Africans will be very greatly worsened if the African Congress is successful in overthrowing the regime in Pretoria or SWAPO is successful in forcing the South Africans out of Namibia.

ORGANIZATIONAL TACTICS

There is no need for the doubtful to depend upon this analysis. African National Congress members, for one, are more than happy to explain their position. Deumi Matabane, Congress spokesman, said in a 1985 television interview that the Congress is not interested in establishing democracy because "we have seen a lot of its weakness." Asked about Communist influence in the Congress he admitted, "We have them." When asked whether whites would be able to keep their property should the South African government be overthrown, he said, "They will maintain what they have, but we are going to make sure that the main pillars of the economy are going to be in the control of the state."[2]

In the meantime, the Congress vows to murder South Africa's white population. They urge blacks to make South Africa ungovernable through violence and are doing their best to train and supply South Africa's blacks with Soviet arms, including grenades and limpit mines. The arms are to be used in white suburbs against civilians. "We send people almost every day (to infiltrate). They are there," Chris Hani, the political commissar of the organization's military wing, has said. "I don't think, when the crunch comes, that very many whites will be prepared to die."[3]

Congress radio broadcasts also urge South African blacks to "identify (black) collaborators and enemy agents and deal with them." They must be eliminated or destroyed and "no mercy should be shown to them." Responding to this call for justice, hundreds of alleged collaborators have been lynched and burned to death.[4]

Typical of Congress tactics was an attack made on the headquarters of the South African Air Force in Pretoria in 1983. A "cream-colored Dodge" pulled into the loading zone on one of the capital's busiest streets, "moments before the rush hour." Six minutes later a bomb destroyed the car, killing nineteen people—mostly black civilians—and injuring more than two hundred.[5] The same strategy was used again in 1985 when, during the rush hour, two car-bomb blasts killed three people in Durban. A *Washington Post* story declared that the attack had "flung automobiles into the air, hurled pedestrians to the ground. . . ."[6]

Other tactics used by the Congress have been the torching of businesses, bombing of railroad stations and tracks, attacks on police stations, a 1980 bank raid in which hostages were killed, and the murders of former National Congress members.

As of 1984, the South African government had acknowledged one hundred and ninety-seven armed attacks in the previous eight years, which included "25 assaults on industrial installations and power stations, 35 assassination attempts, 15 bombs, 30 assaults on police stations, government buildings and military centers and 33 attempts to sabotage railway lines."[7]

SOVIET CONTROL

Moreover, it is not theory that the Soviets control both the African Congress and SWAPO. The U.S. Senate chairman of the Subcommittee on Security and Terrorism declared in 1982 that both the African Congress and SWAPO are Soviet proxies and the Congress has been under the domination of the Communist Party of South Africa since World War II.[8] Defectors from the Congress itself testified in 1972 (during trials of other Congress members) that they had been sent to the Soviet Union and trained for eight years.[9]

Congress supporters, including the World Council, justify their support of this organization by inferring that it is the only organization which truly opposes apartheid. That argument is propaganda. There are many blacks, such as Mangosuthu Buthelezi, Zulu tribal chief and chairman of the South African Black Alliance, South Africa's largest black organization, who also oppose apartheid. Buthelezi's organization supports peaceful change and a democratic structure of one man-one vote political institutions he claims most black Africans also support. The Congress, he charges, rejects the kind of constitutions that "go with Western industrial capitalism."[10]

Buthelezi's view is worthy of consideration. The Zulu nation staged the last armed struggle against the South Africans in 1906, and it was Buthelezi's uncle who founded the African Congress in 1912; Buthelezi's grandfather, King Dinuzulu, was the ANC's first patron.

Further, Buthelezi is a former member of the African Congress and served with ANC heroes Nelson Mandela and Oliver Tambo. Buthelezi claims that the Inkatha, the national cultural liberation movement which he founded in 1975, is structured on the original ideals of the African National Congress—the ideals of nonviolent opposition in which the African Congress believed until it was seduced by Marxism-Leninism.

SWAPO also falsely advertises itself as the only organization fighting South Africa. It is not. There are eleven major political parties which struggle against the South African occupation of Namibia. SWAPO is just the only group which practices terrorism.

Morumba Kerina, SWAPO's cofounder and its first national chairman, confirmed in a 1984 interview that SWAPO is a Soviet-trained army and "an instrument for promoting Soviet interests in Southern Africa." Besides being a Soviet tool, SWAPO is a terrorist organization, Kerina said, charging that SWAPO assassinates its opponents. Documents in the hands of the U.S. government, he said, suggest that Sam Nujoma, now head of SWAPO, issued the order for the 1978 assassination of Chief Clemens Kapuuo, a moderate antiapartheid leader. SWAPO has assassinated many other political opponents, Kerina said.[11]

Over one thousand Namibians, largely black, have been killed or maimed by SWAPO in acts of terror, Kerina charged. SWAPO often places claymore mines along highways, and whole families are abducted in SWAPO raids in order to force the men to fight in the guerrilla army. Many abducted children are taken to Angola and to the Island of Youth in Cuba where they are indoctrinated, he said.[12]

ENCOURAGING SIGNS

The World Council's position on its support for these guerrillas is particularly unjustified if the situation in Namibia is properly understood. SWAPO is not fighting a hopeless situation, nor are they fighting a totally repressive government. A group of Western nations, led by the United States, is attempting to negotiate free elections under United Nations supervision and control. These nations are also attempting to negotiate a ceasefire by both South African troops and SWAPO and restrictions on the South African army and Namibian armed forces.

South Africa originally said it would cooperate, but then said it does not want to withdraw from Namibia (where it has ruled since 1919) until the estimated thirty-five thousand Cuban troops—which prop up the Angolan regime—are committed to leaving. The Angolan government, formerly a Portuguese colony, has been Marxist-Leninist since the late seventies and stays in power with the aid of the Cubans and about fifteen hundred Soviet advisors. South Africa does not want to withdraw until it feels that there is no Cuban threat to Namibia and South Africa. They would also like to see an end to the Cuban and Angolan protection of SWAPO terrorists and their bases.

In the meantime, the South African government has offered to seek legislation in the parliament authorizing an interim administration with limited autonomy. It is now creating, with a commission composed of Namibian political parties, a new constitution. The administration would have a council of ministers and a constituent assembly with the power to pass a bill of rights, set up a constitutional court, and create a council that could draft a constitution. Foreign policy and defense measures would stay under South African control and all legislation would require approval from the administrator general.

An administrator general is now appointed by the South African government, but there are elected bodies which represent, and semiautonomously govern, different parts of the population in the education and public health areas. Apartheid was officially ended in 1978, but whites do enjoy better facilities, and schools and hospitals are largely segregated. The blacks are a much poorer group than the whites, and their education is largely inferior. But there is hope that this situation will change in the foreseeable future.

Spokesmen for the South African government claim they want nothing more than to withdraw from Namibia since South Africa is carrying a "heavy financial burden" by staying in the country. South Africa is supplying 98 percent of the entire Namibian budget, only 37 percent of which is earmarked for the armed forces. The major amount of the budget is for the maintenance of roads, railways, harbors, and schools. More than a billion rands are expended yearly for this budget, they say, more than any resource income they could take out of the country.[13]

SWAPO AND THE SOVIETS

It is very clear that change is not something that SWAPO puts its faith in, nor necessarily a situation which it desires. Kerina represented SWAPO at the United Nations from its beginning in 1959 to 1963, but was forced to leave the organization because of growing Soviet influence. After being banned from returning to Namibia, he was influential in the Botswana independence movement. He is now president of the Namibia Democratic Coalition, which maintains a nonviolent struggle against South African occupation.

SWAPO's representative to the U.S., Kerina pointed out, has said SWAPO is "anti-capitalist." SWAPO's political manual states, "The ideas of socialist orientation . . . have become our way of life. . . . Marxism-Leninism is therefore proving to be the only theory enabling all the oppressed and exploited classes to carry out their historical mission (e.g. the destruction of the rule of capital and of the system of exploitation of man by man)."[14]

Kerina said he can speak "authoritatively" because he was the one who originally began sending students to the U.S.S.R. By the time Kerina began to suspect SWAPO had taken the wrong course it was too late: "SWAPO was by then dominated by cadres trained in the Soviet bloc."[15]

Most of the SWAPO soldiers are Ovambos, a numerous tribe found both in Angola and in Namibia, constituting 51 percent of Namibian tribes. Most men who are willingly recruited into SWAPO, Kerina said, are tricked into believing Radio Luanda and Zambia, which promise free scholarships for SWAPO membership. Once recruited into the ranks, however, they are forced into military training. Many of these soldiers have returned to Namibia and are the source of the growing body of information about life in SWAPO.[16]

Namibian men who flee to refugee camps in Angola, which are administered by SWAPO (and paid for by the United Nations), are also pressed into service. As for those who refuse to serve in the SWAPO army, Kerina said, they are tried by "revolutionary tribunals." The sentence is usually death.[17]

The UN has officially recognized SWAPO as the future government of Namibia, and almost totally finances the organization—to the tune of millions each year. However, the recognition by the Organization of African Unity and the United Nations is a result of Soviet tactics, Kerina said. The Soviets used Libya to push a resolution through the Organization of African Unity for "the exclusive recognition of groups aligned with Moscow, excluding those that were purely nationalistic or pro-Peking. African Unity adopted the resolution after Libya threatened to stop contributing money and materials to the African Liberation Committee," Kerina said.[18]

Kerina's claims have been backed by United Nations documents in which Soviet diplomats have stated they use "active measures" in support of the National Congress and SWAPO. The Soviet document, dated March 31, 1981, states that "the Soviet Union has given and continues to give all-around support to the national liberation movements of southern Africa."[19]

Bulgaria's statements on southern Africa liberation movements is even more interesting. Bulgaria has stated that "Cadres of Southern Africa's national liberation movements are being trained in Bulgaria" and went on to report that its government provides treatment to wounded African National Congress and SWAPO terrorists and other kinds of help, both political and material.[20]

Statements from Hungary and the German Democratic Republic both boast of aid to SWAPO and the National Congress. Hungary stated that anything terrorists do is not terrorism if it is being used against "the colonialist terror of imperialism," and the Democratic Republic boasted that—since 1976—they provided "solidarity goods" worth about "1,000 million marks," food, medicine, medical care for "wounded liberation fighters," clothing, tents, and training for "students and workers." The German Democratic Republic document also emphasized that country's relationship with National Congress president Oliver Tambo and SWAPO chief Sam Nujoma, both whom had visited East Berlin and opened offices in that capital.[21]

It is tragic enough that these groups kill people, but they also teach children to do the same. Many SWAPO camps in Angola, *New York Times* writer Bernard Nossiter reported in 1981, are filled exclusively with children under sixteen who are drilled in Communist propaganda. "Its residents have fled from the war in South-West Africa, and they are heavily indoctrinated to return as guerrillas," Nossiter wrote.[22]

If there was ever any doubt that SWAPO is Marxist-Leninist, Nossiter's story would dispel it. "As the visitors leave," the story said, "a contingent is brought from the adult women's camp. They are a chorus and imitate the breaking of chains. They sing: 'We are determined that Namibia must be free. Marxism and Leninism is our ideology, founded on scientific socialism.' "[23]

THE WORLD COUNCIL SUPPORTS TERRORISTS

Unfortunately, the World Council of Churches cannot claim (should it feel like doing so) it has been deceived concerning the real nature of SWAPO and the African Congress. The World Council has a long history of supporting violent organizations. At the 1975 World Council Assembly in Nairobi an amendment stating that the churches ought not to support the Special Program to Combat Racism, unless there were assurances that funding would not be provided to organizations that would be likely to cause serious injury or the taking of life, was presented. The amendment was defeated 325 to 62, with twenty-two abstentions.

The World Council formally supported ZANU—an organization which sought to overthrow the Rhodesian government. The World Council's support for ZANU was both financial and moral, and all of it was unconscionable. ZANU's tactics were so bloody that the Anglican bishops of Mashonaland and Matabeland charged, in 1973, that it was using "naked terrorism." In a letter of protest to the World Council the bishops said the ZANU guerrillas "came out of the bush, surrounded farmhouses by night, sprayed them with bullets and heavier armaments, wounding occupants, chiefly children, and burning down houses of local Africans."[24]

In 1974 the bishops again wrote the World Council, charging that ZANU had killed eighty-seven civilians. "Far and away the majority of these have been Africans, innocent of any offence and most have been killed with great brutality. Others have been abducted, raped, beaten and disfigured." The bishops also noted "with disgust" that the World Council had granted over six thousand pounds to ZANU that year.[25]

What the World Council did next is even more revealing. ZANU, and other black groups, finally succeeded in ousting the white government from Rhodesia and establishing an interim, democratic government. The interim government was composed of three black nationalist leaders and white prime minister Ian Smith. Its function was to establish a constitutional government which would guarantee the rights of all racial groups. Two of the black leaders, United Methodist Bishop Abel Muzorewa and Congregationalist minister Ndabaningi Sithole (president of ZANU), had been generously funded by the World Council in 1975 and 1976. When they joined the interim government, however, the funding stopped.

Instead, in 1978 the Special Fund to Combat Racism gave the Patriotic Front guerrillas, who were Marxists-Leninists who opposed the interim government, $85,000. This same organization had allegedly massacred thirty-five missionaries and their children over the preceding two years, had murdered two hundred and seven white civilians and seventeen hundred and twelve black civilians. This does not count two hundred and ninety-six civilians killed by terrorist mines. The World Council did not address the charges and did not stop the funding.[26]

When the grant was announced the *Daily Telegraph* of London commented, "In a way one could respect them more (the World Council) if they went to Africa themselves to murder missionaries and children rather than hired a pack of savages to do it for them."[27]

The Presbyterian Church of Ireland subsequently withdrew from the World Council in protest, and the Salvation Army withdrew in 1981 after the grant was announced. They charged that the World Council is guided by "politics rather than the gospel." The Salvation Army asked for "fraternal status" in place of membership, a move which allows them to send advisors to council meetings and to continue cooperation in inter-Christian aid, and medical and ecumenical work.[28]

FRELIMO, another Marxist-Leninist organization, was given over fifty thousand pounds by the World Council before they successfully overthrew the Mozambique government in 1975.

The World Council statements regarding the reaction of member churches to the grants have been cavalier, dismissing members leaving the Council with the comment, "But churches are joining and leaving the Council right along." It added that "No longer does the World Council take its cues only from its constituents in the privileged lands of the north."[29]

Although World Council position papers declare the Special Fund is meant to show the World Council's solidarity for the racially oppressed, it never mentions Vietnam's discrimination against the Chinese living in Vietnam or the persecution of the Miskito Indians in Nicaragua or the murder of groups of African blacks by other blacks. The narrative of abuses of blacks is endless and the atrocities are sickening: murders, tortures, death by burning, death by starvation, in Ethiopia, in Zaire, in Angola, in Mozambique. Uganda alone has accounted for millions of horrible deaths, tribe against tribe, political party against political party; and yet the World Council of Churches has said nothing about the general slaughter.

Further, the World Council does not hesitate to abandon its former allies when it finds other groups for which it has a better liking. When Rhodesian (now Zimbabwe) guerrillas led by Joshua Nkoma and Robert Mugabe, leaders of the aforementioned Patriotic Front, were fighting the interracial interim regime, the Special Fund was generous. Now that Nkoma's Shona tribe are suffering persecution under Mugabe's Marxist-Leninist government, a persecution protested by the country's Catholic bishops, the World Council is silent—and no further money has been forthcoming from the Special Fund for Nkoma.

The most obvious question is whether the World Council can justify its financing of these organizations. In Chapter Two it is asserted that the state is not only justified in defending its population and territory, but obligated to do so. It is asserted that Christians can morally support national defense because under God's law the state is responsible for order and justice. Therefore, does it then follow that the church as a whole can morally and financially support violence which is ostensibly being used to establish freedom elsewhere?

First, there is a difference between Christians and the church. Christians compose the church and hopefully witness to the world: but the church is more than its membership. Christians are perfectly free to fight for freedom anywhere (and obliged to do so for their country in the face of unjust aggression) as citizens of states and of the world. But the church is not the state, nor a citizen of the state. It was established by Jesus to minister to, and evangelize, the world. The church is therefore the Bride of Christ and is not the combined opinions of its members or a participant in their civil duties.

THE LESSON OF DIETRICH BONHOEFFER

Theologian Dietrich Bonhoeffer provided an excellent example of the distinction between Christians as citizens and the Christian church. Bonhoeffer was a German theology professor who believed that the only way to save Christian civilization was to ensure Germany lost World War II. He became a leader in the "Confessing Church," a section of the Lutheran Church in Germany which actively opposed German National Socialism.

In 1939, when Bonhoeffer was thirty-three, he left Germany at the behest of worried friends and went to the United States. He returned after two weeks, however, stating that he did not deserve to take part in the reconstruction of German Christianity after the war if he did not share the persecution of his people. He was arrested in 1943 and was hung at Flossenburg Prison April 9, 1945, a few months before the war ended. Documents had been found which implicated him in the plot to kill Hitler.

Bonhoeffer believed, according to people who were close to him, that it is a "Christian's duty towards God to oppose tyranny, that is, a government which is no longer based on natural law and the law of God . . . and that the Christian must be prepared, if necessary, to offer his life for this. Thus all kinds of secular totalitarianism which force man to cast aside his religious and moral obligations to God and subordinate the laws of justice and morality to the State are incompatible with his conception of life.[30]

"Again, it was typical of Bonhoeffer that he did not commit the Church by his actions. The responsibility was his and not that of the Church, and therefore he cannot, alas, be said to have represented by his action the Confessional Church as a whole."[31]

Bonhoeffer believed that the task and essential character of the church, as differentiated from that of the individual Christian, is working to reconcile the world with God and open its eyes to the reality of the love of God, "against which it is blindly raging."[32] Literally, he saw the church's function as preacher and keeper of the Baptismal and Eucharistic sacraments.[33]

Bonhoeffer further stated that government has a "divine mandate," by law and by "the force of the sword," to preserve the world for the reality of Jesus Christ. "Everyone owes obedience to this governing authority—for Christ's sake," he wrote. Since Bonhoeffer was caught violently opposing his evil and aggressive government, we may suppose Bonhoeffer meant citizens owe obedience to moral governments, which includes supporting national defense. He makes this clear when he declares that governments that are no longer willing to serve the law of God can lay no claim to a divine mandate and must be "made subject to the law of God by the proclamation of the Church."[34]

In other words, the duty of the church is to proclaim the word of God and the duty of the state is to enforce a moral authority that preserves social order. It is not the correct function of the Bride of Christ to finance violence, whether needed or not.

Bonhoeffer even questioned whether Christians as a whole should strive to upset the social order (as differentiated from the totalitarianism he fought), even if that social order is unjust. Saint Paul was quoted extensively by Bonhoeffer, in his book *The Cost of Disciple-*

ship, in sections in which Paul addressed the role of revolution in overturning the social order. Paul, Bonhoeffer pointed out, told the slave not to rebel because he was already free in Christ.[35]

"As a member of the Body of Christ he has acquired a freedom which no rebellion or revolution could have brought him . . . his real meaning is that to renounce rebellion and revolution is the most appropriate way of expressing our conviction that the Christian hope is not set on this world, but on Christ and his kingdom. . . . They (Christians) are bidden to be of good cheer: God himself will use the powers to work for their good and his sovereignty extends even over the powers. This is more than an academic statement about the nature of authority in the abstract. . . . Christ and Christians conquer by service. Failure to realize this distinction will bring a heavy judgement on the Christian . . . it will mean a lapse into the standards of the world."[36]

The concept of "cheap grace," which Bonhoeffer warned against, has been interpreted as an excuse to enter into the world's political battles. What Bonhoeffer really meant by "cheap grace," however, was "the preaching of forgiveness without requiring repentance, baptism without church discipline, Communion without confession, absolution without personal confession. Cheap grace is grace without discipleship, grace without the cross, grace without Jesus Christ, living and incarnate."[37]

Bonhoeffer stressed again and again that the essence of the church was Christ and that had to be manifested in the world in proclamation. The question of whether the church should finance revolution is answered in that assertion. Christ proclaimed triumph over death; giving money that finances death in His name is heresy.

AMERICAN ALLIES

Unfortunately, despite the nature of its activities, the World Council has allies which help it shore up its policies. Some of the organizations which morally support SWAPO and the National Congress are Trans-Africa, Washington Office on Africa, Institute for Policy Studies, the American Friends Service Committee, and the Interfaith Center on Corporate Responsibility.

All of these organizations either receive funds from the National Council of Churches, a mainline church, and/or have been affiliated with churches in their political endeavors. TransAfrica received $28,610 from 1981 through 1983 from the United Methodists and $4,067 in 1984. The Washington Office on Africa was granted $38,750 from 1981 through 1983 and $18,000 in 1984 from the same denomination.

It is not an accident that the Washington Office on Africa has been given special fund grants by the World Council. They were awarded $15,000 in 1982 for programs to "encourage progressive U.S. foreign policy towards southern Africa." TransAfrica received $25,000 from the World Council in 1985.

It is typical of radical organizations to network and cooperate in gathering support for mutual causes. African Marxist-Leninist liberation movements are not an exception. In typical intermovement cooperation, TransAfrica and other radical organizations sponsored a 1981 conference titled "Building Forces Against United States Support for South Africa." Speakers for that conference were, among others, National Congress president Oliver Tambo, third-ranking SWAPO leader Moses Garoeb, and Canon Robert Powell, director of the African office of the National Council of Churches. Other prominent participants were members of the Communist Party, U.S.A. and organizations used by the Soviets.

TRANSAFRICA

There have been many instances in which TransAfrica has declared its support of the Congress and SWAPO, but its actions speak even louder. Keynote speaker at TransAfrica's 1984 dinner was Sam Nujoma, SWAPO leader. The keynote speaker for 1983 was the late Maurice Bishop, formerly Marxist-Leninist prime minister of Grenada. Oliver Tambo has "been sponsored" by TransAfrica. TransAfrica head Randall Robinson and his organization have also spoken out for the Palestinian Liberation Organization and the Marxist-Leninist regimes of Mozambique, Cuba, and Ethiopia.[38]

Nonetheless, TransAfrica's board of directors has included Randolph Nugent and Isaac Bivens of the United Methodist mission board, Oscar McCloud of the Program Agency of the Presbyterian Church (USA), and Charles Cobb, executive director of the United Church of Christ's Commission for Racial Justice. TransAfrica has also been highly successful in legitimizing itself by gathering American support against apartheid. It is responsible for the protests at the South African Embassy in Washington, protests which have included leaders from almost every American mainline church and celebrities of every stripe.

The United Methodists have participated in efforts to help the African Marxists-Leninists. In 1981 they sponsored a "Conference in Solidarity with the Liberation Struggle of the People of Southern Africa." The "people of Southern Africa," to which the title referred, were the African Congress and SWAPO. The United Methodists provided $4,000 in cash for the conference, office space for organizing efforts, staff, and a letterhead which labeled the organizing a United Methodist effort. It also allowed the conference to use the names of prominent United Methodist bishops and officials, many of whom knew little about the conference. The conference coordinator was Carl Bloice, the editor of *People's World*, the West Coast publication of the Communist Party, U.S.A.

Roy Beck, an editor of the *United Methodist Reporter*, attended the New York conference and found that no United Methodists were on the conference steering committee, but the committee did have members of the central committee of the Communist Party, U.S.A. The conference was initiated by the International Committee against Apartheid, Racism, and Colonialism in Southern Africa, a Soviet-front organization.

Beck, who said the conference was a "coming of age" experience for him concerning his attitudes about mainline denominations, questioned why activists who were trying to mobilize support for guerrillas chose speakers who alienate ordinary church members. "It seemed that the conference was designed to alienate," he said. ". . . I found it anti-American, and that's not a tremendous affront to me, to be critical, to be self-critical of the U.S., except that . . . it seemed to me . . . that the anti-Americanism was more important than the anti-apartheid . . . it seemed I heard so much more about how bad the U.S. was than how bad apartheid was."[39]

Ironically, funds and support given to Marxist-Leninist guerrilla movements can be utterly wasted if the purpose is to install permanent Marxist-Leninist governments. The World Council supplied thousands of dollars to Mozambique's guerrillas (FRELIMO) before they successfully overthrew the Portuguese government in 1975. When the Portuguese left, the Mozambique government immediately signed endless pacts and accords with the U.S.S.R. and others in the Eastern Bloc. However, after watching the formerly prosperous Mozambique economy crumble into shambles, President Samora Moises Machel changed direction and is now also signing agreements with the West. There may be eventual political change as well.

That would not necessarily be the case in Namibia, however, should SWAPO triumph there, nor would it necessarily be the case if the National Congress should succeed in conquering South Africa. There has never been a Marxist-Leninist government which was an improvement over its predecessor, no matter how bad that predecessor was. Africa has not been an exception to this rule. Angola under the Portuguese was not a nice place for its black citizens. They were exploited. But under the Marxists-Leninists, it is hell. There is no freedom of speech, Christians are persecuted, there is no freedom of movement, no freedom of the press, and the secret police are more than active.

Further, the Soviets do not finance revolutions as a result of altruism. They expect returns of one kind or another. "The Russians would just as soon see the region burning," one Mozambique official recently told author David Lamb. "The great merit of the West is that it has powers greater than those of the gun."[39]

It is one of the great tragedies in the history of Christianity that the World Council has abandoned its great powers of moral suasion for methods used by its greatest enemies.

TEN

Theories Regarding the Motivation of the Religious Left

This book has attempted to prove that the leadership of the mainline Christian church has established a Religious Left which it leads and finances. It has attempted to prove that the main tenets of the Religious Left are an irrational faith in disarmament, suspicion of American intentions and culture, disapproval of the free enterprise system, and a belief in the goodness of many Marxist-Leninist governments. If that premise is accepted, the question then becomes why the Religious Left chooses to believe these things.

In attempting to examine this matter, several theories are presented. Each was chosen because it has something in it which seemed relevant to the authors. No one theory can hold the whole truth, and some presented here probably hold less than others. Humanity is complicated and answers are elusive, especially when the subject is motivation. "Why?" is the oldest question on earth, the most fascinating, and sometimes the least answerable. Humanity's curse and most distinguished characteristic is that it acts both from the basest and the most saintly of motives. Moreover, there are ten thousand motives for ten thousand persons, even if they are involved in the same political movement.

Nonetheless, it is essential to understand—or attempt to understand—the Religious Left's various motivations. It is useless and futile to merely disagree with this faction, or anyone for that matter, without understanding how they arrived at their conclusions. Argument without understanding tends to lead to stalemate or, worse, name-calling and misleading categorization; it rarely changes anyone's mind. Explanations are not excuses. But at the same time, an attempt at understanding and compassion are sometimes necessary to achieve real change. Unless those attempts are made, there can be no dialogue. Blind dislike also makes it difficult to counter opposing strategies. Labeling someone a Marxist, or other pejorative, rarely helps matters, especially when that person is operating from another premise altogether.

Finally, anything which adds to our knowledge of humanity is valuable, for we are all human. There is no possibility that exists in others, including the Religious Left, which does not exist in us all. It is possible to cry, "I beseech ye in the bowels of Christ, think that ye may be mistaken,"[1] and still recognize our commonality.

This chapter, then, will first examine why a spiritual vacuum appeared in the Christian world, then examine possible motivations for the appearance of the Religious Left. These include the search for meaning, insecurity, alienation from American culture, the secularization of American society, personal instability, self-destructiveness, anger, a tendency for Americans to embark on idealistic crusades, and simple self-interest.

IN THE BEGINNING

First, before mainline Christianity was diverted from its traditional course something happened—theologians discarded traditional Scriptural interpretation. Since Scripture is the foundation of Christianity (the primary way in which the will of God is revealed to humanity), a deep vacuum appeared in the Christian world. The initial process began with the appearance of German "higher criticism" of the nineteenth century—a method of studying Scripture which tends to deny the reality of the supernatural world and ends in rejecting (as unhistorical) miracles and many fundamental Scriptural events.

Author and sociologist Peter Berger explains the acceptance of this and similar liberal philosophies as the rise of a liberalism whose concern is the adjustment of Christianity to the modern world view. Its major result, he believes, has been the "progressive dismantling" of the supernatural foundations of the Christian tradition. Berger believes that liberal theology begs the respect of secular intellectuals whose ideas are accepted as binding. "In other words, Protestant theologians have been increasingly engaged in playing a game whose rules have been dictated by their cognitive antagonists." This has left Christian theology nothing but "hollow rhetoric."[2]

This theological vacuum soon spread to the seminaries—the very places in which Christian clergy learn the intellectual foundation of their faith. A United Methodist seminary, one graduate said in a recent interview, questions faith, questions "everything from the Virgin Birth to the Divinity of Christ." This method is used, he said, to force students to find out what they believe for themselves. The seminary, true to the traditions of the German theologians, does not encourage students to take Biblical events literally.

During his last semester, the student (now a minister) said he and thirty of his fellow-students were asked to write a paper explaining what they believed as Christians. Each student wrote something different. The minister said the main thing he learned at seminary was liberal theologian Paul Tillich's main theme: "God forgive me, I'm a sinner, I could be wrong, I don't know all the answers."[3]

As a result of this method of teaching, one which encourages doubt and questioning, the clergy naturally questions. So much so that in many places in which traditional Christianity is still valued the clergyman has become the "spiritual and psychological outsider in the denomination."[4] One young pastor recently explained that he does not dare tell his congregation what he really believes because they would assume he was guilty of heresy. In these circumstances it is not surprising that the denominations are fast losing membership. If the clergy do not adhere to their faith, it is unlikely their members will be fervent.

Many of the liberal clergy have subsequently become denominational bureaucrats. This is not to say that all denominational bureaucrats are dropout liberal clergy, not even a great percentage. But Christian clergy have set the tone and intellectual atmosphere for their bureaucracies. If the clergy does not believe in orthodox Christianity, it is unlikely that its officials will be any different. And because all faiths tend to enforce orthodoxy, even if at times it is the orthodoxy of unorthodoxy, people who believe differently are not welcomed into its ranks. Bureaucracies tend to hire people with like ideas, and pastors often insist their colleagues accept the liberal ideal.

A good example of this lies in the phenomenon of orthodox clergymen who are outsiders shunned among their peers.[5] There are conferences within the United Methodist Church which are reluctant to take graduates of Asbury Theological Seminary, a conservative school. Moreover, many Protestant seminaries which have obviously taken sides are reluctant to hire professors who graduated from conservative schools, a practice which keeps most seminaries and seminarians on the liberal straight-and-narrow.

This tactic worked better in the past than it does today, although the church is still living with an antiorthodox mandate. Theology's liberal conformity is no longer accepted by dissidents. Instead of producing uniform views, it has created an open rift between liberals and conservatives which has divided both the mainline churches and Roman Catholicism.

The Vatican is highly conservative under the leadership of Pope John Paul II, but a majority of American leadership, including many priests and nuns, are extremely liberal. This situation has led to constant friction between local leadership and Rome. The Episcopal and Presbyterian churches have also seen strain. Some of their congregations have broken off and formed separate denominations.

THE SEARCH FOR MEANING

If we assume that religious liberalism has taken its toll and some Christian leadership has lost its traditional faith, the question then becomes why it transferred its allegiance to another philosophy. Psychologist Viktor Frankl has provided a possible answer. He believes that humanity's greatest drive is its search for meaning, rather than the fulfillment of drives and instincts. When that will to meaning is frustrated, people experience "existential frustration," a "man's concern, even his despair, over the worthwhileness of life." When existential frustration occurs, Frankl points out, people often compensate by striving for power, material wealth, or pleasure.[6]

This is an easy theory to believe. If it were not so, the thousand different creeds and ideologies which mankind has fought over throughout recorded history would never have come into existence; food, sex, and social relationships would have sufficed.

It is also highly probable that persons who have sloughed off their previous, deeply held beliefs (their meaning) would transfer their allegiance to another philosophy instead of more transitory pleasures.

This is particularly true of idealistic and searching Americans, regardless of their religious persuasion. Alexis de Tocqueville, who saw deeper into the American soul in 1835 than anybody since, said that Americans display a "secret disquietude" and "restlessness" that is produced by a lack of boundaries. Everything is possible, thus everything must be tried; therefore content becomes much more difficult.[7] It is reasonable to assume that this sort of institutional "disquietude" makes it more necessary for Americans to find something substantial on which to base a life.

Frankl cited a statistical survey conducted by Johns Hopkins University that proves this point. After forty-eight American colleges were studied, he said, the sociologists found that the goal of 78 percent of all surveyed students was "finding a purpose and a meaning to my life." A statistical survey among Frankl's European students demonstrated that 25 percent felt an "existential vacuum." Among his American students, however, it was 60 percent.[8]

Should Frankl's theory apply to America's Religious Left, however, it still does not explain why errant Christians turned to radical politics to discover their meaning. What appealed? Why was it utopianism which in turn engendered sympathy for Marxist-Leninist societies? What determined that particular choice instead of, for instance, conservative politics or even a belief in science as savior, the secular faith of the nineteenth century?

INSECURITY AND ISOLATION

One answer may be that the religious elite feels alienated and isolated, as apparently does much of the rest of Western civilization. The American founding fathers asserted that all men are born equal and the rights of humanity are given by God, not the state. Those ideas were the beginning of democracy as we know it, a freedom which encourages total individual decision-making. In *Escape from Freedom*, Erich Fromm asserted that this freedom allows individuals to shape their lives as they will, without limit. There are no authorities who force their belief system, their politics, or a preferred way of life on individuals. The same freedom which allows people to grow and choose their way of life, however, also means that many people feel isolated, insecure, powerless, and insignificant. They are swamped with doubts concerning the meaning of their lives.[9]

As a result of these feelings, Fromm said, many humans long to submit to an authority stronger than themselves. They feel the need for "relief from uncertainty, even if it deprives an individual of his (her) freedom."[10]

The need for authority was not always present in the West. Although the mercantile and feudal systems of the Middle Ages (many features of which persisted in some form until the end of the eighteenth century) did not provide even basic subsistence for much of the population of Europe, Fromm asserted, there were great compensations. Work was personal. The craftsman made products and sold them to people he or she knew. While guilds refused to allow their members to compete against each other for more profit, they also provided security for their members. While occupations were foreordained by the social order and family tradition, thus robbing the individual of freedom, there was never the anxiety of choosing what to do with one's life.[11]

Fromm believed that the West has allowed free enterprise to become an impersonal system. It uses individuals as cogs in its "vast machine of distribution," he believed, thus robbing them of a personal relationship to their work. He believed it also forces individuals to sell "themselves" in their work, a result of needing others for employment and profit. This has falsified humanity's relations with each other, he believed, producing alienation, unconscious hostility, anxiety, and the inability of people to understand their feelings.[12]

Some sectors of Christianity, Fromm thought, furthered the process of isolation. The Roman Catholic Church of the Middle Ages stressed the dignity of man, free will, the value of humanity's efforts, the resemblance between God and His creatures, and humanity's right "to be confident of God's love."[13]

But Protestantism, he believed, has forced humanity to face God alone. It can no longer depend on the intervention of the church. Protestantism freed humanity from its dependence on the church's authority and put the responsibility of spiritual welfare on the individual—principles which many believe encouraged the development of democratic capitalism. But Martin Luther and John Calvin, Fromm said, also stressed the powerlessness and personal insignificance of the individual. He believed this feeling has persisted in Western culture.[14]

It is worth mentioning here that the word heard most frequently uttered by both the Left and the Religious Left is "solidarity." It is a word that is used as a pledge to countries and organizations already ruled by Marxists-Leninists, such as "we must show our solidarity with Nicaragua, or Angola, or the African National Conference," and the most familiar word used to describe radical functions. There are solidarity conferences, solidarity marches, and solidarity groups.

Solidarity means, according to the dictionary, "a union of interests, purposes, or sympathies among members of a group; fellowship of responsibilities and interests."[15] It is a word whose meaning and purpose has natural appeal for people who feel isolated.

Fromm did not advocate the destruction of capitalism or Protestantism. He admired the advances humanity made with the help of free enterprise. He saw it as an exchange. Free enterprise provides the way in which humanity can acquire the freedom it needs to develop into complete individuals. At the same time, it takes a security (solidarity) from those same individuals which many of them are still trying to regain. Fromm, who wrote *Escape from Freedom* in 1941, saw the resulting danger as allegiance to fascism, the power which would remove doubt and anxiety. In the latter part of the twentieth century, however, he would probably fear Marxism-Leninism.[16]

If we assume that Fromm is correct, much of Western society is doubtful, fearful, insecure, and hostile. If we assumed that humanity's (including the restless Americans) greatest driving force is to find a meaning which will explain its life, then those two theories correlate. One explains the doubt. The other explains the drive that seeks the answer. Neither theory should be true, of course, of Christians, or other groups who have rooted their lives in a faith which explains the world for them and provides an answer to life's anxieties.

If those who have been securely rooted lose their faith, however, it is psychologically necessary to take on another. This is particularly true when faced with the isolation which modern society imposes. A traditionally faithful person is not prepared to live without belief and cannot live comfortably without the security which the faith has provided. It is difficult enough to live with the normal insecurity which accompanies modern existence—to have a measure of security through a religious creed, then lose it, is comparable to finding oneself orphaned.

The belief system of the Religious Left offers an ideal alternative to the traditional Christian belief system. Working for heaven on earth is similar to working for salvation in the life to come. Both belief systems are other-oriented, idealistic, and give meaning to life.

ALIENATION

Correlating with Fromm's theories are observations made by Paul Hollander, who in *Political Pilgrims* astutely documented the travels of Western intellectuals to Marxist-Leninist countries. The travelers, Hollander found, inevitably admired those societies despite having every rational reason to be horrified. They ignored the suppression of the population, the poverty, and the total lack of intellectual freedom. He attributed their will to believe to their corresponding alienation from Western culture.

A large part of that alienation, he wrote, has its roots in the demand by intellectuals that their culture fulfill their need for belonging and pervasive meaning. Much of the societal criticism which follows their subsequent discontent stems from the ability of intellectuals to openly criticize their culture and the prestige they gain when they do so.

Alienation is also due to the psychological difficulties of living in "complex, mobile, and bureaucratized urban societies" which produce isolation, impersonality, and weakened social ties. That was precisely Fromm's point.[17]

SECULARIZATION

But Hollander also attributed alienation to "the shattering effects of secularization," which have been manifested in the destruction of values which make life meaningful. Hollander quoted author Richard Lowenthal's statement that secularization produces anxiety which "is the direct root of the desperate readiness to look for the missing certainty in a doctrine that expresses a belief in secular salvation in a rationally disguised form. . . ."[18]

There is no doubt that this secularization has taken place in the United States. It is true that there seems to be a significant upswing in religious belief. At the same time, there is also a significant lack of religious observance in the public square. De Tocqueville observed in 1835 that on Sunday, everything in American stopped except church. ". . . on the seventh day of every week the trading and working life of the nation seems suspended; all noises cease."[19] This is no longer the case.

If it is true that secularization is one reason that intellectuals have sought meaning in countries governed by Marxist-Leninist regimes, then we can assume that loss of faith in traditional Christianity by the very people who have chosen to live out its meaning would have doubly shattering effects.

THE SEARCH FOR CERTAINTY

In light of Fromm and Hollander's assertions, it is possible that under the overt assumptions of the Religious Left lie unconscious motives— an unexpressed belief that if its politics are successful, a great force will take control of mankind, eliminating the insecurity and doubt which have plagued it for so long.

Most Christian radicals deny working on behalf of Marxism or totalitarianism, and they are telling the truth. Most Christian radicals do not consciously desire totalitarianism to be visited upon themselves or the world. But after the acceptance by almost all of Western culture concerning the existence of the unconscious mind, it is unreasonable for any educated person to say, "I support this end with my actions, but my actions are not indicative of my meaning."

If church leadership weakens national defense by charging that the United States is at fault in the arms face, advocating unilateral disarmament in the face of a menacing enemy who would most certainly take full advantage of any such situation, then that leadership has worked against the nation's interests. If church leadership attacks a democracy's allies while ignoring or supporting its enemies, constantly attacks the integrity of the nation and its economic system, then that leadership has worked on behalf of that nation's enemies. To then protest its patriotism (or innocence of intent) gives lie to everything science knows about the human psyche.

This does not mean that radicals understand, even unconsciously, the true results of totalitarianism. As Fromm pointed out, humans sometimes see the all-knowing authority as a relief from uncertainty and the loss of freedom as a necessary sacrifice for this end. The unconscious is not aware that the relief from uncertainty will never make up for the loss of freedom.

Humans seem, Fromm asserts, to be in a difficult situation. They do not want uncertainty and isolation, but using an all-powerful authority to end that isolation does not work. ". . . human existence and freedom are from the beginning inseparable . . . for the fact of his (human) separateness cannot be reversed; it is an escape from an unbearable situation which would make life impossible if it were prolonged."[20]

PERSONAL INSTABILITY

Carl Jung also had a theory which could apply to Christian radicals. In *The Undiscovered Self* he wrote that "Everywhere in the West" exist subversive minorities who are mentally unstable and, "sheltered by our humanitarianism and our sense of justice," are ready to light the "incendiary torches." The only thing that stops them, he said, is the reason of the stable portion of the population. Jung believed that the stable portion will not always prevail because most people are not knowledgeable enough about others, or their own state of mind and belief system, to deal with the situation.[21]

The "incendiaries," Jung said, are dangerous because their mental state is that of a "collectively excited group ruled by affective judgments and wish fantasies." Their ideas are dangerous to the general population because they appeal to the resentful and collectively irrational.[22]

It is certainly true that the ideas of the Religious Left appeal to the resentful because they are based in a have-have not mentality. According to the radical Christian, the poor are poor because no one will give them their human rights and the Third World nations are poor because the West has robbed them of their natural resources. As we have seen in previous chapters, these assertions are untrue. They can be characterized as affective judgments and wish fantasy in the sense that the radical's belief system is a result of their need for political ground on which to base a bid for power.

All power is based on some belief which will attract followers. The success of that power bid depends on how much the philosophy appeals to the culture. Radical philosophy does not appeal to most Americans. However, it does appeal to what Peter Berger has characterized as "The New Class"—which consists of those that derive their livelihood from the "knowledge industry." This includes the media, teachers, bureaucrats, and their "centers of power," the universities and foundations. With the help of those who approve and distribute Religious-Left ideas, it seems to have much more power than is based in reality.[23]

The Left does not seem to hold an incendiary torch for our culture—although it showers American society with its stern disapproval and works to weaken its defense structures—but it certainly seems to hold one for others. Violent struggle by Marxist-Leninist revolutionary armies, as we have seen, is inevitably supported by the American mainline church. This support usually manifests itself as constant verbal tirades against whatever government the Marxists-Leninists are attempting to destroy. The most recent example of this has been the activism against the government of El Salvador and South Africa.

SELF-DESTRUCTIVENESS

Another possible answer lies with the urge toward self-destruction often felt by those who do not feel they can escape unhappiness or find their meaning. That theory could explain why church radicals spend as much time attacking their own culture and government as they do. If culture, or the nation, is the expression of the collective self, destroying either or both is one method for destruction of the individuals who live within.

Hollander gives a fine example of such self-destructive urges in the life of radical author Scott Nearing. Nearing rejected America (except to live here). He embraced nearly all Marxist-Leninist societies, going so far as to defend the Soviet invasion of Hungary by arguing that the rebels who had tried to free themselves from Soviet rule were really disgruntled ex-landowners. Nearing, however, must not have been the fool he seemed because he was quoted as explaining that "if the Communists took control in this country (he) would be one of the first to be executed."[24]

Many psychiatrists believe that humans have, to a greater or lesser degree, a death wish as well as an instinct for self-preservation. One instinct sometimes becomes predominant according to the circumstances of a person's life. If a personality has been disappointed and hurt in life, or is simply afraid of it, that person becomes self-destructive and destructive of others. In the extreme this attitude is quite repulsive, as exemplified by the Spanish General Millan Astray whose favorite motto was *"Viva la muerte!"* (Long live death).[25]

Attitudes toward others and attitudes towards self are parallel, Fromm believed. But he pointed out that while people are often conscious of their hostility against others, hostility against the self, except in "pathological cases," is unconscious and is expressed in "indirect and rationalized forms."[26]

ANGER

A simpler explanation for religious radicalism could lie in simple human anger which has directed itself against the most convenient object. Hollander cites author David Potter's observation that anger is often emotionally generated and does not recognize its source. It is therefore not specifically directed toward an object. It is free-floating and ready to express itself aggressively against anything not protected by superior strength or taboos. Thus, ". . . the degree of discontent in any society is not necessarily correlated to the degree of injustice or evil in the institutions of the society. . . ."[27]

We have already established that the main assertions of the Religious Left are based on the struggle between the haves and have nots. The haves (the United States and Western society in general) are allegedly haves which have stolen the goods of the Third World and will not provide a decent living for the poor of the First World due to greed and callousness.

Both of those messages are messages of anger, and are completely opposite of the whole thrust of Christianity. Christ said, "'Thou shalt love the Lord thy God with all thy heart, and with all thy soul and with all thy mind.' This is the first commandment. And there is a second like it: 'Thou shalt love thy neighbor as thyself.' The whole of the Law and the Prophets depends on these two commandments."[28]

When Christ said these words He was quoting the Old Testament (Deuteronomy, chapter six, verse five and Leviticus, chapter 19, verse 18). Those verses state, in effect, that the old law and the new which Christ brought for humanity were both based on the same thing: love from which all other action should stem. Christ did not say the poor are favored, or that resentment and anger toward the wealthy and powerful is justified.

It is possible to argue many things based on Biblical passages. But any argument that ignores the basic thrust of the Christian doctrine of love and forgiveness, or uses individual passages which are taken out of context to validate an attitude which is anti-Christian, is a false argument.

There are no such things as institutions apart from the people who compose them. If we accept that the bureaucracy and leadership of the church display angry attitudes, we must accept that those people are angry.

Hollander strengthened this argument when, citing one explanation of intellectual criticism of Western society, he said that the critics project their individual problems on society, seeking scapegoats for personal grievances, and "blur the boundaries between the personal and social spheres and problems."[29] They vent their discontents and anger on society instead of facing the internal problem. That tendency is strengthened, Hollander suggested, by our society's urge to "politicize" what used to be considered personal problems. Two examples of this, he said, are sexism and homosexuality.[30]

CHILDHOOD ANGER AS POLITICAL INFLUENCE

Human anger flows from many sources, but the most prevalent is childhood experience. The anger that begins in childhood is often unconsciously taken into adult life and shapes all attitudes, including those which are political. People who seem to have firm intellectual attitudes toward political questions are often motivated by unresolved childhood conflicts.

Good examples of this on the American scene are black leaders who give vent to their hatred of America based on alleged political beliefs but are actually acting on (justified at the time) childhood feelings of rejection and persecution. When a black leader goes to Cuba and throws his arms around Fidel Castro, that leader is probably not saying he really approves of Castro or totalitarianism. He is saying that the enemy of his enemy is his friend. Or perhaps he is simply sending a message home: I will not forget . . . or forgive.

It makes little difference that the United States has changed drastically since that leader was a child and that no one in this country is proud of the historic repression of blacks. The emotional life of that leader has never recovered from his initial experiences, and it has shaped all of his subsequent attitudes.

A perfect example of anger expressed in the political arena is that of Commandante Tomás Borgé, Nicaragua's minister of the interior and the head of its secret police. Borgé's rebellion against Somoza and his subsequent Marxism-Leninism can be directly traced to his anger against his mother. He has described his mother as a "social climber," who tried to force him into becoming a priest in order to boost her standing in the community. She tried, he said, to control him to an unhealthy degree.[31]

Borgé said his mother did not allow him to indulge in activities in which other boys were allowed to participate, things as minor as going to the river to swim or going to the movies. "When I was 13, I rebelled completely," he told one reporter. "From then on, I went against my mother's will."[32] About the same time he became involved with anti-Somoza activities, which led to imprisonment at least twice. By the time he was sixteen he was "totally committed."

In an interview Borgé jointly gave with other Sandinistas, Borgé said, "It almost doesn't matter that I grew up in the kind of family where my mother once told me, when I was just beginning to have my political awakening, 'The day you become a Communist, I will fall over dead.'" Borgé said, "And I told her . . . well, I better not tell you what . . ."[33]

"FATHER CARDENAL: Go ahead—what did you tell her, Tomás?

"BORGÉ: I told her that I would not be blackmailed by her gentleness and her naiveté and that I was a Communist. Needless to say, she did not fall over dead."[34]

Nicaraguan President Daniel Ortega is another such example. His father was the product of a liaison between his rich father and the housemaid. The illegitimate birth caused such a scandal in the family that the maid was forced to leave the household without her son. Daniel Sr. grew up an "outcast" who felt "rejected, discriminated against." Daniel Sr. eventually left his rich father's house to make his own life and during the same period began supporting Augusto Cesar Sandino—the Nicaraguan hero and rebel who fought to expel American Marines from Nicaragua. Ortega Sr. was subsequently jailed and tortured by Anastasio Somoza Garcia, the first Somoza in power.[35]

By the time Daniel Jr. was born, the family was in financial straits, Daniel Sr. having lost a job at the formerly U.S.-owned La Esmeralda gold mine. The family later became prosperous, but Ortega, encouraged by his father and brothers, joined the leftist movement. In the late 1960s Ortega went on to bank robbery and assassination.[36] There were real and compelling reasons to rebel against Somoza. However, in this particular case, it is easy to trace the rebellion back to a family grievance which was passed on from father to son.

Ortega did not use the product of his anger, the success of the revolution, wisely. He now suppresses the same people he helped liberate. His grudge against the rich was also made evident in 1979, after the revolution was triumphant. A few days after Somoza was overthrown, Ortega appropriated the house of fellow Somoza opponent Jaime Morales (estimated cost, $300,000), as well as all its contents. When Morales's wife went to her former house to discuss the situation, Ortega's mistress answered the door wearing one of the Morales family's bathrobes.[37]

As Arthur Koestler put it: "A faith is not required; it grows like a tree. Its crown points to the sky; its roots grow downward into the past and are nourished by the dark sap of the ancestral humus. . . . The psychiatrist is apt to forget that smooth adjustment to a deformed society creates deformed individuals. The reformer is equally apt to forget that hated, even of the objectively hateful, does not produce that charity and justice on which a utopian society must be based."[38]

Koestler knew this personally as his affiliation with the Communist Party had roots which reached "back into childhood." Although his father failed at business, Koestler was still showered with gifts, which induced feelings of guilt. He developed a strong dislike for the rich because they were able to buy things without a guilty conscience.

"Thus I projected a personal predicament onto the structure of society at large."[39]

Although there are valid reasons for political rebellion, many do begin in personal anger. It then follows that many supporters of revolution are similarly motivated.

ZEALOUS IDEALISM

A much more innocent explanation lies within the American character. We as people have always been idealistic crusaders. Anyone who doubts this should meditate on the abolitionist movement, the Civil War, the prohibitionist movement, the civil rights movement, the anti-Vietnam War movement, the (active) antiapartheid movement.

All of these movements were based on the highest of ideals; but most of them were carried out by people who only examined one side of the question and did not have the patience to plot a strategy of gradual change. American zealots not only want change, they want it right now—even when immediate change brings more problems than it solves. The lone exception was the civil rights movement, which was an idea whose time was long overdue.

Yuji Aida, a professor at Kyota University in Japan, has explained how the Japanese view Americans. They are a "strange, inexplicable" people, he wrote, citing what he sees as "naive sanctimoniousness," the tendency to look at issues only in shades of black and white, a "tunnel vision" which is forced on others. "Once Americans get a bee in their bonnet, they are convinced they are absolutely right." Aida cited the drive for a Equal Rights Amendment, the movement for racial equality, amnesty for illegal aliens, and the fight against whaling as "hysterical."[40]

Aida's choice of movements to characterize the hysteria he perceives is debatable, but his view of the American character is insightful. He was just as insightful about the Japanese character. His countrymen are skeptical and opportunistic, he said, American's opposite. "We know all about ideals, but to us they are merely the face we show others. We have no intention of defending them to the end. And we do not become missionaries. We leave that to young hotheads, eccentrics and fanatics." Aida also added hypocrisy to his list of Japanese characteristics.

As Aida inadvertently pointed out, all nationalities are not similarly idealistic and prone to crusades. But Americans are, and we do frequently indulge ourselves. Many American Christians undoubtedly turn to radical politics for this reason. Clark Pinnock, one such idealist who became involved in the Sojourners movement, later explained his turn toward radicalism as having had a dream, "a utopian dream for a society of brotherhood and peace; a society with equality and justice for all. . . . We believed that corrupt capitalistic society had to be totally dismantled, and replaced by a more humane order based on love and simple living."[41]

Because America seemed to represent the world's violence, racism, and materialism, Pinnock said, America became "our nightmare." Pinnock said he did not realize at the time how much the revolt against American values was a revolt against his, and his political ally's, position in the advantaged class. Since the system was evil, they hated those who were successful. Since they were successful, they hated themselves. "Radicalism served to take away the guilt I felt for being born into a secure and comfortable middle class home and nation."[42]

Thereafter, socialism was "embraced," Pinnock said, and corporate America, Washington foreign policy, and industrialization were attacked. Marxist-Leninist societies were also praised, and all blame for the world's ills was placed on the United States.

The radical evangelicals accepted an Anabaptist theology to help them justify this stance, Pinnock said. It taught that America was "a fallen order" with which Christians could not compromise. One of its firmest beliefs was that violence was wrong at any time, and it emphasized the necessity for utopian communities. Pinnock said he did not believe, at the time, that his viewpoints were political, but theological.

Pinnock said he renounced radical politics after having noticed that there were things in democracies that are positive and worthy of support. "Gradually it dawned on me," Pinnock wrote, "that I had been misperceiving the world. . . . "[43]

It is probable that many people now involved in radical politics have also accepted an Anabaptist theology and misperceive the world. Many of Pinnock's former beliefs sound very much like the attitudes espoused by the current Religious Left, and many of them may be based on similar misperceptions.

HYPOCRISY AND SELF-INTEREST

It is possible, when searching for truth, to look too deeply into the human psyche. Sometimes the answer is on the surface, or is entwined with things we already know about human nature. For instance, many people hold untrue or illusionary beliefs about themselves because it is easier and more comfortable for them to do so than face the truth.

There are Christians who cheat on their business partners during the week and the Internal Revenue Service on April 15, but choose to believe themselves righteous because they piously attend church every

Sunday. On the same note, it was once fashionable for members of the political Left to work in Cuba's sugar cane fields at harvest—a gesture which undoubtedly made the two-week peasant feel self-sacrificing, revolutionary, and part of a greater whole.

The Rev. Isaac Rottenberg was on the staff of the National Council of Churches in the 1960s and 1970s. He has accused the National and World Council of Churches of working for their own self-interest and of repeatedly displaying "a spirit of partisanship and power politics that contradicts their claims and that eventually must lead to the charge that the ecumenical ship is sailing under false colors."[44]

Rottenberg said that during the years in which he served as chairman of the executive committee of the NCC's Office on Christian-Jewish Relations, "the political infighting between the various offices was fierce (as is the case today). But open personal confrontation for the purpose of honest dialogue was carefully avoided. Why? Because the interest in scoring political points by passing certain resolutions at Governing Board meetings was greater than the interest in speaking out of a common faith."[45]

Rottenberg said people at the NCC want "more than anything else" to be perceived as "prophetic, as people who question conventional wisdom as well as entrenched institutions." Rottenberg points out, however, that the prophetic spirit must be informed by the "Protestant principle," which implies self-criticism.[46]

Unfortunately, Rottenberg has observed a siege mentality in the ecumenical movement (of which the NCC is the primary component). He has predicted that if dissent continues being viewed as "bad faith and when criticism is automatically seen as a surrender to 'the Right,' the inevitable result will be a movement that is isolated from its own constituents, estranged from American society, insecure about its position and increasingly strident toward those who are perceived to be 'the enemies.'"[45]

It is valuable to remember that institutions are sometimes caught in traps of their own making. They take extreme positions from which it is difficult to retreat or simply identify those positions with the institution itself. Thus, any retreat to a more popular stance is identified with the death of the institution. Moreover, the more numerous the staff of any institution, the more difficult it is to gain a consensus for change. This may be the trap in which the National Council presently finds itself.

So, why does the Religious Left identify itself with totalitarians? Why does it seemingly work against its country's interests? There is no one answer. It is important to remember, however, that people are psychological beings before they are anything else. The source of human attitudes and beliefs is rarely based totally in the intellect. If a person believes absurd things it is generally not because that person has been tricked, or is stupid, but because that person wants to believe. There is a reward for believing the absurd thing that is not available when facing the truth.

Unfortunately, it is also rare for someone who has worked for mistaken causes and believed false concepts to recant. Such courage is unusual.

Therefore, argument and presentation of facts will not change a majority of the Religious Left. The only way in which its influence on the church can be lessened is to stop its funding or remove its leadership from positions within the denominations.

ELEVEN

Is Reform Possible?

Is reform possible?

Many contend that the Religious Left dominates the mainline church to such an extent that change is unlikely. As of 1986 this has proven to be the case. Denominational leadership has been so resistant to change, even when under pressure, that many church members have either left their denomination in despair or pretended that the problem does not exist. The Religious Left has controlled the church by default.

Still, change is possible if one of two things happen. There must either be spiritual renewal within the church, or church membership must force change by exerting financial pressure on its leadership and bureaucracies.

Much of the problem thus far has been with the character of mainline church leadership. A large percentage of them are moderates. They are decent people who genuinely love the church and believe in traditional Christian teaching. They were chosen for their position because they are conscientious. However, they are usually consensus personalities who cling to safety. They tend to jump on the most popular bandwagon regardless of its worth. This pervasive timidity has been disastrous because it has made them vulnerable to manipulation. At the same time, though most of them believe in traditional Christian teaching, they have lost the fervency which would have strengthened their resistance to the politically radical.

In many ways the radicals have demonstrated more integrity than the moderates. Most radicals are willing to risk their reputation for what they believe. They are not afraid to be controversial and to take unpopular positions. What they believe, however misguided, they believe fervently. As a result, they have influence far above what their numbers would justify.

It would seem that conservatives, which represent a majority of members in most mainline denominations, could have stymied a Religious Left with which they totally disagree. Their fervency is unquestionable. But the conservatives have held only marginal positions of influence during the last fifty years. They have been, in large part, unsophisticated and less educated than their liberal rivals. This cost them respect and made their presence a frequent embarrassment to the liberal-moderate coalition which controls the mainline church hierarchy.

Conservatives also hurt themselves because many insisted on a faith which is merely a validation of American culture or a conservative political party. Many of them have insisted on a self-centered, ritualized Christianity which rejects the value of other cultures. This attitude, in turn, produced insularity and an unconcern for the world at large.

This situation is changing. The conservative movement is now producing scholars who have a broader theological outlook, a more compassionate attitude, and who are personally more sophisticated.

Therefore, the hope of the church may be with a new coalition of conservatives who certainly have the desire to produce change and moderates who have the power to do so. This can only come about, however, if leadership rediscovers the urgency of its Christian mission or is forced to see the conservative point of view.

As difficult and slow as the process may seem, both renewal and pressure on moderate church leadership can only begin with one source—the individual church member. Reform will not take place if it does not begin in local congregations. The church needs to be reformed from the bottom up. When local members become concerned enough to realign their spiritual lives, and caring enough to seek the same for their church, real change will take place. The local church is the place where everything begins. Only when members believe so heartily in the traditional message that they will allow no other, will their churches take courage. Only then will conferences, synods, assemblies, and dioceses be changed. Only then will leadership be reformed.

As for pressure, there is no one leader who will suddenly appear and solve the problem. The reform movement now in place, as represented by various organizations cited in Chapter One, constitutes a minority of mainline membership. It cannot force reform because it does not have the numbers to do so. It must have the active support of Christian membership who share its views and of those who are willing to exert themselves for what they believe. Pressure, like renewal, begins with the individual. When individuals care enough to become actively involved in denominational reform, when they care enough to begin that reform on the local church level—even when it costs them friends, time, trouble, and conflict—then there will be change.

A national financial boycott may be necessary to get the attention of church leadership. Positive bureaucratic change probably will not begin until the carte blanche funding is stopped. Perhaps local churches should consider putting funds (missions, church and society, etc.) in escrow until they receive satisfaction that their grievances have been heard and reform is underway.

If there is continued financial backing for controversial programs, laity has no excuse for complaint. Traditionally, when complaints are made about questionable denominational programs the response has been that people must not be unhappy because they continue their financial support. Leadership does not reveal that pastors may be facing professional difficulties if their congregations do not support all program funding. Bishops do not appreciate pastors who oppose the status quo. Nonetheless, pastors who allow themselves to be pressured to support questionable programs, and congregations who care more for their comfort than for their principles, are responsible for the results.

As harsh as a boycott may appear, there is a precedent. Denominational bureaucracies have already set the example. They have recently called for a grape boycott, and there have been boycotts against Campbell's Soup and Nestlē. If it is ethical for liberals to boycott, then it must also be ethical for moderates and conservatives. A national committee of concerned lay persons and pastors from each denomination should be formed to organize the boycott, should it be necessary, and to educate the membership concerning the abuse in denominational programs.

There has been much said in this book about what the Christian church should not have done and what it should not believe. This said, there is room to consider what the church and its leadership should be about.

- The church and church leadership should be humble. Experience in denominational leadership or bureaucratic decision-making does not create an expertise in the military, political, or economic arenas. The church should speak out concerning principles and recognize that sincere, intelligent Christians may disagree as to how the principles should be applied.

- A prophetic church will always speak for freedom and human rights. The authentic Christian attacks all that degrades humanity. This not only includes poverty, it also includes oppression—oppression from the Left, as well as oppression from the Right.

- The leadership of the church, its clergy, and its theologians must witness to the transcendence of the church. They must refute the view that the church is a "human institution to be understood in sociological terms and employed for sociological purposes."[1] Christian leadership and all Christians, if they wish to remain a part of the church of God, must proclaim that the church is "divinely constituted and divinely guided on its pilgrimage toward a kingdom that is not of our manufacture."[2] When the transcendence is once again recognized, the church will be freed from earthly ideologies to which it is now held captive.

- The Christian church should do everything in its power to bring about genuine reconciliation between people, classes, and nations. This mission for reconciliation is not the same as a mission for pacifism or appeasement. It should be witness to the possibility of brotherhood through a God whose "peace passes all understanding."

- More than anything else, before any other mission, before any other duty, the Christian church must proclaim to a suffering world that "neither death, nor life, nor angels, nor principalities, nor things present, nor things to come, nor powers, nor height, nor depth, nor anything else in all creation, will be able to separate us from the love of God in Christ Jesus our Lord."[3]

The cost will be high for those who insist on these guidelines and these spiritual truths and no other. Pastors must be willing to sacrifice promising careers, and lay members must be willing to live in the midst of controversy. Bishops must be willing to be criticized by their peers and be charged with disloyalty. Reform will not come easily, but it will come if enough Christians are willing to sacrifice for the sake of truth and integrity.

If they are not willing to do so, then the church has truly been betrayed.

Radical Organizations

This section is an attempt to inform the reader where large amounts of church tithes are distributed and to give an adequate description of organizations receiving those funds. Most major denominations do not provide a financial disclosure detailing their expenditures, so the information has had to be obtained back to front—in other words, to find out how the organizations are funded instead of decoding church budgets. Because most of the organizations in question do not reveal their funding sources and budgets, the funding information presented here tends to jump years. It may have been possible to discover funding for an organization for 1981, but not 1982, or to reveal funding for 1982 and 1984, but not for 1983. There are many instances in which funding for only one year was confirmed or denominational giving was confirmed, but it was impossible to confirm the amount.

Any information about grants provided by the National Council of Churches has been particularly hard to obtain, as they refuse to open their books to investigating organizations. In contrast, the United Methodist Church now provides a detailed financial disclosure report every year. This accounts for our detail on United Methodist funding.

This is by no means a complete list of unsuitable organizations funded by the church, but only some of the more blatant examples. If all were listed, they would fill the whole book, not just one appendix.

One further note: except for instances involving personal quotations, particularly serious charges, or large bodies of material from one source, this appendix is not footnoted. Sources of information have been too numerous to list. Most quotations drawn from organizational material are not footnoted, although there has been an effort to identify the publication. Addresses of each organization have been provided, when possible.

- IMPACT is a Washington lobbying organization composed of church and quasichurch groups who lobby exclusively for left of center causes. IMPACT also has twenty-one state offices scattered around the country and about fifteen thousand members nationwide. The organization is sponsored by agencies of sixteen mainline denominations—including those of the American Lutheran Church, the Lutheran Church in America, the Roman Catholic Church, the United Church of Christ, the Presbyterian Church, U.S.A., the United Methodists, the American Baptist Church, U.S.A., the Reformed Church, and the Episcopal Church—who finance the organization through grants. And the price is not small.

The United Methodist Board of Global Ministries paid almost $60,000 to be an IMPACT member between 1981 and 1983 and gave another $17,158 to IMPACT grass-roots organizations. The United Methodists gave a total (including local chapters) of $14,500 in 1984. Each sponsoring agent has a place on the board of directors. Some of the causes IMPACT has lobbied for are the ratification of the SALT II treaty, defeat of the MX missile program and the Strategic Defense Initiative, cutoff of funds to the Nicaraguan contras, and budget increases for federal poverty programs.

IMPACT has much influence, chiefly because it mobilizes its grass-roots membership to fiercely lobby on issues which it thinks important. IMPACT makes sure all fifteen thousand members, and the sponsoring agents, know when issues will come up before Congress and who to lobby in order to influence the vote. The results of these tactics are obvious. Sen. Lawton Chiles (D-Florida) floated a proposal to the Senate budget committee, in 1983, to cut federal food stamps. Chiles dropped the proposal after his office was flooded by calls from angry Florida constituents. Those constituents had been alerted by IMPACT.[1]

The *Religious News Service* quoted Florida church activist Karen Woodall on the matter. "We have a telephone tree, and so we contacted our key contacts around the state and they called their contacts, saying it was urgent that they call Senator Chiles' office. Then we called other religious groups that also have telephone trees, and set up an appointment in Washington to reinforce those calls." An aide to Chiles told the *News Service* that the activists had "really turned on the heat."[2]

There is nothing wrong with participatory democracy, which requires lobbying, but it is a different matter if churches are spending money on a lobbying organization which does not reflect the views of a majority of its members.

IMPACT's address is 110 Maryland Avenue, N.E., Washington, D.C. 20002.

- *NACLA*, the North American Congress on Latin America, advocates Cuban-type socialism and is blatantly anti-American. Its ideological draft statement admits NACLA sought the support of those "who not only favor revolutionary change in Latin America but also take a revolutionary position toward their own society. . . ." The organization supports El Salvador's Marxist guerrillas and Nicaragua's Sandinista government, a fact the organization admits.

Many of the North American Congress staff members have written books which are used by university Latin America Studies Departments. This is unfortunate because the Congress is the conveyor of much false information. In a 1982 Congress publication, *Target Nicaragua*, the writers claimed that anti-Sandinista forces were responsible for the deaths of Miskito Indian leaders. Further investigation, however, reveals that the Sandinista government, not the contras, have been responsible for the deaths of thousands of Indians, the theft of their lands, torture, and thirteen "relocation" camps where nine thousand to fifteen thousand Indians are presently being kept against their will.

In interviews with past and present Congress members for Helen Shapiro's "NACLA Reminiscences: An Oral History," from *NACLA Report on the Americas*, one Congress activist said he believed NACLA was conceived with two purposes. "One was Latin America specifically, but the other more general one was the political use of information . . . consequently, along with demystifying research, NACLA also had a contrary emphasis of developing expertise on the left."

NACLA founders and employees rarely differ from the organization's attitudes. Founder John Gerassi served as director of the U.S. branch of the Bertrand Russell International War Crimes Tribunal. The Tribunal accused the U.S. of Vietnamese genocide. He has also been a regular contributor to the *National Guardian*, the Communist weekly, and wrote a book titled *Ven Ceremos, the Speeches and Writings of Che Guevara*.

The Presbyterian Hunger Program gave NACLA $10,500 in 1980 for a Agribusiness Project of the North American Congress on Latin America. It then promptly produced a publication titled *Agribusiness in the Americas*, which stated that "It is only in societies organized along socialist lines—where production and distribution is organized by the principle of social equality rather than private profit—that the possibility of ending hunger exists. China is a dramatic example."

The Congress was credited by Philip Agee—a former CIA agent who has made a career out of revealing names of active intelligence officers—with having helped him undermine the CIA. Agee is now suspected of being an agent of the KGB and is persona non grata in this country. CIA station chief Richard Welch was murdered in Athens after Agee published his name in *Counter-Spy*. The Congress was on the original steering committee for the Committee in Solidarity with the People of El Salvador (CISPES), the American branch of the El

Salvadoran Marxist guerrillas. (See listing later in this Appendix.) NACLA's address is 151 W. 19th Street, New York, N.Y. 10011.

MONEY - In fiscal year 1983 the Lutheran Church U.S.A. gave NACLA $8,000, the National Council of Churches gave $8,000, the Maryknoll Fathers and Brothers gave $7,000, and the Presbyterians gave $5,000. From 1976 through 1981 the Congress was given grants totaling $26,500 by the Presbyterian hunger money. Ironically, according to its own financial statements, NACLA participates in the capitalism it so much despises. It owns shares in several corporations. In 1984 the Methodists contributed $1,000 more to North American Congress coffers.

● *The Washington Office on Latin America*, or WOLA, is pro-leftist and acts as a liaison between radical groups in Central America and church groups, congressmen, labor unions, and the media, often bringing Latins to testify before Congressional committees. The organization has grown in influence and specializes in influencing Congress with reports, publicity, and seminars.

Former civil rights activist Bruce Cameron, formerly one of the most effective lobbyists on Capitol Hill for leftist human rights organizations, said, at one time, that WOLA was "nothing but a shill for the Sandinistas."[3] Cameron, who now supports the anti-Sandinista rebels, has recanted his statement but maintains that some WOLA employees and other human rights organizations and activists are biased on behalf of Marxist-Leninist regimes. "There's a litmus test they have established for themselves," Cameron says of WOLA and of the human rights "community" in general. "They can't move toward the center, but they can move all the way to the left." The "community" is also intolerant of dissenters. When Cameron began to air his new views, he lost his position at the Foreign Policy Education Fund and the Human Rights Political Action Committee.[4]

The credibility of Cameron's statements is verified when WOLA's actions are examined. WOLA and the Institute for Policy Studies (to be discussed later in this Appendix) can be credited for bringing, before the 1979 overthrow of Somoza, Nicaraguan government official and erstwhile priest Ernesto Cardenal to the U.S. to speak on behalf of the Sandinista movement. He was ostensibly attending an Institute for Policy Studies Latin American Round Table program, designed to aid in the formulation of alternative U.S. policy toward Latin America.

In 1985 WOLA, in conjunction with Representative Samuel Gejdenson and attorneys for Reichler and Applebaum, the Nicaraguan government's official registered agent in the United States, released a report on alleged contra atrocities. The report was assembled by attorney Reed Brody and law student Jim Bourdeloin, who spent four months in Nicaragua. The National Forum Foundation charged in May 1985, however, that the report was compiled with the full cooperation of the Sandinistas, and the attorneys' transportation through the countryside, as well as their housing and office space were all provided by the Nicaraguan government.[15]

The report was submitted to the House Foreign Affairs Subcommittee on Western Hemisphere Affairs and the aforementioned groups. A second fact-finding group was then assembled for another trip. It included, among others, WOLA representatives, Rep. Gejdenson, the attorneys, the former chief council to the Senate Foreign Relations Committee under the chairmanship of Frank Church, interpreter Valerie Miller, a two-year resident of postrevolutionary Nicaragua and author of a book on the infamous literacy campaign, and human rights lawyer-activist Donald Fox.[6]

Fox later admitted that his Nicaraguan-born wife, now a U.S. citizen, went to Managua with the group in order to visit her family—at WOLA's expense. Mrs. Fox's brother is a high-ranking official in the Nicaraguan Foreign Ministry in Rome.[7]

The group naturally uncovered no discrepancies in the original report, and only bothered to corroborate ten of the almost one hundred and fifty affidavits. When the group returned to Washington they called, with much publicity, for a congressional investigation into the alleged contra atrocities. Nobody mentioned the help they received from the Sandinista government.[8]

Brody later admitted getting help in living and working arrangements from the Sandinistas, but denied Sandinista interference as he searched for witnesses. The Reagan Administration later revealed, however, that four incidents which he claimed had been carried out by the contras had, in fact, happened before the contras were an organized force; six atrocities were perpetrated by a contra, but one who had acted on his own and later been executed by his own people. A religious couple that Brody claimed had been murdered by the contras were actually murdered by Nicaraguan secret police.[9]

Two former WOLA employees must certainly have been sympathetic to the Sandinistas. Kay Stubbs and Sophia Clark are now employed by the Nicaraguan Foreign Ministry.

WOLA boasts of having, on its board of directors, among others, nuns and an official of the U.S. Catholic Conference. Thomas Quigley, the official, is also heavily involved with the Inter-Religious Task Force on El Salvador and Central America. WOLA itself was on the original steering committee for the Committee in Solidarity with the People of El Salvador (CISPES), the following organization.

WOLA's address is 110 Maryland Avenue, N.E., Washington, D.C. 20002.

MONEY - Executive director Joe Eldridge, an ordained United Methodist minister, has had salary paid by the United Methodist Board of Global Ministries and $99,000 of the $420,000 WOLA budget comes, or has come in the past, from the United Methodists, American Baptist Churches, U.S.A., The American Lutheran Church, The Episcopal Church, The Mennonite Central Committee, The National and World Council of Churches ($19,100 in 1981 from the National Council and $5,860 from the World Council), the Presbyterian Church, and seventeen different Catholic orders and organizations. In 1981 it received $41,500 from the Maryknoll Fathers alone. In 1984 the United Methodists contributed $1,850. In 1980 WOLA received $35,000 from the Maryknoll Fathers, $10,250 from the Capuchin Missions, and $7,500 from the World Council of Churches.

- CISPES, or the *Committee in Solidarity with the People of El Salvador*, is a Communist-created organization formed to gather support for El Salvador's Marxist-Leninist guerrillas. It has an interesting history because it is the only organization known to have open ties to Marxists-Leninists. The organization was created in February 1980 by Farid Handal, brother of Shafik, El Salvador's Communist Party chief and a sometime member of the guerrilla organization which is seeking to overthrow the government. The Handals are Palestinians who have ties to the Palestinian Liberation Organization, which, in turn, supplies the Salvadoran guerrillas with arms.[10]

Handal created CISPES as a result of Soviet resolve to create foreign support for the insurgents in El Salvador. The details of his February trip to the United States were found among papers captured at a guerrilla safe house in El Salvador, and the House Permanent Select Committee on Intelligence subsequently published excerpts.[11]

According to the papers, Handal first consulted with the Cuban Mission to the United Nations who offered to help Handal and advised him to consult with "progressive" Congressmen, among them Ron Dellums of California, to make his trip appear more "natural and in that way protect my visa." Handal reported that Dellums is "Black, but very progressive." Dellums has long been associated with radical organizations. The United States Information Agency released documents captured in Grenada after the invasion that reveal Dellums had a close tie with the Marxist-Leninist Bishop government. Two of Dellums's staff traveled to Cuba shortly after the invasion and allegedly broadcast anti-American statements over Radio Havana.[12]

Handal wrote in his report that Dellums's "political counselor made known that my visit could not have arrived at a better moment. They were interested in better understanding the situation in El Salvador because they were ready to do battle against the hawks who have today strengthened their position and influence in the Senate and Congress of the U.S.A. . . . Monday morning the offices of Congressman Dellums were turned into our offices. . . . Everything was down there." Handal also officially met with the Congressional Black Caucus.[13]

He then met with members of the Directorate of the American Communist Party and with the person "responsible for the U.S. Peace Council." The "peace council" is, according to American intelligence, a Soviet front organization.[14]

That person was Sandy Pollack, and she proposed a national conference under the auspices of the U.S. Peace Council, the National Council of Churches, Amnesty International, the Washington Office on Latin America, and unions. "The objective of the conference is to establish a support mechanism for the solidarity committees and to help create solidarity committees in those states where they do not exist yet." After having met with representatives of the National Council of Churches, Handal wrote that "they were eager to collaborate."[15]

When the Reagan Administration issued a White Paper on El Salvador in 1981, which included a report on Handal's trip to the United States, Philip Agee, the CIA defector, organized a news conference; he then denounced the documents, claiming they were forged by American intelligence. The fact that Agee claimed the documents are forgeries is almost proof in itself that they are genuine.[16]

CISPES has more than lived up to Handal's expectations, having created a strong pro-Marxist (and anti-American) network that constantly lobbies Congress. There are over one hundred and twenty affiliate CISPES committees around the country.

In keeping with methods used by its founder, in 1980 CISPES circulated a forgery labeled "Dissent Paper on El Salvador and Central America." It was supposedly a State Department document from officials who disagreed with department policies about Central America. The authors supposedly warned that support for the El Salvadoran government would end with disaster and America would eventually be forced to use military might. The forgery was later printed (and presented as authentic) in the newsletter for the Religious Task Force on El Salvador, the Institute on Policy Studies and mentioned in columns by Anthony Lewis of *The New York Times* and Flora Lewis of the same publication. Flora Lewis later apologized to her readers and said she had been fooled about the document.[17]

CISPES associates, at least, seem willing to risk everything for what they believe. Carroll Ishee, formally with the African Liberation Support Committee of Vancouver, Seattle and San Francisco, was killed in the summer of 1984 while fighting with the Salvadoran guerrillas. His wife is Levaun Ishee, a Southeast regional coordinator for CISPES.[18]

CISPES has had considerable success recruiting help for the guerrillas among influential Americans. In 1983, three hundred of New York's affluent attended a $100 per plate benefit dinner for, supposedly, medical aid for the "liberated" areas of El Salvador. The $30,000 would be used in projects supervised by the guerrillas. The dinner was organized by CISPES and aided by a committee of entertainers and other celebrities headed by television actor Ed Asner. Speakers included Harry Belafonte, guerrilla member Mario Valasquez, and former Congresswoman Bella Abzug.

CISPES has also cosponsored events with the National Council of Churches, Jesse Jackson's Operation PUSH, and numerous religious organizations. Bruce McColm of Freedom House, a conservative think-tank and information broker, has charged that the United States Peace Council (the Soviet front organization) has also helped finance CISPES.

CISPES is located at 930 F Street, Washington, D.C. Its mailing address is Box 50139, Washington, D.C.

MONEY - CISPES was granted over $2,000 by the United Methodists between 1981 and 1983 and $500 in 1984. The United Methodist financial disclosure statement described CISPES as a "broad coalition organ of churches and individuals opposed to intervention in El Salvador. Its purpose is to educate the U.S. public regarding the reality of the situation in El Salvador." Many major denominations have also contributed.

- EPICA, *The Ecumenical Program for Inter-American Communication and Action*, was given funds by the United Methodist Board of Global Ministries, in 1982, to produce a booklet that was to be titled *A Population Primer on Grenada*. The title was later altered to *Grenada: The Peaceful Revolution*. In one chapter called "The Election Question" the text reads, "General elections would threaten the revolutionary process by inviting outside interference through financial contributions or covert manipulations." EPICA was, naturally, one of the loudest voices protesting the U.S. invasion in 1983.

The National Council of Churches has contended that EPICA's anti-American publications provide "a forum for Christians in other countries to speak to Christians here." After a study of EPICA publications, however, the Institute on Religion and Democracy concluded that almost everything in them was written by United States residents. EPICA is frankly pro-Sandinista and pro-Cuban.

Interestingly enough, EPICA founder Phillip Wheaton has contributed to *Counter-Spy*. Wheaton met with Farid Handal when Handal visited the United States when first organizing CISPES, a fact that he later admitted. EPICA was on the original CISPES steering committee.

EPICA is located at 1470 Irving St., NW, Washington, D.C. 20010.

MONEY - EPICA was given, in 1981, $19,260 by the National Council of Churches, $2,500 by the World Division of the United Methodist Board of Global Ministries.

- *The Center for Constitutional Rights* was founded in 1966 by three leaders of the National Lawyer's Guild, William Kunstler, Morton Stavis, Arthur Kinoy. Also taking a hand were the late Ben Smith, a registered agent of the Cuban government, and Peter Weiss. Weiss served from 1962-1972 as president of the American Committee on Africa, the principal U.S. support group for the African Marxists-Leninists. The National Lawyer's Guild is the largest U.S. affiliate of the International Association of Democratic Lawyers, the Soviet-controlled front for lawyers. The Association was organized with the assistance of the Soviet government in 1936 as a front operated by the Communist Party, U.S.A. The U.S. government also recognizes the Guild as a Soviet front organization.

The 1974-1975 annual report describes the Center's mission as a struggle against "illusory democracy," and Kunstler has described the Center's work as "endeavoring to bring down the system through the system."[19]

Favorite tactics include attempts to provide legal defense to accused terrorists—everyone from members of the Baadar-Meinhoff gang to the Marxist-Leninist Puerto Rican Socialist Party. The defense in such cases is used not only to defend the accused, but to attack the United States. When the Center defended Puerto Rican Socialist Party member Delfin Ramos, who was charged with possession of stolen explosives, the Center defense team stated that they were "representing Ramos in such a way as to not only expose the government's political motivations for the prosecution, but to reveal the oppressive nature of the colonial relationship. . . ." This organization has instituted legal suits designed to help the Marxist-Leninist guerrillas of El Salvador and the Cuban government and has published material touting the Sandinistas of Nicaragua. One of the articles published in the Center's newsletter, *Fight The Right*, in May 1981, was titled "Reagan's Reign of Terror."

The Center's address is 853 Broadway, New York, New York, 10003.

MONEY - The United Methodist Board of Global Ministries padded the Center's $170,000-plus (as of 1981) budget with $5,500. In 1982 they reduced funding to $3,445, but in 1983 increased funding to $14,302. The amount for 1984 went up to $23,000. It should not surprise anyone that the board is helping finance the Center because Global Ministries official Peggy Billings has been on the Center's board of trustees.

- *Clergy and Laity Concerned* was very active in the nuclear freeze campaign and works against every U.S. weapons system ever devised. In an undated fund and membership raising letter, Clergy directors accused the U.S. of "playing politics with food—not only tolerating but encouraging repressive governments that starve their poor . . . our government gets involved because we are assured cheap labor, access to national resources in these countries, and unopposed exports of agricultural products to the United States."

The statement went on to imply that the United States is responsible for the infant death rate in the Dominican Republic. Clergy's attitude is not surprising if you know that in its 1970 description of themselves, Clergy said it was involved in a struggle "against American imperialism in every corner of the world." Several of CLC's leading members, however, signed an ad attacking Joan Baez because she dared to criticize Vietnam for its human rights record after the fall of South Vietnam.

The description of Clergy in the United Methodist Board of Global Ministries' grant book says, "It establishes nationwide campaigns which prove to be powerful tools in changing government policies. It analyzes and works to change the misuse of American corporate government and military power."

The United Methodist Board of Global Ministries apparently thinks so well of Clergy that it encourages Clergy to teach Sunday school. In 1982 the Board gave Clergy $2,000 to provide children's programs for annual interchurch seminars held every Sunday for a month. "Training sharing with religious educators in the Eugene (Oregon) area; cooperation with vacation church schools on peace and justice themes; and workshops for church school staffs from individual congregations."

A Clergy document titled "History of Clergy and Laymen Concerned about Vietnam" (the original name) stated, "From its inception, Clergy has been deeply indebted to the National Council of Churches for its cooperation and assistance. Clergy has had offices in National Council of Churches facilities, has used NCC printing and addressing equipment and services, and has utilized the non-profit organization tax exemption of the NCC. In addition, the NCC has been extremely understanding about money due them from Clergy during times of financial difficulty." The paean and the help is not difficult to understand if you know that the NCC originally founded Clergy.

The organization's address is 198 Broadway, New York, New York, 10038.

MONEY - Between 1981 and 1983 the United Methodist Board of Global Ministries granted the American branch of Clergy $40,800 (Clergy has a half-million dollar budget) and gave a further $8,610, in 1983, to the Philippines branch of the Clergy and many thousands more to Clergy state offices. Clergy was also given $11,000 by the Presbyterian Hunger Program. In 1984 the United Methodist Church contributed $30,500 for one year alone.

- *A Coalition for a New Foreign and Military Policy* has fifty-five members, a majority of which are churches or quasi-church groups. Not all, however. A Coalition Disarmament Working Group has had, as members, the Institute for Policy Studies Militarism and Disarmament Project, a far-left think-tank with questionable connections (see elsewhere in this Appendix); the U.S. Peace Council, which is, as previously stated, according to American intelligence, a Soviet front; the National Center to Slash Military Spending, run by Pauline Rosen, a veteran Communist Party activist; the National Lawyer's Guild, another Soviet front according to U.S. intelligence; Women's Strike for Peace, a Soviet front; and two unions expelled from the AFL-CIO as Communist Party fronts, the United Electrical Workers and the West Coast International Longshoremen and Warehouseman's Union of Harry Bridges.

The Coalition is much like Clergy and Laity Concerned. They deplore all American involvement in Central America and their newsletter boasted, in 1984, that "we are very close to shutting down the U.S. covert operations against Nicaragua . . . together we can stop this dirty, secret war and make a major change in U.S. foreign policy. . . ." The newsletter went on to ask the reader to contact one of nine "swing votes" in the Senate. Such tactics are very successful because legislators are unable to tell that the grass-roots support which has been mobilized is part of a radical organization. The Coalition has also campaigned against almost every defense program ever funded by Congress.

In the Coalition's "Disarmament Guide" the writers state, ". . . the next time you hear exaggerated stories about Soviet intentions and 'worse case' scenarios, think how frightening the world must look to a Soviet military planner—faced with an economically and technologically superior adversary (the U.S.) which perpetually pushes for an advantage in the arms race, which has intervened militarily or through its intelligence agencies in Indochina, the Dominican Republic, Cuba and Iran, to name but a few."

The organization's address is 720 G Street, Washington, D.C. 20003.

MONEY - The Coalition was given over $28,000 between 1981 and 1983 from various agencies of the United Methodist Board of Global Ministries and $8,100 for 1984.

- *The Religious Task Force on Central America* is a relentlessly pro-Sandinista, pro-El Salvadoran guerrilla organization whose steering committee is composed almost entirely of Catholic clergy and officials, including Tom Quigley, an official of the U.S. Catholic Conference (see Chapter Eight).

The organization, which receives church funds, attacks the Nicaraguan bishops for their anti-Sandinista attitudes. A typical paragraph from their literature is as follows, "The Nicaraguan Bishops' Pastoral Letter on Reconciliation, which was read in most parishes on Easter Sunday and included a call to dialogue with those who have taken up arms against the government, has provoked a wave of protest here. . . . Many were angered by the fact that the bishops, when they address the theme of reconciliation, fail to mention that the suffering and violent death of so many Nicaraguans is a direct consequence of U.S. support for the counter-revolutionary movement. . . ."

According to sources in Nicaragua, the only protests that were heard over the Bishops' 1984 Easter Sunday letter were those of the Sandinista government. The Task Force was on the original CISPES steering committee.

The Task Force address is 1747 Connecticut Avenue, N.W., Washington, D.C. 20009.

- *The Inter-Religious Task Force on El Salvador and Central America*, founded by the National Council of Churches, wrote a background study on El Salvador which states that the Democratic Revolutionary Front, the Marxists-Leninists, are considered "the legitimate representative" by a majority of the people of El Salvador. This statement is not true. The guerrillas have very little support from Salvadorans. The Task Force was an original member of the CISPES steering committee.

The organization's address is 475 Riverside Drive, Room 622, New York, New York, 10115.

MONEY - The Task Force was funded in 1981 by the United Methodist Board of Global Ministries for $4,950. The agency gave them $500 in 1982, $3,000 in 1983, and $7,150 in 1984. In 1983 the National Council gave the Task Force a $1,000-grant to compile and mail information for "Central America Week" which churches were urged to observe in March 1983.

- *Theology in the Americas*, or TIA, had a conference in Detroit in 1980 which dealt with exploring a "creative socialist alternative" in America. However, TIA's main thrust is liberation theology. The United Methodist Board of Global Ministries' description of TIA, in its 1983 list of grants, says, "TIA continues to challenge the theological mainstream by basing theological reflection within the struggles of the poor and oppressed." To prove its appreciation the board gave TIA $67,115 from 1981-1983 and $13,200 in 1984. TIA was given $1,400 by the Latin American Division of the National Council of Churches in 1981.

TIA's address is room 1244-AA, 475 Riverside Drive, New York, New York 10115.

- *The Indochina Consortium of the World Council of Churches* spent over $1 million dollars in 1979 and 1980, including approximately $100,000 from the Presbyterian Hunger Program, to support the "long term plan of setting up a new economic zone in Lam Dong." Church World Service, part of the National Council, sent $400,000 to this project, $10,000 of which was contributed by the Disciples of Christ. The new economic zones are forced resettlement camps which often offer nothing but starvation to the people settled there. The Vietnamese consider the new economic zones a death sentence, and hundreds of thousands became "boat people" and died on the high seas trying to avoid them (and other horrors).

The funding of these "new economic zones" are the equivalent of the Episcopalians and the National Council of Churches donating funds to Nicaragua's "relocation" camps for Miskito Indians, which they did do. The Episcopalians gave $10,000 in 1985. The funds might give a degree of comfort to the people in the camps, but it is highly questionable whether American Christians should help totalitarian governments build prisoner-of-war camps.

- CAREE, *Christians Associated for Relationships with Eastern Europe*, is one of the most interesting organizations which has received church money. It is affiliated with the National Council of Churches Europe Committee of the Division of Overseas Ministries. According to the U.S. Central Intelligence Agency and the West German Office for the Protection of the Constitution, CAREE's close working partner, the Christian Peace Conference, is a Soviet front organization. The CIA believes that Christian Peace Conference president Bishop Karoly Toth of the Reformed Church of Hungary is a KGB agent.

CAREE began its life as the U.S. Committee for the Christian Peace Conference. The group changed its name to CAREE in 1972, after a crisis caused by the 1968 Soviet invasion of Czechoslovakia. Despite the name change, however, the Conference is very much CAREE's partner organization. Members of both organizations are present on each other's boards and committees and send delegations to sister gatherings, work together on projects and mutually contribute to the other's financial well-being.

CAREE's 1984 annual meeting was chaired by Christoph Schmauch, also a member of the Christian Peace Conference's International Secretariat and a native of East Germany. Schmauch also runs the World Fellowship Center in Conway, New Hampshire. (That organization was founded by a member of the World Peace Council and the Peace Council is, according to the U.S. Government, a Soviet front. Founder Willard Uphaus was once sentenced to a year in jail for not producing records of guests who had met at the Fellowship Center.) CAREE's annual meeting was also attended by Philip Oke, the United Nations representative to the Christian Peace Conference, and Bruce Rigdon, a member of the Conference working committee and a staffer at the National Council of Churches. Rigdon is chairman of the new National Council's Committee on U.S.A.-U.S.S.R. Church Relations, which sends delegations from the U.S. to the Soviet Union, usually church bureaucrats and leadership, which generally come back with praise for religious freedom in the Soviet Union.

CAREE, sponsors Christian-Marxist dialogues both in the U.S. and internationally and organizes exchanges with individuals and teams from Eastern Europe churches, including the U.S.S.R.

Had the State Department not labeled the Christian Peace Conference a Soviet front organization, average readers of Peace Conference material would probably have come to that conclusion on their own.

The Conference invariably (like the World Council of Churches) takes the Soviet line. Some of the more blatant examples are found when reading Conference literature.

The Peace Conference statement on Afghanistan is typical. The subtitle reads, "The achievement of the April revolution in the Democratic Republic of Afghanistan needs our international solidarity." The text claims that the Soviets were invited into Afghanistan by a reformer government because "the forces of the old feudal regime have attempted to stop and reverse the progressive development. . . . In view of these promising tendencies in Afghanistan we consider all attempts to disrupt this development from some of its neighboring countries as being oriented against the interests of the Afghan people and constituting a dangerous threat to peace in Asia and the world at large."

The rest of the statement is similar, blaming the U.S. for its attitude on the invasion, claiming American attitudes lead to "dangerous international tensions" and urging the U.S. to take its "responsibilities" seriously by ratifying the SALT II treaty and cancelling new weapons systems.

CAREE's office is located at 475 Riverside Drive, New York City.

MONEY - The United Church of Christ, the United Methodists, the Presbyterians, the Mennonites, the National Council of Churches, and the U.S. Catholic Conference have all donated funds to CAREE. The United Methodists gave $1,500 in 1984.

- *The Institute for Policy Studies* is an effective and subversive "think-tank" whose mission seems to be discrediting American policies any way it can—advising total disarmament, forcing the dismantling of U.S. intelligence agencies, attacking American culture, defending the Soviets (as mere reactionaries to American aggression), and touting terrorist groups.

   The multimillion-dollar agency "can be described as an enormous intelligence operation practicing both covert action and subversion. It is itself an adaptation of the multi-national corporation, and serves as an 'imperial' nerve center, with endless subsidiary operations that in turn influence and shape a whole series of ostensibly independent groups."[20]

Radical associates of the IPS and their activities have been so extensive it is impossible, in an appendix, to list them all. Among the highlights, however (almost all culled from Rael Jean Isaac's "America the Enemy—Profile of a Revolutionary Think Tank," published in

1980 by the Ethics and Public Policy Center) have been things as diverse as:

Orlando Letelier: Letelier was an associate at IPS and also the former ambassador to the United States from Chile under Allende's government. He was found to be an apparent Cuban agent after his death. Columnist Jack Anderson revealed soon after Letelier's murder by car bomb that papers were found in his briefcase which proved he had received $1,000 a month from Havana for his work. Interestingly enough, during the 1980 trip to establish CISPES, Farid Handal met with Isabel Letelier of the IPS, widow to Orlando Letelier.

Typical of IPS, following Letelier's death, the Institute appointed Tariq Ali to Letelier's former position at the Transnational Institute, IPS's European office. Ali is the British leader of the Trotskyite Fourth International, an organization which maintains contacts with international terrorist organizations. So unsavory are Ali's activities that he has been barred from entering the U.S., France, India, Japan, Turkey, Thailand, Hong Kong, and Bolivia. He has been quoted (in *Newsweek*, January 14, 1974) that "We are dedicated to achieving socialism all over the world and not through peaceful revolution." Interestingly enough, other Transnational Institute employees have been Michael Klare, a leading member of the North American Congress on Latin America (which we have already examined), and Basker Vashee, who was a member of ZAPU, a Marxist guerrilla group which operated in Rhodesia.

IPS co-founder Marcus Raskin is a member of the Organizing Committee for the Fifth Estate, which published *Counterspy*. *Counterspy* is the anti-U.S. intelligence publication which published names of U.S. intelligence personnel. In Agee's *Inside the Company: CIA Diary*, he wrote of the debts he owed to several people who gave him information. One of those people was Michael Locker, who later became a director of an IPS spin-off group and a member of the IPS Ad Hoc Working Group on Latin America.

Not content to merely help a traitor, IPS has also produced two of its own films which seek to discredit American intelligence. The 1979 IPS catalog billed one as revealing "heretofore unknown information about CIA practices and policies."

IPS fellow Saul Landau has made two propaganda films about Cuba, *Report from Cuba*, and *Fidel*. According to the Council for Inter-American Security, the proceeds from its premiere showing in San Francisco in 1969 went to the Black Panther Defense Fund.

IPS has helped support the Middle East Research and Information Project (MERIP), which in turn supports the major Middle East terrorist groups. Employees of the IPS are editors of MERIP Reports. MERIP has used IPS facilities for its meetings, and IPS fellow Eqbal

Ahmad has fund-raised for IPS. IPS has also offered courses on the Middle East taught by MERIP staffers.

Despite these highly public activities, there has been no hue and cry about IPS activities. It employs about seventy-five full-time scholars, visiting fellows, research and staff assistants and has a budget of about $2 million dollars. IPS enjoys prestige in Washington and has produced a flood of studies and publications that are targeted for Congressmen. They usually advise the cutting of defense programs.

As in all leftist organizations, IPS associates and directors are closely allied with like-thinkers. Peter Weiss, associated with the Center for Constitutional Rights, is vice-chairman of the Samuel Rubin Foundation, the principal source for IPS funding, and also the chairman of the IPS board of trustees. When Samuel Rubin died in 1978, IPS founder Raskin said he had been one of those who dared to "call themselves revolutionary." Cora Weiss, wife of Peter Weiss, is head of the Riverside Church of New York's "peace" program, which was discussed in Chapter Two.

Policy Studies' address is 1901 Q Street N.W., Washington, D.C. 20009.

MONEY - IPS received $20,000 in 1979 from the United Presbyterian Hunger Program and was granted $23,800 by the United Methodists, for various projects, between 1981 and 1983. It received $13,120 from the Methodists in 1984.

A spin-off of IPS, the "anti-Zionist" Middle East Research and Information Project has also had grants bestowed upon it. The project was given $8,500 by the United Methodist Board of Global Ministries between 1981 and 1983 and $555 in 1984.

- *The American Friends Service Committee,* which was originally a Quaker organization, describes itself as "non-sectarian," but rooted in Quaker belief. It is, in actuality, a pacifist organization which works tirelessly for disarmament. "AFS staff and volunteers work in communities across the country to enlist local citizens in the campaigns for disarmament, to challenge national priorities, and demand conversion from nuclear weapons production to peacetime production," their brochure states.

The brochure continues, "AFSC's grassroots peace education network is perhaps the most potent network of its kind in the U.S." Since $3.4 million is spent by the Friends for those programs, potence is likely. Why churches feel the need to give to an organization which is already so affluent is a mystery. Unless, of course, they are just lending a kind of moral support.

In January 1984, the Committee issued a news release that

charged "political repression" had been growing in the Caribbean since the United States invaded Grenada. The release claimed that "news coverage of important political events is sparse. Indefinite detention without charges and without trial is permitted under Grenadian law and some 35 persons are currently under political detention."

Those charges—made shortly before American troops were withdrawn from Grenada—may or may not be true. What is interesting is that the Friends not only said nothing about horrible human rights abuses under Marxist-Leninist Maurice Bishop's regime, but actually supported it. Those abuses were much worse than the unsubstantiated charges made by the Friends. Under the Grenadian Marxists-Leninists, all independent news media were forced to close, editors were jailed, and the jails were full of political prisoners that Bishop, with the help of Cuban friends, tortured.

According to the Heritage Foundation, the Friends cannot plead ignorance. They charge that Friends members were in Grenada six months prior to the invasion, in position to see what the revolutionary government was doing. The Friends, however, made no report on the abuses of Bishop's regime and according to documents seized by American troops during the invasion, they had ties to Bishop's regime.

Service Committee headquarters is located at 1501 Cherry Street, Philadelphia, Pennsylvania, 19102.

MONEY - The Friends received $98,000 of its 1984 $18.4 million budget from churches, including the United Methodists, Presbyterians, Episcopalians, Lutherans, Church of the Brethren, and various Catholic orders. About $151,000 came from Quaker organizations.

- The Board of Global Ministries' national division in 1983 gave the *Fellowship of Reconciliation*, a pacifist organization that opposes American defense policies, $2,700. According to the description, it works for peace, civil liberties, social justice, and through the development of nonviolent alternatives in resolution of conflict. The women's division gave $200, but described the organization as an agency opposed to capital punishment.

Reconciliation is located at Box 271, Nyack, New York 10960.

- *The Interfaith Center on Corporate Responsibility's* main assertion has been that international corporations, and big business in general, are somewhat akin to robber barons. The Center has noted ". . . four root causes of hunger: unjust economic systems, insufficient food production, population growth and patterns of consumption among the affluent." The organization, discussed in detail in Chapter Three, is a coalition of seventeen Protestant denominations and one hundred and seventy Catholic orders.

MONEY - The ICC was granted $195,634 by Global Ministries in three years, from 1981 through 1983 and $58,887 in 1984. It is also financially supported by every other mainline organization.

The Interfaith Center is located at 475 Riverside Drive, New York, New York 10115.

- *The National Conference of Black Lawyers* was granted $2,000 between 1981 and 1983 from Global Ministries and $10,000 alone in 1984. But the conference is affiliated with the International Association of Democratic Lawyers, which the CIA says is a Soviet front organization. Lennox Hinds, the conference director, is the permanent representative for the Democratic Lawyers to the United Nations. Not content with that, United Methodists gave $10,000 to the Affirmative Action Coordinating Center in 1983 to "plan, formulate and implement programs and policies to assure affirmative action and equality in employment." The Affirmative Action Center was established by the National Conference of Black Lawyers.

The Conference is located at Georgetown University Law Center, 600 New Jersey Avenue, Washington, D.C. 20001.

- *Agricultural Missions*, a department of the National Council of Churches, got over $114,000 in 1982 and 1983 from United Methodist General Board of Global Ministries and received $37,906 in 1984 from different Methodist agencies. According to a Global Ministries report, however, Agricultural Missions' main function is supporting "local indigenous movements that tended toward total liberation of rural people—spiritual, economic and political."

Missions staff are liberation theologians at best. In their 1981 annual report, missions staff maintain that the cause of underdevelopment are "powerlessness of people and colonialism." The mission sees its duty as "decolonialism," which means "Liberation both from the objective conditions of colonialism, i.e., the exploitative relationship between countries, as well as from its subjective manifestation. . . . Agricultural Missions has two constituencies: 1. the rural poor who are engaged in their own liberation and 2. churches and church agencies in North America. . . . We have arranged face to face contacts between the churches and persons who are directly involved in people's liberation struggles."

Missions is located at 475 Riverside Drive, New York, New York 10115.

- *The Nuclear-Free and Independent Pacific Movement* was given $300 by the United Methodist Board of Global Ministries in 1983. As mentioned in Chapter One, that organization had much success in 1984 when New Zealand, which had been heavily lobbied, forbade American ships carrying nuclear arms from their ports.

Maybe the church tired of the Pacific issue because in 1984 the Methodists gave $10,000 to the Nuclear Free Zones in the Religious Community. Whether this organization means they won't allow MX missiles in the sanctuary or Pershing missiles near the parsonage is unclear.

- The National Council of Churches, the United Methodist Church (through the Women's Division of Global Ministries), the Presbyterians, and the Episcopal Hunger Program joined forces to fund a group called the *Institute for Food and Development Policy*. The Presbyterians had given, as of 1983, $52,500. The Institute "resource guide" on hunger, published with a grant from Agricultural Missions of the National Council, states that only in Socialist countries has hunger been "effectively" overcome.

- *The Religious Task Force Mobilization for Survival* got a total of $4,500 in 1982 and 1983 from the United Methodist Board of Global Ministries and $1,000 in 1984. The group supports disarmament activities.

As important as money is, it does not tell the whole story—alliances between church bureaucracies and leftist organizations are also highly influential. The Coalition for a New Foreign and Military Policy is, according to its newsletter, affiliated with the American Baptist Churches U.S.A., Department of Church and Society of the Christian Church (Disciples of Christ), Church Women United, U.S. Peace Section of the Mennonite Central Committee, Washington Office of the Church of the Brethren, National Assembly of Women Religious, and the National Council of Churches.

It also enjoys affiliations with the National Federation of Priests Councils, National Office for Jesuit Social Ministries, Sisters of Joseph of Peace, Union of American Hebrew Congregations, Board of

Homeland Ministries and Office of Church in Society of the United Church of Christ, Board of Church and Society and Global Ministries (Women's Division) of the United Methodist Church, U.S. Washington Office of the United Presbyterian Church, Washington Office for the Episcopal Church.

It was also affiliated, of course, with many left-of-center organizations, such as the American Friends Service Committee, Center of Concern, Clergy and Laity Concerned, Fellowship of Reconciliation, War Register's League, and the Washington Office on Africa.

Witness for Peace advisory members include Richard Barnet of the Institute for Policy Studies, Angela Berryman of the American Friends Service Committee, and George Webber of Clergy and Laity Concerned.

These alliances are not just on paper, but are active associations. For instance, during the November 1983 March on Washington, which was primarily a protest against the Administration's Central American policies, most of the following groups marched together and/or officially endorsed the march: the National Council of Churches, the United Church of Christ, the Unitarians, United Methodists, Church Women United, the Jesuits Province of New York, the Maryknoll Fathers and Sisters, the National Office of Jesuit Social Ministries, and the U.S. Catholic Mission Association.

Also marching or endorsing the march were the U.S. Catholic Conference, two different orders of Catholic sisters, Sojourners, the Washington Office on Latin America, Clergy and Laity Concerned, EPICA, the North American Congress on Latin America, the Institute on Policy Studies, the Cuba Resource Center, the American Friends Service Committee, the Communist Party, USA, Communist Workers Party, CISPES, and the National Council of Soviet American Friendship.

EPICA, the National Council of Churches, and the Washington Office on Latin America cosponsored a 1980 Democratic Revolutionary Front (the El Salvadoran guerrillas) speaking tour.

Worse, under the sponsorship of the National Conference of Black Lawyers and the National Lawyers Guild, CISPES, The Washington Office on Latin America, the North American Congress on Latin America, and TransAfrica supplied speakers for "War Crimes Tribunals on Central America and the Caribbean." It was America who was being tried.

Held in October 1984 at Columbia University, the "trial" was divided up into different "crimes": "The conspiracy to deny the peoples of the region their right to self-determination," "Planning and waging aggressive wars, overt and covert," etc., etc. The first paragraph of the news release reads, "Nearly forty years after the Nuremberg Trials a group of Americans are once again examining evidence of war crimes and atrocities. This time, however, it is the U.S. government that is being charged with violations of international law."

America, of course, was found guilty.

The alliances are so strong that one organization has even been known to advertise another, or to work in tandem. The Justice and Peace Office of the Maryknoll Fathers and Brothers, who constantly work against American presence in Central America, put out an "action alert" in August 1983. In it, justice and peace officials asked that their readers "write, call or visit" their senators while at home for the summer recess urging them to ban all covert aid to the contras, and urged the reader to also "make use of your local media." But for further details, the alert said to contact the Coalition for a New Foreign and Military Policy.

Most left-of-center organizations have boards of directors and advisory committees which are full of officials from other left-of-center organizations, creating a united front instead of separate entities. The Washington Office on Latin America's (WOLA) Board of Directors and Advisory Council has, among others, officials from the NCC, the American Friends Service Committee, the Board of Global Ministries, Maryknoll Fathers, and other Catholic orders, and the ubiquitous Thomas Quigley (U.S. Catholic Conference). Isabel Letelier, of the Institute for Policy Studies, is also a member.

CAREE, an organization whose associations are so suspicious that they should give most people pause, boasts of having had as members former Methodist bishop and National Council of Churches president James Armstrong and Bryan Hehir, an official at the U.S. Catholic Conference. When asked about his membership, Armstrong said he had only lent his name, but had never been involved in CAREE and knew little about it.

Letter from Kalmin Smith Regarding his Witness for Peace Tour of Nicaragua

October 14, 1985

". . .There were a few other incidents that happened on the tour that I failed to mention in our conversation that may be of interest to you:

". . .We spent much time with the faculty and administration of the Latino Americano Biblico Seminario in San Jose. Those individuals had nothing positive to say about the Methodists of Costa Rica. They stressed liberation theology and economics. They were angry that the Methodist congregations of Costa Rica were reluctant to accept their graduates who were trained in liberation theology. Indeed, they admitted that because liberation theology is unpopular with local congregations, their enrollment was less than half of what it had been. Victorio Aroya who teaches sociology at the seminary and who supports liberation theology explained that the seminary was fundamentalist until the 1960s when the 'student body broadened.' Since then it was expelled from the Evangelical Alliance of Costa Rica because of its tilt toward liberation theology and accusations that the seminary had links to violent leftist groups. Victorio was bitter that Methodists in Costa Rica emphasized individual salvation rather than 'social justice.' (It is important to note that the Methodist bishop told us Costa Rican Methodists emphasize helping others through schooling, distribution of food and other aid to the poor, etc. When the critics of Methodists in Costa Rica say Methodists aren't for social justice, they mean Methodists don't like Marxist ideology.) He was also bitter that the most popular preacher in Costa Rica is Jimmy Swaggart through his television ministry. Victorio also complained that 'Evangelicals (Protestants) in Central America are receiving money from the U.S. to support pastors who are non-political.' He made it clear that he prefers

American dollars be directed toward preachers who actively share his political views.

"On October 18 we visited the Instituto Teologico de America Central Intercongregacional which is a Catholic seminary. I asked the priest in charge of the seminary if liberation theology brings non-believers to Christ or if its emphasis on materialism and political action pulls persons away from the church? The priest responded in Spanish. He said that liberation theology does not make new Christians and that many who accepted liberation theology had left the church for political activities. That statement was translated in the same way by the three individuals in our group who were fluent in Spanish. Yet one member of our group who is extremely pro-liberation theology and pro-Sandinista insisted that those three individuals had translated incorrectly. This individual speaks no Spanish at all. This incident told me more than I really wanted to know about the leftist world view of some of the members of our group. Clearly, they wished only to hear their preconceptions affirmed.

"On Sunday, October 21, we attended the 'people's church' Santa Maria de Los Angeles (in Nicaragua). I found the Mass and the church interesting because this particular church has long been associated with the Sandinistas and the revolution. The head priest is Uriel Molina who is one of the leaders of liberation theology in Nicaragua. We were told that the people's churches were the churches of the people and presumably the most popular with them. Yet, this church wasn't much more than half full and that included three bus loads of Americans, most of whom seemed enthusiastic supporters of the Sandinistas. I was appalled by the political murals in the church which displayed weapons and violent acts. The priest (not Molina) based his homily on the biblical story where Jesus said to render to God what is God's and to Caesar what is Caesar's. According to the priest, while God is paramount, there is to be no separation of church and state. Therefore Christians should be involved in the Sandinista revolution since giving oneself to Caesar (the Sandinistas) was the same as giving oneself to God.

"Anti-Semitism seems to me to be widespread in the Sandinista government. Everywhere we went, I asked what happened to the Jews? Surprisingly, this seemed to irritate some of the 'liberal' traveling companions who found it indelicate to ask such questions of our hosts. The outspoken anti-Semitism of Joel (the tour guide) was particularly troubling and there was some discussion about this among the members of our group on October 22. On October 23, we visited the Seminario Teologico Bautista (Baptist Seminary). I once again raised that irritating question about Jews. The response of the students and faculty with whom we met was that the seizure of the Jewish synagogue was a legitimate act by the Sandinistas because the synagogue was used as a rallying point for counterrevolutionary forces. They expanded on that subject to say that many churches were centers of resistance to the revolution and that Sandinista mobs understandably took the churches and the temple to express their dissatisfaction. To me, this seemed to be a rationalization or even normative prescription for violent acts against religious groups and individuals who disagree with a government. Despite these astonishing comments about the relationship between religion and politics, our visit to the seminary ended with a tearful statement by one of the pastors in our group in which he told the Nicaraguans that he was a Christian before he was an American and that he would share their grievances in America with his congregation. I agree with that pastor that the fundamental principles of Christianity should limit the action of states. But he seemed to miss the point that the seminarians we talked to clearly were Sandinistas first and Christians second.

"One other insight of our visit to the Baptist Seminary seems important to me. We were told that for a time the Seminary exclusively taught liberation theology, but when that happened, local congregations in Nicaragua refused to accept its graduates. So now, they provide a 'balanced' approach to theological studies. I don't understand how so many Americans convince themselves that liberation theology is the theology of the people when we have received repeated testimony that the people reject clergy trained primarily in liberation theology.

"We also met with Miguel D'Escoto on October 22. One of the other groups we saw at the Catholic church was also there. I noted that the Americans there jumped up and applauded when he entered the room as though he were our President or our Bishop. Most of the questions directed toward him were such soft balls as 'Why does the U.S. fear the Sandinista Revolution?' I asked D'Escoto if he believed Mondale would have a different policy toward Nicaragua than Reagan. He responded that the Democrats would be 'more open' toward Nicaragua and he was certain that Mondale would never invade Nicaragua. He specifically urged us to vote for Mondale and against Reagan. Later that evening Joel angrily promised that the Latin population in the U.S. would begin terrorist operations if the U.S. invaded Nicaragua. Even later Joel said that he did not advocate terrorism against the U.S. but he was just describing what he believed would happen.

"On October 24, we met with Rene Nunez, Secretary General of the Sandinista Front at the Ministry of the Interior which is the department responsible for police-type functions including the secret police. We were joined by another group and, while waiting for Nunez, a few members of our group amused themselves by asking the other group to guess which of us was a Republican. Needless to say, I was offended to be singled out by my fellow Methodists while sitting in the headquarters of the secret police of a country hostile to our own. At that meeting, one of the clergy in our group found it necessary to make an insulting comment about the U.S. Ambassador in the presence of Nunez.

"On October 25, we visited the Central American Historical Institute. At the Center we met Kathy Gander (a Canadian)and Ria Riesner (an American). Both women expressed pride that their Washington office was involved in briefing Walter Mondale for his foreign policy debate with President Reagan. This institute claims to be the source of independent and objective information. Kathy Gander said they were journalists after truth and not partisans. But at the end of our interview, Ria Riesner announced a rally to be held at the U.S. Embassy to protest U.S. policy and support the Sandinistas. She invited us to participate. Some of our group did participate in that rally. I asked Ria Riesner if her invitation gave the lie to their claims to be independent and objective purveyors of truth. She said 'no.'

"We did visit *La Prensa* as a result of my complaining (along with a few others) about the lack of balance on the tour. As our bus pulled out of the driveway, we met a parade of about 500 Sandinista-organized individuals marching to *La Prensa* to protest the paper. They carried plastic FSLN flags and had obviously been organized by the government or the party which is the same thing. *La Prensa* had not been permitted to publish by the government on Monday of the week we visited the office. It is continuously censored—one wonders who should rightfully protest to whom. Of course, anyone protesting at FSLN headquarters would be jailed or beaten or chased away very quickly. But not surprisingly, several members of our party shouted and cheered to the marchers to show their solidarity with the Sandinistas. Some flashed the V (victory) sign and begged for Sandinista flags. This shameful event was a repeat of what happened the first full day we were in Nicaragua when we were caught up in a larger demonstration. What would the United Methodists of Michigan think if they had seen that sight? Christ's church will undoubtedly survive the foolishness of these uninformed Americans. But the short-term impact on the United Methodist Church can only be negative.

"One other incident of interest. We met with Peggy Hiener. She and her husband serve as United Methodist missionaries in Nicaragua. Both work for CEPAD. Her husband works in forestry but was in the States at the time we visited. I asked Peggy if she ever evangelized. She said 'no.' If someone brings up the subject of religion, she will talk with them. Otherwise, no. Frankly, this admission astounded me.

Later, I had the opportunity to read several of the letters that Mr. Hiener sends to the States for circulation in Methodist churches. Many of them read more like Sandinista propaganda than the kind of letters from missionaries I am used to reading. . . ."

Letter from Robert Gillette

East European correspondent for the Los Angeles Times,
currently stationed in Warsaw,
regarding Soviet efforts to influence Americans

August 20, 1985

". . .You asked how does the KGB convince American religious groups, or their delegations, that there is freedom of religion in the Soviet Union.

"Simple American gullibility—an unwillingness to believe that seemingly sincere, hospitable, mature adults would lie to them—is part of the answer, although probably only a small part. As the Marquis de Custine, the French traveler, wrote after touring Russia in 1839, 'Any traveler who lets himself be indoctrinated by the locals could traverse the length and breadth of (Russian) empire and return having done nothing but tour a sequence of facades.'

"There is a risk, however, of giving the Soviet authorities more credit than they deserve for 'indoctrinating' innocent Americans. Many of the Americans in question—members of religious or peace delegations (which contain a sizable component of clergy)—appear unusually open or vulnerable to manipulation, far more so than a randomly selected group of Americans might be. A few, for whatever reasons, are simply old-fashioned fellow travelers.

"Their psychology, or mindset, is complex. But it probably explains to a large extent why they have gone to the trouble and expense of visiting the Soviet Union in the first place. (Billy Graham is a special case, as noted below.) Many of these visitors—but not all—are the latest in a long line of 20th century Americans and West Europeans who have distinguished themselves by a capacity to tour a totalitarian society and find little or nothing objectionable about it. Among their predecessors are Vice President Henry Wallace, who visited a forced labor camp in Siberia in 1944 and found it splendid, and U.S. Ambassador Joseph Davis, who pronounced the purge trials of the 1930s a model of jurisprudence.

"From my contacts with American religious and peace groups, often at Soviet-sponsored press conferences which they held at the end of their tours, several characteristics stood out, especially among the organizers and leaders. Chief among these features were large egos, a loss of faith in American institutions, and an abiding fear of nuclear war that seemed to numb the critical faculties of otherwise intelligent people.

"Some appear simply to have lost all semblance of faith in the good intentions, let alone the truthworthiness, of the American government and the press. Sweeping assertions of a kind that these people would reject out of hand if offered by an American, such as President Reagan's description of the Soviet Union as an 'evil empire,' are rather willingly accepted when offered by the 'victims' of such attacks.

"These visitors are quick to accept, for instance, Soviet assertions that the American press paints a uniformly distorted (that is, negative) view of life in the Soviet Union. They show little evidence of having read much, or carefully, about the country. But when it nevertheless fails to conform to a simplistic image they carry in their minds—when they see no guns on the streets to oppress the people, and a few splendidly restored churches open for services—it is not hard for their Soviet hosts to persuade them that the totality of what they have read has been deliberately distorted. Oppression, of course, is not easy to see from the window of a tour-bus, but these people seem not to appreciate this.

"Their hostility was often quite evident during the courtesy briefings the U.S. embassy would give on Soviet affairs. Journalists, some of whom had lived in the Soviet Union for three or four years and spoke fluent Russian, were dismissed as hopeless cold warriors by casual visitors who spoke no Russian and whose total exposure to the Soviet Union consisted of a two-week guided tour.

"In addition to an eroded faith in America, members of these touring groups also bring with them a deep fear of nuclear war which their Soviet hosts play upon, often quite crudely, but not without effect. Concomitant with this fear is an intense need to believe that the Soviet Union is, as it insists, a benign and peaceful nation concerned only with its own security and with making a better life for its own citizens. Were this not so, some American visitors have said, there would be 'no hope' for the future.

"Their obsession with the threat of war, and its effects on their powers of perception and reasoning, call to mind Milovan Djilas' explanation for the blind veneration of Josef Stalin that guided him and most other faithful communists until the 1950s. In his 'Conversations with Stalin,' the former Yugoslav leader wrote that:

"'In actual fact what happened to the Yugoslav Communists is what has happened to all throughout the long history of men who have ever subordinated their individual fate and the fate of mankind exclusively to one idea: unconsciously they described the Soviet Union and Stalin in terms required by their own struggle and its justification.'

"Official Soviet church organizations have enhanced their own image of usefulness in the eyes of the state by conveying an image of reason and peaceableness to foreign visitors, some of whom seem almost desperate to seize upon this happy vision. To conclude that there is also freedom of religion in the Soviet Union is but a small step further.

"Given this mindset, it also requires no great logical leap to accept the primacy of preventing nuclear war over certain values that have traditionally set Western nations apart from Russia—freedom of faith and expression, the rule of law, the dominance of individual liberty over the rights of the state. Soviet churchmen and others contend that this is all quite irrelevant in face of imminent nuclear war. They had reduced their debatable thesis to catchy slogans about preserving the 'sacred right to life' as the leading imperative of the age, thus sidestepping questions about the quality of that life.

"In so doing, state-controlled Soviet church organizations, in reaching out for contact with Western groups like the U.S. National Council of Churches, are peddling the old 'Better Red than Dead' viewpoint in new, more sophisticated packaging.

"I found with startling regularity that visiting American clerics had not only accepted much of this slippery reasoning but reacted with an offended tone when the subject of human rights activists like Andrei Sakharov came up in our conversations. Sakharov, as it happens, contends that civil liberties and arms control—and thus the 'sacred right to life'—are inextricably linked. For unless the Soviet people can learn something about their own government's foreign and military policies, and speak freely about them, they can have no hope of influencing these policies. And in the absence of public pressures on the Kremlin, Sakharov contends, there is little hope for meaningful arms control. Few of the American clerics I encountered in Moscow seemed sympathetic with this view, however.

"So the task before Soviet officials is not, for the most part, a very challenging one: tell the visitors what they long to hear, play on their obvious fears, on their suspicion of American institutions, and stroke their egos.

"In many instances, groups of visiting Americans these days consider themselves not simply tourists but emissaries building bridges of understanding where professional diplomacy has failed. Their hosts are only too happy to reinforce this self-image, and also to point out that the role of 'citizen diplomat' carries with it certain obligations.

"For one thing, to find fault with the Soviet Union, and certainly to bring up such internal matters as human rights issues, is to identify oneself as 'anti-Soviet' and therefore not truly interested in peace. Over and over, visitors are told that Western accusations of religious and political oppression are groundless slanders propagated by the opponents of detente. To dignify such charges by repeating them is not only insulting behavior for 'guests,' but contrary to the spirit of detente.

"Sometimes a small number of dissenters would appear in the American groups, who privately expressed dismay at the fallibility of their companions. But they tended not to be represented among the leadership, and in the interest of group harmony they usually kept their silence. The majority, on the other hand, react defensively to suggestions that they are being treated to a propaganda show, while some dismiss the possibility with a light-hearted joke. I recall one American woman last year who arrived at the offices of the official Soviet Peace Committee in Moscow to take part in a news conference wearing a button that read, 'Another KGB Dupe.'

"For more sophisticated visitors, who recognize that religion is not entirely free in the Soviet Union, there is another, more sophisticated approach.

"In a quiet moment, a Soviet cleric—a functionary of the state, but a cleric nonetheless—will draw the visitor aside to explain in hushed and private tones how valuable this kind of contact is to the various Soviet churches, and how it reinforces their legitimacy in the eyes of the state. For verisimilitude, the cleric may let it be known that he personally opposes the war in Afghanistan, that the church is working in its quiet way to press for disarmament, and so on.

"It is probably true that these contacts are good for the Soviet churches, but only when Soviet churchmen can demonstrate the even greater usefulness of the church as an instrument of state propaganda.

"For there is a small request that goes with these quiet assurances to American visitors. 'Please,' they say, 'don't spoil priceless contacts among us by raising issues of human rights. Of course we have problems, much exaggerated in the Western press, but we're working on them in our own quiet way. Don't make it harder for us.'

"This is a soft and seductive pitch. Its purpose is to draw American religious groups into a conspiracy of silence. Combined with an assiduous stroking of egos at exhausting rounds of banquets, seminars and guided tours, it often seems to work.

"Moreover, visiting Americans, with little apparent appreciation of the strictures placed on religious practice, are often surprised and dazzled by the splendor of an 18th century Orthodox church, its professional choir and Sunday services. So you see, they're told, fresh from a banquet in which their hosts have toasted peace and the unity of mankind, we do have freedom of religion.

"In fact, the Soviets abandoned the wholesale closure of churches as counterproductive after Khrushchev closed some 10,000 houses of worship before his ouster in 1964. The official policy now takes a longer view, seeking to encourage a natural process of decay or attrition. It is roughly akin to the girdling of a tree with an iron band of restrictive laws, while the soil is poisoned by compulsory instruction of atheism in the schools and through youth organizations.

"Most of the ways in which this is done should be familiar: By denying the church its normal social and spiritual role in the community, outside the church proper; by prohibiting religious instruction for children under age of 18; by severely restricting the supply of religious literature (especially the Bible and Koran); by arresting those who seek to proselytize; by penalizing white-collar professionals and students (though generally not peasants and blue-collar workers) who are found to attend services, and in many other ways—few of them visible to the casual visitor.

"That many faiths—especially the more fundamental Protestant faiths—have nevertheless managed to grow in this hostile environment is a matter of concern, and a source of discouragement, to the authorities, who tend to blame it on clumsy and ineffectual atheist propaganda. (See the *Los Angeles Times*, 16 May 1982, p. 1. Please note crucial typo: at one point it should read that "young men and women are now (as opposed to not) turning back toward religion. . . .")

"You also ask whether Soviet Baptists feel betrayed by Billy Graham. I don't know—I haven't interviewed any recently—but they certainly have good reason to feel that way. The report you cite is completely plausible.

"As I noted above, Billy Graham is a special case. Graham's behavior on his two trips to the Soviet Union was regarded by many in the foreign diplomatic community as craven, but consistent with his apparent goal: to win Soviet approval to preach to large audiences in a 'Christian Crusade,' and to obtain permission to have some of his books published in the Soviet Union.

"To these ends, Graham and his aides have sought to assure Soviet officials that he not only would avoid giving any offense, but could be of positive help to the authorities in dealing with recalcitrant Pentecostalists and other sects that have refused to submit to official controls.

"According to a Western diplomat who spoke at length with a

Graham aide after his most recent trip to the Soviet Union, Graham has told Soviet officials that he would 'understand' if certain passages in his books are deleted in Soviet editions. Graham, the aide said, went on to note that his writings could help the Soviet authorities deal with 'emotional' fundamentalists because his books counsel against emotionalism and in favor of compliance with the law. The morality of the law seems not to matter.

"I saw Billy Graham in action in Moscow in 1982. The courage of his admirers, and the behavior of the man they admired, made for quite a contrast.

"One of the more vivid memories I have from four years in the Soviet Union was the bright, cool Sunday morning when Graham spoke at Moscow's only Baptist church. Uniformed and plainclothes police had blocked off Maly Vuzovsky, the narrow side-street where the church is located. Admission was by invitation only. A fair number of bona fide church members were there (some with tape recorders) and so were burly KGB security people, all dressed alike.

"Outside, behind a metal barrier, some 300 people had gathered in hopes of catching a glimpse of Graham, and perhaps hearing a word from the man whose books they read—at great risk—in illegal, hand-typed '*samizdat*' editions. Oddly enough, they were all from outside of Moscow. Some had come from as far as Siberia, spending days on the train and a sizable part of a month's salary to hear Billy Graham preach. Among them were sturdy, ruddy-cheeked farm people from the Ukraine and Byelorussia and a contingent of nervous but deter-mined teenagers from Tula, south of Moscow.

"Why no one from Moscow itself? Because the Voice of America had broadcast Graham's schedule, and thereupon the Soviets had changed his appearance from afternoon to morning. Muscovites, un-aware of the schedule change, assumed they could show up a few hours beforehand and still catch a glimpse of the great American evangelist. But those who came from afar, with no place to spend the day (or the previous night) except in a train station, went directly to the church and were prepared to wait the entire day for a glimpse of Billy Graham. They did not get it.

"To pass the time, they sang hymns. The police repeatedly or-dered them to be quiet, and they simply ignored the police. Graham, meanwhile, was about 50 yards away, inside the church, delivering a sermon in which he urged the worshippers to obey their government. (He professed later not to have seen a banner unfurled in the balcony in front of him appealing for world attention to Baptists imprisoned in Soviet labor camps.)

"Outside, the crowd began asking whether Graham would come out to see them. I told several that I didn't know, but that I would try to find out. Slipping back into the church through a side entrance, I found Graham's advance man and told him of the several hundred followers waiting patiently outside, singing hymns. Would Graham acknowledge their presence?

"The aide said he didn't know, but that 'we're running 20 minutes behind schedule, and security is tight.'

"Security from what, he didn't say.

"Shortly, Graham emerged from the same side entrance, out of sight of the crowd. I approached him as he stepped into the back seat of his black Chaika limousine, identified myself and told him (as I wrote in my notebook) that '300 of your followers from all over the country are waiting to see you just down the street at the police barriers. They've been singing hymns for an hour now, they read illegal editions of your books, and they want to know if you will step down and see them. Will you?'

"'Oh?' Graham replied, with a quick smile. 'I didn't know that.'

"Then he closed the car door and settled back into the seat, as the car shot off in the opposite direction.

"Graham's attitude toward Western correspondents during that visit was one of barely disguised hostility. We spelled controversy, and controversy was the last thing he wanted. Among other things, we kept asking him if he planned to visit the seven Siberian Pentecostalists who at that point had been living almost four years as religious refugees in a ground-floor room of the American embassy, where they had fled seeking exit visas in 1978. Graham avoided the question at first, but finally consented to visit and pray with them.

"But not before extensive negotiations with the Pentecostalists on the circumstances under which this meeting would be conducted. Anxious to avoid offending his Soviet hosts, Graham insisted that the meeting be brief, and that Western journalists be barred from taking pictures of the scene. These tough little Siberians, who had endured 20 years of harassment by the Soviet authorities, did not give in easily. As they parlayed with Graham's aides, the evangelist himself waited tensely, and not at all happily, upstairs in the office of the deputy chief of mission, Warren Zimmermann.

"When the meeting finally took place, after more than half an hour of negotiation, the curtains in the refugees' little ground-floor window were draw in compliance with Graham's demand that prying news cameras not be allowed to record the scene. A brief reading of passages from the Bible ensued in chilly atmosphere, and the session ended after a few minutes.

"I was not in the Soviet Union during Graham's most recent visit. But according to diplomats and colleagues who followed his progress, it was much the same, as Graham sought to avoid 'controversy' at all costs.

"According to a diplomat who spoke later with his aides, Graham had a narrow brush with controversy at a small church in the Siberian city of Novosibirsk, but emerged unsullied.

"At one point in the service, a woman raised a banner calling attention to religious believers imprisoned for their faith. 'Fortunately,' the aide confided, 'the (Soviet) security people got to her quickly, and she went down without a scream.'

"That comment, I think, says all one needs to know about Billy Graham in the Soviet Union.

". . .I would also recommend reading Robert Conquest's book, *Kolyma: the Arctic Death Camps* (Viking Press, 1978, ISBN 0-670-41499-0). See Chapter 8, 'A Clownish Interlude' for classic examples of Soviet deceptions practiced on distinguished visitors. . . ."

Chapter One

1. A good example of this type of thinking was published in *MissioNEWS*, a publication of the General Board of Global Ministries of the United Methodist Church, in its March 1982 issue. In an article titled "Mission to the World," Randolph Nugent, Jr., general secretary of Global Ministries, said, when discussing the Christian mission, "However, on the other hand, when we look at the world today and study the history of Christian missions, we realize how much harm was done as well as good. When we look also at the other religions of the world and see so much in them that is obviously of God and which grows so naturally and harmoniously out of the cultures of the people, we are no longer confident that we are in possession of all the good news."

2. "U.S. Threat to Peace Concerns Bishops," by Roy Beck, *The United Methodist Reporter*, May 10, 1985.

3. Personal interview, July 1985.

4. "An Analysis of the Christian Left in the United States," by Kathleen Schultz, *Monthly Review*, July/August 1984.

5. *Ibid.*

6. *Ibid.*

7. *Ibid.*

8. *Ibid.*

9. "The Bishops As Pawns, Behind the Scenes at the U.S. Catholic Conference," by Dinesh D'Souza, *Policy Review*, Fall 1985.

10. *This World*, Fall 1984.

11. *Ibid.*

12. *Ibid.*

13. *Op. cit.*, "The Bishops As Pawns," by Dinesh D'Souza.

14. *Ibid.*

15. *Ibid.*

16. "Where Are the Hungry? Where Do They Reside?," *The Presbyterian Layman*, May-June 1985.

17. Personal interviews with members of the Antiguan Embassy, in Washington, and with members of the U.S. State Department, names withheld by request; "Bird Clobbers Church," article in the *Outlet* newspaper, Antigua, April 26, 1985; "U.S. Church Group Barred," article in the *Carribean Contact*, Antigua, May 1985; United Methodist Communications *News*, April 26, 1985.

18. *Report from Cuba*, United Methodist Church of the Dakotas area, June 1977.

19. Remarks made by Valladares at the Institute on Religion and Democracy while accepting the Religious Freedom Award, October 1983, printed on July 17, 1983 on the editorial page of *The Washington Post*.

20. Personal interview with Tedla, November 1984.

21. "The Curious Politics of Ecumenism," by Richard Ostling, *Time* magazine, August 22, 1983.

22. *Ibid*.

23. "A National Survey of Episcopalian Laity, Clergy, Bishops, Convention Deputies and Alternates," by The Gallup Organization, Inc., 53 Bank Street, Princeton, New Jersey, August 1985.

24. Presbyterian panel, February 1985, Research Unit of the Support Agency, The Presbyterian Church, 475 Riverside Drive, New York, New York, 10115.

25. "Study Shows Bishops' Political Stands Divisive Issue for Laity," by William Bole, *Religious News Service*, March 4, 1986.

26. "Past Imperfect: History and the Prospect for Liberalism-I," by William Hutchison, *The Christian Century*, January 1-8, 1986.

27. "Denominational America and the New Religious Pluralism," by Wade Clark Roof and William McKinley, *The Annuals of the American Academy of Political and Social Science*, Religion in America Today, July 1985.

28. *Ibid*.

29. *Ibid*.

30. "Discord in the Church," by Richard Ostling, *Time*, February 4, 1985.

31. A typical example of this is Father Conrado Balweg, the "renegade priest" of the Philippines. It is believed he fights with the New People's Army. According to the Associated Press, as of Spring 1985 Balweg had a $11,000 price on his head. Another example is the late Father Camilo Torres of Colombia, one of the founders of liberation theology, who, when he finished his work on the subject, joined the Marxist-Leninist guerrillas and was killed in an ambush at El Carmen in 1966.

32. *Commentary on the State of Religion in the U.S. Today*, Gallup Poll, by George Gallup, Jr., 1984.

33. *Ibid*.

34. *All Faithful People: Change and Continuity in Middletown's Religion*, Theodore Caplow, et. al., University of Minnesota, 1983, passim.

35. *Commentary on the State of Religion in the U.S. Today*, by George Gallup, Jr., 1984.

36. Panel Seeks to Shape New Image and Understanding of NCC Role, by Elliott Wright, *Religious News Service*, May 17, 1983.

37. Addresses for the organizations are: Good News, P.O. Box 150, Wilmore, KY, 40390; Presbyterian Lay Committee, 1245 N. Providence Road, Media, PA, 19063; Presbyterian United for Biblical Concerns, R.D. 4, Pottstown, PA, 19464; Biblical Witness Fellowship, Box 9327, Knoxville, TN; The Prayerbook Society of the Episcopal Church, 120 Village Square, Suite 2, Louisville, KY, 40243.

38. *Democracy in America*, Volume One, by Alexis de Tocqueville (New York: Harper and Row, 1966), p. 277.

39. *Ibid*.

Chapter Two

1. "False Gospel Almost Took Over in Grenada," by Ted Seymour, *Presbyterian Journal*, May 16, 1984.
2. "More Religious Groups Criticize Nation's Action Against Grenada," by *Religious News Service*, October 31, 1983.
3. Press release from the United Church of Christ Office of Communication, by Hiley Ward, November 2, 1983.
4. "Grenada Collective Action," from *Gist*, a publication of the Bureau of Public Affairs, Department of State, January 1984.
5. ". . .Backward Christian Soldiers," by Bill Reel, *New York Daily News*, October 17, 1983 and personal interview, Spring 1985.
6. *Ibid.*
7. "Analysis of the Church in Grenada," from the Ministry of the Interior, Butler House, St. George's, July 12, 1983, "Top Secret."
8. *Ibid.*
9. "False Gospel Almost Took Over in Grenada," by Ted Seymour, *The Presbyterian Journal*, May 16, 1984.
10. "Grenada Collection Action," from *Gist*, a publication of the Bureau of Public Affairs, Department of State, January 1984.
11. *Ibid.*
12. *Ibid.*
13. "The Episcopal Church and 'The Arms Race,'" by Mrs. Dorothy Faver, *The Christian Challenge*, August 1981.
14. "Archbishop Reiterates Speech in Catholic Northwest Progress," a reprint from the *Catholic Northwest Progress*, newspaper for the Catholic Archdiocese of Seattle, July 2, 1981.
15. "Catholics Crucify Nuke Arms Policy," by John Trinkl, *Guardian*, December 16, 1981.
16. "Bishop Raps 'Just War,'" by Bob House, *National Catholic Register*, November 22, 1981.
17. "Catholic Bishop's Leaders Oppose MX and Reagan 'Star Wars' Defense," by *Religious News Service*, June 27, 1985.
18. "Sign of God's Grace Seen in President's Nuclear Arms Speech," by Roy Beck, *United Methodist Reporter*, November 27, 1981.
19. *Ibid.*
20. *Ibid.*
21. "UM Bishops Ask Senate to Refuse Funds for MX Missile," *Newscope*, March 22, 1985.
22. *False Presence of the Kingdom*, by Jacques Ellul (New York: Seabury Press, 1972), pp. 187, 188.
23. *Christianity and Power Politics*, by Reinhold Niebuhr (New York: Scribner, 1940).
24. Speech delivered to the Episcopal Church's National Conference on Peacemaking, Cathedral of St. John, Denver, Colorado, April 28, 1983, published in *Jubilee*, "Making Distinctions About Making Peace," Volume I, Number I.

25. *Ibid.*
26. *Ibid.*
27. *Ibid.*
28. *Op. cit.*, *False Presence of the Kingdom*, by Jacques Ellul, p. 43.
29. Speech delivered to the Episcopal Church's National Conference on Peacemaking, Cathedral of St. John, Denver, Colorado, April 28, 1983, *Jubilee*, Volume I, Number I.
30. *Ibid.*
31. *"Peace and Freedom: Christian Faith, Democracy and the Problem of War,"* by George Weigel, pubished by the Institute on Religion and Democracy, 1983.
32. *Ibid.*
33. *Ibid.*
34. "A Perspective for Christians on Military Preparedness," by Francis Schaeffer, *Intercessors for America Newsletter*, November 1, 1982.
35. *Ibid.*
36. "Why the Church Is Not Pacifist," by Michael Novak, *Catholicism in Crisis*, June 1984.
37. *Ibid.*
38. Quoted in *ibid.*
39. "Perceptions of the Adversary: A Problem for Peacemaking," from the Peace Section, *Washington Memo*, published by the Mennonite Central Committee, November-December 1981.
40. "Independent Soviet Peace Movement: Official Reaction," by Sergei Batovrin. Copies can be obtained by writing to Helsinki Watch Committee, 36 W. 44th Street, Suite 911, New York, NY 10036.
41. *Ibid.*
42. *Ibid.*
43. "The New Soviet Apologists," by Arch Puddington, *Commentary*, November 1983.
44. *Ibid.*
45. *Ibid.*
46. *Breaking With Moscow*, by Arcady Shevchenko (New York: Alfred A. Knopf, 1984), p. 19.
47. "The Awful Logic of Genocide," by John-Francois Revel, *National Review*, October 4, 1985.
48. "5 Soviets Now Fighting with Rebels Tell Their Stories," by Arthur Bonner, *The New York Times*, published in the *Houston Chronicle*, November 30, 1985; "From Russia, With Hate," by John Barron, *Reader's Digest*, November 1985.
49. *"Tears, Blood and Cries, Human Rights in Afghanistan Since the Invasion 1979-1984,"* the U.S. Helsinki Watch Committee report on Afghanistan, 26 W. 44th Street, New York City 10036.
50. "The Modern Barbarians," by L. Thomas Walsh, from *Armed Forces Journal International*, July 1980.
51. *Op. cit.*, "5 Soviets Now Fighting with Rebels Tell Their Stories," by Arthur Bonner.

52. *Op. cit.*, "Tears, Blood and Cries, Human Rights in Afghanistan Since the Invasion 1979-1984."

53. *Ibid.*

54. *Ibid.*; also, *To Die in Afghanistan*, Helsinki Watch Asia Watch, December 1985.

55. "The New Holocaust," by Rosanne T. Klass, *National Review*, October 4, 1985.

56. "Remaking Afghanistan in the Soviet Image," by Richard Bernstein, *The New York Times Magazine*, March 24, 1985.

57. "Trained as a Terrorist at Age Nine," by John Barron, *Reader's Digest*, August 1985.

58. Quotes 1 and 2, "Crossroads for the Freeze," by Jim Wallis, *Sojourners Magazine*, January 1983; quote 3 from *Sojourners Magazine*, November 1982, pp. 11, 12.

59. "A Sojourner Returns," an interview with Clark Pinnock by the Institute on Religion and Democracy, *Briefing Paper*, January 1985.

60. *Ibid.*

61. *Ibid.*

62. *Ibid.*

63. *Ibid.*

64. *KGB Today*, by John Barron (Pleasantville, NY: Reader's Digest Press, 1983), p. 283.

65. *Op. cit.*, "Why the Church Is Not Pacifist," by Michael Novak.

66. *Ibid.*

Chapter Three

1. "Politics and Baby Formula in the Third World," by Ernest Lefever, *The Wall Street Journal*, January 14, 1981.

2. *Draft: A Study Document, Economics and Theology Covenant Group*, United Church of Christ, August 1984.

3. *Conscience and Dividends, Churches and the Multinationals*, by Thomas Oden, published by the Ethics and Public Policy Center, 1985, pp. 8, 9.

4. "The Corporation Haters," by Herman Nickel, *Fortune*, June 16, 1980.

5. *Ibid.*

6. "The Shaping of an Issues Strategy," remarks by Rafael Pagan, president of Nestlé Coordination Center for Nutrition, before the Public Relations Student Society of America, New York, October 25, 1983.

7. *Ibid.*

8. *Ibid.*

9. Personal interview, February 1986.

10. "The Nestlé Controversy—Another Look," by John Sparks, a publication of Public Policy Education Fund, Grove City, Pennsylvania, 1982.

11. *Ibid.*

12. *Op. cit.*, "The Corporation Haters," by Herman Nickel.

13. "The Taming of NESTLE," by Fred Clarkson, *Multinational Monitor*, April 1984.

14. Personal interview, Spring 1985.

15. *Ibid.*

16. "The Corporation Haters," by Herman Nickel, *Fortune*, June 16, 1980.

17. *Ibid.*

18. Personal interview with INFACT official Doug Clement, February 1986.

19. *Op. cit.*, *Conscience and Dividends, Churches and the Multinationals*, by Thomas Oden.

20. "Scientists Challenge the Center on Corporate Responsibility of the National Council of Churches," a press release issued by Scientists and Engineers For Secure Energy, Inc., April 5, 1984, 570 Seventh Avenue, Suite 1007, New York, NY 10018.

21. *Op. cit.*, *Conscience and Dividends*, by Thomas Oden, pp. 47, 48, quoting *ICCR Agribusiness Manual* (New York: Interfaith Center on Corporate Responsibility, 1978).

22. *Ibid.*

23. *Op. cit.*, "The Corporation Haters," by Herman Nickel.

24. "Transnational Monitor," from *Development Forum*, September 1984.

25. *Op. cit.*, *Conscience and Dividends*, by Thomas Oden, p. 89.

26. *Ibid*, p. 89, using reference from *The Corporation: A Theological Inquiry*, edited by Michael Novak and John Cooper (Washington: American Enterprise Institute, 1981).

27. Economics and Theology Study Group, United Church of Christ, August 1984.

28. The exact quote (p. 7) reads; "The doom of the wealthy man, whose only description is given in economic terms in Luke, is a difficult notion for those of us who are wealthy (and nearly all Americans are wealthy in global terms) to grasp. We are tempted to think of this parable as being about the need for more charity or a little more kindness or about our own 'spiritual poverty.' When we hear it thus, we neatly avoid even considering the pointed message of Jesus that those who are wealthy while others suffer in poverty face the judgment of God."

29. *Op. cit.*, Economics and Theology Study Group, United Church of Christ, August 1984.

30. *Ibid.*

31. "Catholic Social Teaching and the U.S. Economy," *origins*, NC documentary service, November 15, 1984.

32. *Ibid.*

33. "Planning for Sustained Community," by Gar Alperovitz, a paper prepared for Catholic Social Teaching and the American Economy, a symposium on the proposed pastoral letter, December 12-14, The University of Notre Dame.

34. "Briefs," from *Religion and Democracy*, a newsletter of the Institute on

Religion and Democracy, September 1984; "Protestant Leaders Testify to Catholic Bishops Committee on the U.S. Economy," by the *Church Economic Programs Information Bulletin*, published by the Institute on Religion and Democracy, September 15, 1984.

35. "Second Draft of Pastoral Has New Focus on Middle Class," by William Bole, *Religious News Service*, October 7, 1985.

36. "Bishop: Capitalism Doesn't Profit Faith," by Lisa Ellis, *Dallas Times Herald*, November 12, 1985.

37. *The Spirit of Democratic Capitalism*, by Michael Novak (New York: Simon and Schuster, 1982), pp. 248, 249.

38. *Ibid.*, page 240.

39. "The Report of the Task Force to Review Policies, Strategies and Programs of the United Presbyterian Church Related to Transnational Corporations," issued in 1983.

40. "Technology Not Answer to Ecological Problems, Says Theologian," *Newscope*, July 22, 1983.

41. "3rd World Sermon Notes," from *Church Economic Programs Information Service Bulletin*, June-July 1984, published by the Institute on Religion and Democracy, Washington, D.C.

42. "WCC Takes on MNCs in Asia," *CESPIS Bulletin*, published by the Institute on Religion and Democracy, March 1984.

43. *Churches and the Transnational Corporations: An Ecumenical Program*, a report to the Central Committee of the WCC from the Committee on the Church's Participation in Development, July 1982, p. 25.

44. *The Good News Is That the Bad News Is Wrong*, by Ben Wattenberg (New York: Simon and Schuster, 1985), p. 151.

45. *Ibid*, pp. 150, 151.

46. *Losing Ground, American Social Policy 1950-1980*, by Charles Murray (New York: Basic Books, 1984), p. 14.

47. *Op. cit.*, *The Good News Is That the Bad News Is Wrong*, by Ben Wattenberg, p. 154.

48. *Ibid.*, p. 159.

49. *Op. cit.*, *Losing Ground, American Social Policy 1950-1980*, by Charles Murray, p. 58.

50. *Ibid.*, pp. 125-134.

51. "Mending Broken Families," an editorial from *The New Republic*, March 17, 1986.

52. *Time*, "Redefining the American Dilemma," November 11, 1985, p. 33.

53. *Op. cit.*, *The Spirit of Democratic Capitalism*, by Michael Novak, p. 14.

54. *Ibid.*

55. *Ibid.*

56. *Ibid.*

57. *Ibid.*, p. 16.

58. *Ibid.*

59. *Ibid.*, p. 17.

60. *Ibid.*, p. 16.
61. "A Few Home Truths About Latin America," *Commentary* magazine, February 1985.
62. *Ibid.*
63. *Ibid.*
64. *Ibid.*
65. "Human Needs and Satisfactions," a global survey by Gallup International, London, England, 1976, pp. 211, 212.
66. "Report of the Task Force to Review Policies, Strategies and Programs of the United Presbyterian Church Related to Transnational Corporations," a task-force report requested by the 1979 General Assembly Mission Council of the United Presbyterian Church, p. 28.
67. *Ibid.*, p. 29.
68. *Ibid.*, p. 30.
69. *Ibid.*, pp. 4, 5.
70. *Ibid.*
71. *Ibid.*
72. *Report of the Infant Formula Task Force to the 1984 General Conference*, the United Methodist Church.
73. *Ibid.*
74. *Ibid.*

Chapter Four

1. "Why Ethiopia Is Starving," by Ralph Bennett, *Reader's Digest*, May 1985.
2. "Ethiopia's Kremlin Connection," *Backgrounder*, The Heritage Foundation, January 17, 1985.
3. *Ibid.*
4. *Op. cit.*, "Why Ethiopia Is Starving."
5. "What the West Must Do," By Dereje Deressa, condensed in the *Reader's Digest*, May 1985.
6. News in Brief, *Religious News Service*, December 26, 1984.
7. *United Methodist Communications News*, by Tracy Early, December 14, 1984.
8. "Relations Sour Between Ethiopia and Western Food Donors," by Clifford May, *The New York Times*, February 18, 1985; "Ethiopia's Cynical Regime," an editorial by the editors of *The Washington Post*, January 18, 1985; "Murder by Hunger," an editorial by the editors of *The Wall Street Journal*, January 10, 1985; "Resettlement's Heavy Toll," from *Time*, February 10, 1986; "Resettlement Kills More People Than Famine," from *The Presbyterian Layman*, March/April 1986.
9. *United Methodist Communications News*, by Tracy Early, December 14, 1984.

10. "Bishops Appeal for Hunger, Peace," from *News & Comment*, February-March 1985.

11. *Op. cit.*, "Ethiopia's Kremlin Connection," *Backgrounder*.

12. In 1977 employees of Church World Service, a division of the National Council of Churches, told the Congressional Subcommittee on International Organizations that the Vietnamese were doing a good job in their reeducation camps. After describing the good food and making other favorable comments they concluded, "It would seem that the entire process of reeducation is one reflecting the government's commitment to encouraging and enabling people to exercise their rights, restored as full participants in Vietnam's future." As a matter of documented fact, "reeducation kills." The prisoners are used as cheap labor and torture is the norm. The prisoners are given very little to eat and most of what they get is, by normal standards, uneatable. Because they are often too weak to work well, they are often punished. Tran Nhu, a survivor of "reeducation," was sent to Camp Xuan Giang in North Vietnam in 1966. There were two thousand and six hundred prisoners. By 1971 there were only twenty-three of the original two thousand and six hundred left alive. See *Human Rights in Vietnam*, hearings before the Subcommittee on International Organizations of the Committee on International Relations, House of Representatives, 95th Congress, 1st session, June 16, 21st and July 26, 1977, pages 61, 70-74 to verify the testimony. See also "Reeducation Kills," by Tran Nhu, *Freedom at Issue*, July-August 1985 to verify facts about reeducation camp.

13. "The Jackson Tour," by Fred Barnes, *The New Republic*, July 30, 1984.

14. From Cuban government newspaper *Granma*, July 15, 1984.

15. *Op. cit.*, "The Jackson Trip," by Fred Barnes.

16. "Cuba Courts Black Churches," *Information Digest*, August 3, 1984.

17. *Ibid.*

18. *Granma*, July 15, 1984.

19. *Ibid.*

20. *Ibid.*

21. *Op. cit.*, "Cuba Courts the Black Churches."

22. "Holy Fools," by Charles Krauthammer, *The New Republic*, September 9, 1981, quoting from September, 1981 issue of *One World*.

23. "Introducing Cuba," by Mary Lou Suhor. *Cuba: People-Questions* (New York: Friendship Press, 1975).

24. *Ibid.*

25. "Castro and the Narcotics Connection" (a summary of government findings), The Cuban American National Foundation, 1983.

26. *Ibid.*

27. "The Narcotics-Terrorism Connection," by Rachel Ehrenfeld and Michael Kahan, *The Wall Street Journal*, February 10, 1986.

28. "Inside Castro's Prisons," by Armando Valladares, *Time*, August 15, 1983.

29. *Ibid.*

30. "Human Rights Violations in Cuba," by Richard Shifter, *Catholicism in Crisis*, March 1985.
31. *Ibid.*
32. *Ibid.*
33. "Church Activism," from *Midstream*, March 1984, quoting from "Spirituality and Struggle for Fullness of Life," by Eugene Stockwell, *Missiology*, January 1979.
34. "China: People-Questions," *People and Systems* (New York: Friendship Press, 1977).
35. *Ibid.*
36. "Chinese Christians Caught in Government Crackdown," *Response* magazine, January-February 1984.
37. "A Church in Crisis Weeps and Prays," *Time*, September 17, 1984.
38. *Ibid.*
39. *The God That Failed*, edited by Richard Crossman (Chicago: Regnery Gateway, 1949), p. 15.
40. *Ibid.*, p. 16.
41. *The Challenge of Marxism, A Christian Response*, by Klaus Bockmuehl (Downers Grove, IL: InterVarsity Press, 1980), p. 17.
42. *Political Pilgrims*, by Paul Hollander (New York: Harper Colophon Books, 1983), p. 7.
43. *Chronicles of Wasted Time*, by Malcolm Muggeridge (New York: William Morrow and Company, 1973), p. 244.
44. *Sun Never Sets*, by Malcolm Muggeridge (New York: Random House, 1940), p. 79.
45. *Op. cit.*, *Political Pilgrims*, by Paul Hollander, p. 336.
46. "Jews and American Politics, 1984 and After," a portion of which was by Paul Gottfried, *This World* magazine, Winter 1985, Number Ten, p. 33.
47. "The Politics of Charity," by Doug Hostetter and Michael McIntyre, *The Christian Century*, September 18, 1974.
48. "Are We One Nation Under God?," by Peggy Billings, *Response* magazine, June 1975.
49. Personal interview, Fall 1984.
50. "Jonas Savimbi on the Angolan Struggle," *National Catholic Register*, December 9 and 16, 1979.
51. *Ibid.*
52. *Life in All Its Fullness*, by Phillip Potter, published by the World Council of Churches publishing house, Geneva, Switzerland, 1981, p. 85.
53. *Marxism*, by Thomas Sowell (New York: William Morrow and Company, 1985), p. 25.
54. *Ibid.*
55. *Ibid.*
56. *Ibid.*
57. *Ibid.*
58. *Ibid.*

59. *Ibid.*
60. *Ibid.*
61. *Nomenklatura*, by Michel Voslensky (New York: Doubleday, 1984).
62. *Ibid.*, pp. 325, 326.
63. "Why Gorbachev Is Worried," by Tom Bethell, *National Review*, October 4, 1985.
64. *Modern Times*, by Paul Johnson (New York: Harper and Row, 1983), pp. 676, 677.
65. *Ibid.*, pp. 714, 715.
66. "Marxism Practically Dead in Eastern Europe," by Kitty McKinsey, Knight-Ridder News Service, printed in the *Lexington Herald-Leader*, November 3, 1985.
67. *Op. cit.*, "Why Ethiopia Is Starving," by Ralph Bennett.
68. *Ibid.*
69. *Ibid.*
70. "What the West Must Do," by Dereje Deressa, *Reader's Digest*, May 1985.
71. "The Second Revolution," *Time*, September 23, 1985.
72. United Methodist Board of Global Ministries *MissioNEWS*, May 1982.
73. *Op. cit.*, *The God That Failed*, edited by Richard Crossman, pp. 17, 35.
74. *Ibid.*, p. 68.
75. *Ibid.*
76. "Communism and the Left," reprint of a speech by Susan Sontag made February 6, 1982, at Town Hall in New York City, published in *The Nation*, February 27, 1982.
77. Quoted in *op. cit.*, *Marxism*, by Thomas Sowell, p. 166.

Chapter Five

1. Photograph printed in *Silent Testimony of the Persecuted Church*, newsletter of the International Representation for the Council of Evangelical Baptist Churches of the Soviet Union, Inc., November 1984.
2. *Ibid.* From the text.
3. "The Church of the Russians," by Michael Bourdeaux, *KNS*, Number 204, July 19, 1984; "The National Council of Churches and The U.S.S.R.," by Joshua Muravchik, *This World*, Fall 1984, Number Nine.
4. *Ibid.*
5. *Op. cit.*, "The National Council of Churches and the U.S.S.R.," by Joshua Muravchik.
6. "In the Soviet Paradise," from the editorial page of *The Washington Post*, June 25, 1984.

7. Personal interview with spokesmen for the International Representation for the Council of Evangelical Baptist Churches of the Soviet Union, Inc., Summer 1985.

8. "A Word from Georgy Vins," from *Silent Testimony of the Persecuted Church*, November 1984.

9. *Op. cit.*, "The Church of the Russians," by Michael Bordeaux, quoting from the Parisian *International Herald Tribune*, June 22, 1984.

10. "A Question of Faith-II," by Peter Reddaway, published in the *Baltimore Sun*, September 13, 1984.

11. "Soviet Abuse of Psychiatry Continues," by Ludmilla Thorne, *Freedom at Issue*, July-August 1985.

12. "U.S. Visitors Praise Status of Religion in Soviet," by Seth Mydans, *The New York Times*, June 21, 1984.

13. A Marxist-Christian encounter is usually an attempt to find similarities between Marxism and Christianity. Unsurprisingly, much of the time people who participate in these encounters find these similarities. CAREE is not the only organization to sponsor encounters. One was held at the University of Northern Iowa in 1984. It featured U.S. Communist Party theoretician Herbert Aptheker, U.S. Peace Conference representative Terry Provance (the Peace Conference is a Soviet front organization according to U.S. intelligence), and professors from Catholic schools such as Holy Cross and Loyola. The titles of the speeches and workshops were interesting. One was called "A Catholic Who Became A Communist," another was "Kindred Humanistic Commitments in the Views of Jesus and Marx," and "Karl Marx and Pope John Paul II on Labor."

14. *Op. cit.*, "The National Council of Churches and the U.S.S.R.," by Joshua Muravchik.

15. "Bishop Feodosy, Russian Orthodox Church, Appeals to Brezhnev," translated by *Religion in Communist Dominated Areas*, published in Vol. XXII, Nos. 10, 11 and 12, 1983.

16. *Ibid.*

17. *Ibid.*

18. *Op. cit.*, "The National Council of Churches and the U.S.S.R.," by Joshua Muravchik.

19. "The Trial of Father Alfonsas Svarinskas," RCDA publication, Volumes 4, 5, & 6, 1983, translation from *Chronicle of the Catholic Church in Lithuania*, Number 58, May 22, 1983.

20. *Ibid.*

21. *Ibid.*

22. "Why Romania No Longer Deserves to be Most Favored Nation," by Juliana Geran Pilon, *Backgrounder*, a publication of the Heritage Foundation, Number 441, June 26, 1985.

23. "Center Watches Soviet Religious Life," by the Associated Press, printed in the *Longview News-Journal*, June 15, 1985.

24. *The Undiscovered Self*, by Carl Jung (New York: Mentor, 1957, 1958), pp. 29, 30.

25. "The Fifth Seal," speech by Michael Bordeaux to the "Freedom of

Religion, Human Rights and Detente" symposium, Vienna, May 1983.

26. "Men Have Forgotten God," Aleksandr Solzhenitsyn, address upon receiving the Templeton Prize for Progress in Religion, May 10, 1983. Printed in *National Review*, July 22, 1983, p. 874.

27. "Secular Inhumanism," by Michael Bordeaux, *Policy Review*, September 1985.

28. *Op. cit.*, "The Fifth Seal," speech by Michael Bourdeaux.

29. *Ibid.*

30. *Op. cit.*, "The National Council of Churches and the U.S.S.R.," by Joshua Muravchic.

31. According to Arcady Shevcheko, author of *Breaking with Moscow*, Arbotov's institute in Canada is a front for the KGB.

32. *Op. cit.*, "The Fifth Seal," a speech by Michael Bordeaux.

33. *Op. cit.*, "Secular Inhumanism," by Michael Bourdeaux, remarks by Bordeaux at the Religious Liberty Conference, held at the Institute on Religion and Democracy, Washington, Summer 1985.

34. *Ibid.*

35. *Ibid.*

36. *KGB: The Work of Soviet Secret Agents*, by John Barron (New York: Bantam Books, 1974), p. 49.

37. *Ibid.*

38. "NBC Airs Soviet Propaganda," printed in *Accuracy in Media*, March 1984, p. 1.

39. "Soviet Religious Leader Urges U.S. to Respond to Peace Talks," by Marjorie Hyer, *The Washington Post*, May 22, 1984.

40. *Op. cit.*, "Men Have Forgotten God," an excerpt from a speech delivered by Aleksandr Solzhenitsyn.

41. "Visiting Soviet Clergy Asked About Christians in Prison," by Willmar Thorkelson, *Religious News Service*, May 14, 1984.

42. *Op. cit.*, "The Fifth Seal," by Rev. Michael Bourdeaux.

43. *Ibid.*

44. *Ibid.*

45. *Op. cit.*, "U.S. Visitors Praise Status of Religion in Soviet," by Seth Mydans.

46. "Farewell to Leningrad," by Marcus Sloan, *Houston Chronicle*, June 30, 1985.

47. "Soviets Show the Facade of Peace," by Robert Gillette, *Los Angeles Times*, August 12, 1984.

48. *Ibid.*

49. *Ibid.*

50. *Ibid.*

51. *Op. cit.*, *KGB: The Secret Work of Soviet Secret Agents*, by John Barron, pp. 119-122.

52. "Soviet Religious Life Surprises and Disturbs American Visitors," by Antero Pietela, *Religious News Service*, June 20, 1984.

53. *Op. cit.*, *The God That Failed*, edited by Richard Crossman, pp. 177-188.

54. *Ibid.*
55. *Ibid.*
56. *Op. cit.*, "Soviets Shows the Facade of Peace," by Robert Gillette.
57. *Op. cit.*, "The Fifth Seal," a speech by Michael Bordeaux.
58. *Ibid.*
59. *Ibid.*
60. "Fact Sheet: The Soviets, the Churches and the Media," by Alan Thomson, July 23, 1984, from the National Council of American Soviet Friendship, Inc., 162 Madison Avenue, 3rd Floor, New York, New York 10016.
61. *Op. cit.*, "The Trial of Father Alfonsas Svarinskas."
62. *Ibid.*
63. *Ibid.*

Chapter Six

1. "A Clash of Wills—Radical Priests Are Squaring Off Against Church Hierarchy in War-Torn Nicaragua," by Chris Hedges, *The Dallas Morning News*, March 2, 1986.
2. *A Theology of Liberation*, by Gustavo Gutierrez (Maryknoll, NY: Orbis Books, 1973), p. 151.
3. *Jesus Christ Liberator: A Critical Christology for Our Time*, by Leonardo Boff (Maryknoll, NY: Orbis Books, 1973).
4. *Op. cit*, "A Clash of Wills," by Chris Hedges.
5. *Doing Theology in a Revolutionary Situation*, by Jose Miguel Bonino (Philadelphia: Fortress Press, 1975), p. 162.
6. "Liberation in Nicaragua: The Theology of the Sandinista Revolution," by Edward Lynch, *A Thesis Presented to the Graduate Faculty of the University of Virginia in Candidacy for the Degree of Master of Arts*, Woodrow Wilson Department of Government and Foreign Affairs, University of Virginia, 1983, quoting from "The Cult of Revolution in the Church," by John Eppstein, *Our Sunday Visitor*, 1974.
7. "Instruction on Certain Aspects of the 'Theology of Liberation,'" by Cardinal Joseph Ratzinger and Archbishop Alberto Bovone, prefect and secretary of the Vatican Congregation for the Doctrine of the Faith, printed in *Origins*, NC documentary services, September 13, 1984, Volume 14, Number 13.
8. *Op. cit.*, "Liberation in Nicaragua: The Theology of the Sandinista Revolution," by Edward Lynch.
9. *Ibid.*
10. *Ibid.*
11. The Letter of Paul to the GALATIANS, 5:19-23, *Holy Bible*, Revised Standard Version.
12. Gustavo Gutierrez, quoted originally in *Christianismo y Marxismo en*

la Teologica de la Liberacion, by Fernando Moreno Valencia (Editorial Salesiana, 1976), p. 35.

13. *Op. cit.*, *A Theology of Liberation*, by Gustavo Gutierrez, p. 26.
14. As quoted in "Nicaragua: First Test for Liberation Theology," by Hunberto Belli, The Puebla Institute, *Occasional Bulletins*, January 1985, Number 6.
15. *Ibid.*
16. "Both Sides in El Salvador Seek Legitimacy Through Church," by Chris Hedges, *The Dallas Morning News*, March 3, 1986.
17. *Ibid.*
18. "The Case Against Liberation Theology," by Michael Novak, *The New York Times Magazine*, October 21, 1984.
19. "Are Multinationals a Menace to the Third World?" by John Sparks, a special report of the Public Policy Education Fund, Inc.
20. *The Spirit of Democratic Capitalism*, by Michael Novak (New York: Simon and Schuster, 1984), p. 230.
21. *Ibid.*
22. *Op. cit.*, *A Theology of Liberation*, by Gustavo Gutierrez.
23. *Ibid.*
24. "Instruction on Certain Aspects of the 'Theology of Liberation,'" signed by Cardinal Joseph Ratzinger, prefect of the congregation, and Archbishop Alberto Bovone, secretary of the congregation, *Origins*, NC documentary service, September 13, 1984.
25. *Ibid.*
26. *Ibid.*
27. *God, Revelation and Authority*, Carl Henry (Waco, TX: Word Books, 1976), p. 240.
28. *Ibid.*
29. "Liberation Theology," by Cardinal Joseph Ratzinger," *Catholicism in Crisis*, September 1984.
30. *Ibid.*
31. *Ibid.*
32. *Ibid.*
33. *Ibid.*
34. *Ibid.*
35. *Ibid.*
36. *Ibid.*
37. *Op. cit.*, *"Instructions on Certain Aspects of the 'Theology of Liberation,'"* signed by Cardinal Joseph Ratzinger and Archbishop Alberto Bovone.
38. *Ibid.*
39. Ratzinger said that the core of Marxist *theory* is denial of liberty and human rights. As we have seen in the last chapter, it is not Marxist theory which insists on these matters, but the interpreters of Marxist theory which have used the doctrine for their own ends.
40. *Nicaragua, Land of Sandino*, Thomas Walker (Boulder, CO: Westview Press, 1981), p. 99.

41. *Op. cit.*, "Liberation in Nicaragua: The Theology of the Sandinista Revolution," by Edward Lynch, quoting from House Committee on Foreign Affairs, Special Central American Economic Assistance, 1979, pp. 52-58.

42. *Ibid.*, quoting from *Guardians of the Dynasty*, by Richard Millet (Maryknoll, NY: Orbis Books, 1977), pp. 11-13; quotes are from introduction by Miguel D'Escoto.

43. *Ibid.*, quoting from *Special Central American Economic Assistance*, a publication of the House Committee on Foreign Affairs, 1977, p. 57.

44. *Op. cit.*, *Nicaragua, Land of Sandino*, by Thomas Walker, pp. 87, 88.

45. *Ibid.*, "Liberation in Nicaragua: The Theology of the Sandinista Revolution," by Edward Lynch, p. 74.

46. "Gloom But Not Yet Doom," *Time*, May 14, 1984.

47. *Op. cit.*, "Liberation in Nicaragua: The Theology of the Sandinista Revolution," by Edward Lynch, p. 76.

48. "The Churches in the Nicaraguan Revolution," by Michael Dodson and T. S. Montgomery, from *Nicaragua in Revolution*, edited by Thomas Walker (New York: Praeger Publishers, 1982), p. 161.

49. *Op. cit.*, "Liberation in Nicaragua: The Theology of the Sandinista Revolution," by Edward Lynch, p. 77.

50. *Op. cit.*, "The Churches in the Nicaraguan Revolution," by Dodson and Montgomery, from *Nicaragua in Revolution*.

51. *Op. cit.*, "Liberation in Nicaragua," by Edward Lynch, quoting from Walker's *Land of Sandino*, p. 100; "Nicaragua, the Revolution Takes Hold," by Wayne Cowen, from *Christianity and Crisis*, May 12, 1980; *op. cit.*, "The Churches in the Nicaraguan Revolution," by Dodson and Montgomery from *Nicaragua in Revolution*.

52. *Op. cit.*, *Nicaragua, Land of Sandino*, by Thomas Walker, p. 99.

53. *Op. cit.*, "Liberation in Nicaragua," by Edward Lynch, quoting from Dodson and Montgomery in *Nicaragua in Revolution*.

54. "Church Protests in Philippines Met with Greater Repression," by Richard Cimino, *Religious News Service*, December 19, 1984.

55. "Philippine Bishops Fail to Agree on Pastoral," by Gregg Jones, *National Catholic Register*, August 4, 1985.

56. "The New Khmer Rouge," by Ross Munro, *Commentary*, December 1985.

57. *Ibid.*

58. *Ibid.*

59. *Ibid.*, and "Rural Philippines Church Grapples with Rural Crisis," by A. Lin Neumann, *National Catholic Reporter*, March 30, 1984.

60. *Op. cit.*, "The New Khmer Rouge," by Ross Munro.

61. *Ibid.*

62. *Ibid.*

63. *Ibid.*

64. "Options in the Philippines, Part Two," by John Whitehall, *Freedom at Issue*, May-June 1985.

65. *Op. cit.*, "Rural Philippines Church Grapples with Rural Crisis," by A. Lin Neumann.

deduct calls
to Lynn / Canoga Way
motel

Canoga Park

7435 Wimetka
#109

1:00

rt. on Wimetka
Sherman Way
818 3~~~~~ - 341-9700

66. "Progressive Bishop Says Non-violence Is the Only Answer in the Philippines," by William Bole, *Religious News Service*, October 28, 1982.
67. *Op. cit.*, "Liberation in Nicaragua: The Theology of the Sandinista Revolution," by Edward Anthony Lynch.
68. *Ibid.*
69. *Ibid.*
70. *Op. cit.*, "Liberation in Nicaragua," by Edward Lynch, quoting Anne Fremantle's *The Papal Encyclicals in Their Historical Context* (New York: Mentor Omega, 1963), p. 168.
71. *Ibid.*, Freemantle, p. 233.
72. "Liberation Theology and the Pope," by Michael Novak, *Commentary*, June 1979.
73. Quoted in "The High Costs of the Dependency Theory Myth," by Lawrence Harrison, *Catholicism in Crisis*, September 1984.
74. *Ibid.*
75. *Ibid.*
76. "Latin America and the Spanish Tradition," by L. John Van Til, *Special Report Number 17*, Public Policy Education Fund, Inc., February 1982.
77. "Why Latin America Is Poor," by Michael Novak, *The Atlantic Monthly*, March 1982.
78. *Ibid.*
79. First Seminar of the Dominican Interprovincial Conference of Latin America Costa Rica—1983—final document, translated by George Dyer, O.P. Province of St. Martin de Porres, U.S.A.
80. "Rejecting Liberation Theology Termed 'Act of Blasphemy,'" by Roy Beck, *United Methodist Reporter*, November 2, 1984.
81. "Distortion in Korean Study Materials Claimed," by Roy Beck and Roberta Sappington, *United Methodist Reporter*, October 5, 1984.
82. "Efforts Made to Clarify Korean Church Situation," by Roy Beck, *United Methodist Reporter*, December 28, 1984.
83. "Evil Is Never a Road to Good," religion section, by Richard Ostling, *Time*, February 18, 1985.

Chapter Seven

1. "In Nicaragua," by Mario Vargas Llosa, *The New York Times Magazine*, April 28, 1985, p. 36.
2. *Ibid.*
3. *Ibid.*
4. *Ibid.*
5. *Ibid.*
6. *Ibid.*

7. *Ibid.*
8. "The Treatment of the Nicaraguan Indians by the Sandinista Government," *Freedom at Issue*, May-June 1982, Number 66.
9. *Ibid.*
10. "A Witness to Genocide," by Stedman Fagoth Muller, *Free Trade Union News*, March 1982.
11. *Ibid.*
12. "The Treatment of the Nicaraguan Indians by the Sandinista Government," *Freedom at Issue*, May-June 1982, Number 66.
13. *Op. cit.*, "A Witness to Genocide," by Stedman Fagoth Muller.
14. "The Treatment of the Nicaraguan Indians by the Sandinista Government," *Freedom at Issue*, May-June 1982, Number 66.
15. "The Unreported War Against the Sandinistas," by Bernard Nietschmann, *Policy Review*, Summer 1984, p. 32.
16. Personal interview with Professor Bernard Nietschmann, Department of Geography, University of California at Berkeley.
17. "Among the Miskitos," by Joan Frawley, *Policy Review*, Spring 1984,, p. 50.
18. "The Unreported War Against the Sandinistas," by Bernard Nietschmann, *Policy Review*, Summer 1984.
19. *Ibid.*
20. *Some Actions and Situations That Violate the Human Rights of the Miskito, Sumo, and Rama Indians of the Atlantic Coast of Nicaragua.* Dated November 9, 1982, Puerto Lempira, Honduras, Central America. It is signed by Tilleth Mullins, Enrique Lopez, Sigfrid Williams, Wigglif Diego, and Cirilio Wilson. This statement has never been published as far as we know. It was sent to the Institute on Religion and Democracy (Washington, D.C.) in 1983 by tribal elders.
21. *Ibid.*
22. *Ibid.*
23. *Op. cit.*, "A Witness to Genocide," by Stedman Fagoth Muller.
24. *Op. cit.*, *Some Actions and Situations That Violate the Human Rights of the Miskito, Sumo, and Rama Indians of the Atlantic Coast of Nicaragua.*
25. These statements were never published as far as we know. The Indian council sent them to various organizations in the United States in 1982 and 1983, apparently hoping they would be published and arouse public opinion.
26. *Ibid.*
27. *Ibid.*
28. *Ibid.*
29. *Ibid.*
30. Statement Before the Organization of American States Inter-American Commission on Human Rights, on the Situation of the Indians in Nicaragua, Presented by Bernard Nietschmann, October 3, 1983.
31. *Ibid.*
32. *Ibid.*

33. *Ibid.*
34. "Moravian-Sandinista Dialogue," by Margaret Wilde, *The Christian Century*, May 11, 1983.
35. "An Open Letter to Moravians in North America Concerning Nicaragua and the Miskito People," by Rev. Joel Gray, *The North American Moravian*, June-July 1984.
36. *Op. cit.*, "Moravian-Sandinista Dialogue," by Margaret Wilder, *The Christian Century*, May 11, 1983.
37. Personal interviews, April 1986 with Bernard Nietschmann; also, "North American Indians Assert Sandinistas Bombed Villages," by Stephen Kinzer, *The New York Times*, February 11, 1986.
38. "Persecution of Christian Groups in Nicaragua," *White House Digest*, February 29, 1983, source of which was "Communicado Oficial de la Direccion National del FSLN sobre la Religion," *Barricada*, October 7, 1980.
39. *Ibid.* Also, "U.S. Aides Condemn Nicaraguan Curbs on Civil Liberties," by Bernard Weinraub, *The New York Times*, October 17, 1985; "Reform the Contras," by Robert Leiken, *The New Republic*, March 31, 1986.
40. "Nicaragua's Popular Church: Just Another Party Organ?" by Joan Frawley, *The Wall Street Journal*, February 22, 1985.
41. "The Sandinista Regime Today," by Humberto Belli, *Freedom at Issue*, November/December 1982.
42. *Ibid.*
43. "Nicaraguan Harvest," by Mark Falcoff, *Commentary*, July 1985.
44. *White House Digest*, "Persecution of Christian Groups in Nicaragua," February 29, 1984, quoting Cardinal Obando y Bravo, "Comments on the Papal Letter," *La Prensa*, Managua, August 14, 1983.
45. *Ibid.*
46. "The Battle for Democracy in Nicaragua," *Backgrounder*, The Heritage Foundation, March 14, 1984.
47. *Op. cit.*, "In Nicaragua," by Mario Vargas Llosa.
48. *Ibid.*
49. *Nicaragua: A Revolution in the Family*, by Shirley Christian (New York: Random House, 1985), p. 227.
50. *Ibid*, pp. 211, 212.
51. "The Subversion of the Church in Nicaragua," an interview with Miguel Bolaños-Hunter, a *Briefing Paper* published by the Institute on Religion and Democracy, December 1983.
52. Statement by Julio Cesar Montes Aranda, former Sandinista, found in letter written by Congressman Willian E. Dannemeyer, 39th District of California, to Rev. David Preus, presiding bishop of the American Lutheran Church, July 2, 1984.
53. "Human Rights Violations and Religious Persecution in Nicaragua," *Policy Forum*, October 1984, National Forum Foundation publication.
54. *Christians Under Fire*, by Humberto Belli (Garden City, MI: Puebla Institute, 1984), p. 45.

55. "The Subversion of the Church in Nicaragua," a *Briefing Paper* interview published by the Institute on Religion and Democracy, Washington, D.C., December 1983.
56. *Ibid.*
57. *Ibid.*
58. *Op. cit.*, *White House Digest*, "Persecution of Christian Groups in Nicaragua."
59. *Ibid.*
60. *Ibid.*
61. *Ibid.*
62. "Despair and Fear in Managua," by David Asman, *The Wall Street Journal*, March 25, 1985.
63. "A Nicaraguan Catholic Priest Swears His Innocence of Charges of Sedition: A Statement by Father Luis Amada Peña," *Occasional Bulletins*, The Puebla Institute, October 1984.
64. "Prelate Charges Sandinistas Seek to Oust Catholic Church," *The Washington Post*, June 23, 1984.
65. "The Expelling of Ten Catholic Priests From Nicaragua: An Interview with Rev. Santiago Anitua, S.J.," *Occasional Bulletins*, The Puebla Institute, October 1984.
66. *Ibid.*
67. *Ibid.*
68. "The Subversion of the Church in Nicaragua," *Briefing Paper* interview of Miguel Bolaños-Hunter, by the Institute on Religion and Democracy, Washington, D.C., December 1983.
69. *Ibid.*
70. *Ibid.*
71. *Ibid.*
72. *Op. cit.*, *White House Digest*, "Persecution of Christian Groups in Nicaragua."
73. "Miguel Obando: Independent," by Joan Frawley, *The National Catholic Register*, May 12, 1985.
74. *Op. cit.*, *Christians Under Fire*, by Humberto Belli, p. 50.
75. *Nicaragua: Revolution in the Family*, by Shirley Christian (New York: Random House, 1985), p. 231.
76. "Nicaraguan Repression: Church Reports Differ," by William Bole, *The Lutheran*, November 17, 1982.
77. *Op. cit.*, *Christians Under Fire*, by Humberton Belli, p. 50.
78. "Persecution of Protestants in Nicaragua: The Neglected Story," by Humberto Belli, 1983.
79. *U.S. Government Foreign Broadcast Information Service*, Central America, August 2, 1982, p. 7.
80. *Op. cit.*, Humberto Belli, "Persecution of Protestants in Nicaragua: The Neglected Story."
81. Letter from Salvation Army LTC Ernest Miller.
82. "Church officials in Nicaragua Said Arrested, Harassed," by Roy Beck, *United Methodist Reporter*, November 15, 1985.

83. "The Lonely Struggle of a Nicaraguan Priest," by Trevor Armbrister, *Reader's Digest*, April 1986.
84. *White House Digest*, quoting *The Wall Street Journal*, by Shoshana Bryen, August 24, 1983; "The Sandinista War on Human Rights," *Backgrounder*, The Heritage Foundation, July 19, 1983.
85. *Ibid.*, "The Sandinista War on Human Rights."
86. Speech by Prudencio Baltodano during "Religious Persecution in Nicaragua," seminar held by the Outreach Working Group on Central America, the White House, May 4, 1984.
87. *Ibid.*
88. *Ibid.*
89. "Nicaragua's State Security: Behind the Propaganda Mask," an interview with Alvaro José Baldizon Aviles by the Institute on Religion and Democracy, *Briefing Paper*, September 1985.
90. *Ibid.*
91. "El Tigrillo: Portrait of a Contra," by Trevor Armbrister, *Reader's Digest*, October 1985, p. 99.
92. "Christians in the Sandinista Revolution," a speech given by Geraldine de Macias, January 20, 1983 at the Institute on Religion and Democracy, Washington, D.C.
93. *Op. cit.*, "The Subversion of the Church in Nicaragua," interview with Miguel Bolaños-Hunter.
94. *Ibid.*
95. "Nicaragua's Popular Church: Just Another Party Organ?" by Joan Frawley, *The Wall Street Journal*, February 22, 1985.
96. "Spiritual Awakening Occurring Behind Prison Walls in Nicaragua," by Kate Rafferty, *The Forerunner*, July 1984.
97. *Ibid.*
98. *Ibid.*
99. *Ibid.*
100. "'Constant Surveillance' Claimed in Nicaragua," by Roy Beck, *United Methodist Reporter*, December 27, 1985.
101. "Mottesi 'Peace Crusade' Marks Great Victory for Nicaraguan Christians," *Open Doors News Service*, February 1984.
102. *Ibid.*
103. Personal interview, October 4, 1985.
104. *Ibid.*
105. *Ibid.*
106. *Ibid.*
107. *Ibid.*
108. "The Sandinista Regime Today," by Humberto Belli, *Freedom at Issue*, November/December 1982.
109. *Op. cit.*, White House Digest, "Persecution of Christian Groups in Nicaragua."
110. *Op. cit.*, "The Sandinista Regime Today," by Humberto Belli.
111. Broadcast from Nicaragua, American Broadcasting Company, by Peter Collins, April 20, 1984.

Chapter Eight

1. Signing were Catholic bishops Maurice Dingham, Walter Sullivan, Walter Schoenherr, P. Francis Murphy, Thomas Gumbleton; United Methodist bishops Leontine Kelly, C. Dale White, Kenneth Hicks, Ernest Dixon, Joseph Yeakel, Melvin Talbert; Episcopal bishops Paul Moore, Harold Hopkins, William Davidson, Lyman Ogilby, L. Shannon Mallory, H. Coleman McGehee; UCC president Avery Post, NCC general secretary Ari Brower, and president Philip Cousins.
2. "Religious Groups Orchestrate Opposition to 'Contra' Aid," by Gerry Fitzgerald, *The Washington Post*, April 23, 1985.
3. *Ibid.*
4. *Ibid.*
5. Personal interview with Dean Brown, October 9, 1985.
6. The United Methodists gave Witness for Peace $20,000 in 1984 and the Presbyterian Women's Opportunity Fund donated $10,000 for the same year. This is just the tip of the iceberg of Witness for Peace funding by American churches.
7. Personal interview, October 2, 1985.
8. *Ibid.*
9. "Pilgrims for Peace," by Alfredo Lanier, *Chicago* magazine, October 1984, p. 207.
10. *Ibid.*
11. *Ibid.*
12. *Ibid.*, p. 209.
13. Personal interview, October 2, 1985.
14. *Op. cit.*, "Pilgrims for Peace," by Alfredo Lanier, p. 207.
15. *Ibid.*
16. *Ibid.*
17. Personal interview, October 2, 1985.
18. "'Witness For Peace': Pawn for Oppression," by Alejandro Bonaños-Geyer, *Voice of Nicaragua*, published by the Nicaraguan Information Center, November 1985; and "A Closer Look at 'Witness for Peace,'" by Peter Flaherty, *The Presbyterian Layman*, November-December 1985.
19. *Ibid.*
20. "A Shield of Love," by Joyce Hollyday, *Sojourners*, November 1983.
21. "Observations of the West Michigan Central American Trip," by Kalmin Smith, *Michigan Christian Advocate*, November 12, 1985.
22. Personal interview with Kalmin Smith, October 9, 1985.
23. *Ibid.*
24. *Ibid.*
25. Personal interview with Rader, October 9, 1985.
26. "Tomás Borgé, Charismatic Jailer," by Merle Linda Wolin, *Los Angeles Herald Examiner*, May 5, 1985.
27. *Ibid.*
28. "Ex-Sandinista Official Says Visiting Religious Groups Deceived," by William Bole, *Religious News Service*, October 4, 1985.

29. *Ibid.*
30. Personal interview with Andrew Zuniga, president of the Confederation of Professional Associations of Nicaragua (CONAPRO), based in Managua, Nicaragua.
31. *Op. cit.*, "Ex-Sandinista Official Says Visiting Religious Groups Deceived," by William Bole.
32. "The Speaker and His Sources on Latin America," by Philip Taubman, *The New York Times*, September 12, 1984.
33. "Catholic and Other U.S. Church Groups Oppose Reagan's Hard-Line Policy on Central America," by Gerald Scib, *The Wall Street Journal*, December 8, 1983.
34. *Ibid.*
35. "Nicaraguan Church Official says USCC Staffer Hindered Bishops," by Joan Frawley, *National Catholic Register*, September 9, 1985.
36. "USCC Latin Policies Under Review After Bishops' Trips," by Joan Frawley, *The National Catholic Register*, March 31, 1985.
37. "Remembering a Bishop," by Tom Quigley, *The Witness*, Volume 63, September 1980.
38. "Catholic Groups Differ With Pope Over Nicaragua," by Joanne Omang, *The Washington Post*, July 23, 1984.
39. "U.S. Group: Religion Not Under Attack in Nicaragua," by David Anderson, United Press International, July 28, 1984.
40. "John Paul II's Visit to Managua," by Charlene Muir, *The Churchwoman*, Summer 1983.
41. "Nicaraguans Face Divided Loyalties," by Liston Pope, Jr., *The Catholic Times*, December 2, 1983.
42. "Religion Focus of Conflict Between Sympathy-torn Nicaraguans," by Gary MacEoin, *National Catholic Reporter*, August 12, 1983.
43. *Ibid.*
44. It is dated November 19, 1982. Copies can be obtained by writing the Nicaraguan Information Center, P.O. Box 607, St. Charles, MO 63301.
45. John Paul's letter was quoted in Bolaños's letter.
46. Personal interview, October 4, 1985.
47. "Nicaragua's Popular Church: Just Another Party Organ?" by Joan Frawley, *The Wall Street Journal*, February 22, 1985.
48. Personal interview, Fall 1984.
49. "Rome Superior Threatens 'Rebellious' Nicaraguan Jesuits," by *Religious News Service*, July 16, 1984.
50. *Op. cit.*, "Nicaraguan's Popular Church: Just Another Party Organ?" by Joan Frawley.
51. "The Subversion of the Church in Nicaragua," a *Briefing Paper* interview with Miguel Bolaños-Hunter by the Institute on Religion and Democracy, December 1983.
52. "Nicaragua's State Security: Behind the Propaganda Mask," a *Briefing Paper* interview with Alvaro Baldizon Aviles by the Institute on Religion and Democracy, September 1985.
53. "Who Speaks for Nicaragua's Evangelicals?," an interview with Kate

Rafferty of Open Doors by the Institute on Religion and Democracy, *Briefing Paper*, January 1985.

54. *Ibid.*
55. Personal interview with Geraldine de Macias, October 9, 1985.
56. *Ibid.*
57. "Sanctuary Network Burgeoning in U.S.," by Robert Tomsho, *The Dallas Morning News*, October 27, 1985.
58. "The Sanctuary Movement: A Time for Reappraisal," from *Religion and Democracy*, a newsletter of the Institute on Religion and Democracy, March 1985.
59. "We Can't Allow All Salvadorans to Stay," by Senator Alan K. Simpson, *The Washington Post*, July 10, 1984.
60. *Ibid.*
61. *Ibid.*
62. *Ibid.*
63. *Ibid.*
64. "Sanctuary," by Daniel Ritchie, *Eternity*, June 1985.
65. "The Sanctuary Movement: A Time for Reappraisal," *Religion and Democracy*, the newsletter of the Institute on Religion and Democracy, March 1985.
66. "Rebels Terrorize Local Officials in El Salvador," by Chris Hedges, *The Dallas Morning News*, May 12, 1985.
67. "Steady Progress in El Salvador," *The Backgrounder*, a publication of The Heritage Foundation, February 2, 1983.
68. "American Catholics Are Being Used on El Salvador," by Georgie Anne Geyer, *The Washington Star*, March 31, 1981.
69. *Op. cit.*, "We Can't Allow All Salvadorans to Stay," by Sen. Alan K. Simpson.
70. Personal interview, Spring 1985.

Chapter Nine

1. "The WCC Finances Violence to Combat Racism," an editorial by editors of *Christianity Today*, November 20, 1981.
2. "Followers of Lenin Will Reap Spoils of South Africa," by Richard Viguerie, *Houston Chronicle*, August 28, 1985.
3. "Blacks in S. Africa," by Marcia Kunstel, *The Dallas Morning News*, August 29, 1985.
4. *Op. cit.*, "Followers of Lenin Will Reap Spoils of South Africa," by Richard Viguerie.
5. "South African Rebels Make Comeback," by Glenn Frankel, *The Washington Post*, January 1, 1984.

6. "Terrorist Bomb Kills 3, Injures 22 During Rush Hour in South Africa,"
by Allister Sparks, *The Washington Post*, April 4, 1985.
7. *Ibid.*
8. "Soviet, East German and Cuban Involvement in Fomenting Terrorism
in Southern Africa," *Report of the Chairman of the Subcommittee on
Security and Terrorism to the Committee on the Judiciary United
States Senate Ninety-Seventh Congress, Second Session, November
1982*.
9. "TransAfrica, a Lobby of the Left," a publication of The Lincoln
Institute for Research and Education, Washington, D.C., 1985.
10. "Who Speaks for South Africa's Blacks?," by Mangosuthu Buthelezi,
The Washington Post, November 27, 1985.
11. "The Democratic Option in Namibia," a *Briefing Paper* interview with
Professor Mburumba Kerina by the Instutute on Religion and
Democracy, April 1984.
12. *Ibid.*
13. Personal interviews, names withheld by request.
14. *Op. cit.*, "The Democratic Option in Namibia."
15. *Ibid.*
16. *Ibid.*
17. *Ibid.*
18. *Ibid.*
19. U.N. General Assembly Document A/CONF.107/5, May 5, 1981,
supplement A/CONF.107/5Add.1.
20. *Ibid.*
21. *Ibid.*
22. "Namibian Refugees Get a Dose of Politics with Aid," by Bernard D.
Nossiter, *The New York Times*, April 1, 1981.
23. *Ibid.*
24. *The Fraudulent Gospel, Politics and the World Council of Churches*,
by Bernard Smith, published in the United States by the Church
League of America, 1977, in Great Britain by the Foreign Affairs
Publishing Company, Ltd., 1977.
25. *Ibid.*
26. *Amsterdam to Nairobi, The World Council of Churches and the Third
World*, by Ernest Lefever, published by the Ethics and Public Policy
Center, 1978.
27. *Op. cit.*, "The WCC Finances Violence to Combat Racism."
28. "Salvation Army Out of World Council," by United Press
International, *Chattanooga News-Free Press*, August 25, 1981.
29. "Grants to Groups Combating Racism: Facts and Rationale," a
statement by the World Council of Churches, 1978, reprinted in
appendix to *Amsterdam to Nairobi*, by Ernest Lefever, published by
the Ethics and Public Policy Center, 1979.
30. *Memoir*, by G. Leibholz, foreword to *The Cost of Discipleship*, by
Dietrich Bonhoeffer (New York: Macmillan, 1959).
31. *Ibid.*
32. *Ethics*, by Dietrich Bonhoeffer (New York: Macmillan, 1949), p. 205.

33. *Op. cit.*, *The Cost of Discipleship*, by Dietrich Bonhoeffer, pp. 225, 226.
34. *Ibid.*
35. *Ibid.*, pp. 234, 235.
36. *Ibid.*
37. *The Cost of Discipleship*, translated by R. H. Fuller, rev. ed. (New York: Macmillan, 1960), p. 36.
38. *Op. cit.*, "TransAfrica, A Lobby of the Left."
39. Personal interview, Fall 1984.
40. "Mozambique's Move Away from Marxism," by David Lamb, *Reader's Digest*, April 1985.

Chapter Ten

1. Written by Oliver Cromwell in a letter to the General Assembly of the Church of Scotland, August 3, 1650.
2. *A Rumor of Angels: Modern Society and the Rediscovery of the Supernatural*, by Peter Berger (New York: Doubleday Anchor, 1970), pp. 9, 10.
3. Personal interview, name withheld by request.
4. "Does Christianity Have a Future—Part II," by James Hitchcock, *New Oxford Review*, July-August 1980.
5. *Ibid.*
6. *Man's Search for Meaning*, by Viktor Frankl (New York: Pocket Books, 1984), pp. 121-123.
7. *Democracy in America*, Volume II, by Alexis de Tocqueville (New York: Vintage Books, 1945), pp. 144-146.
8. *Op. cit.*, *Man's Search for Meaning*, by Viktor Frankl, pp. 121, 122, 129.
9. *Escape from Freedom*, by Eric Fromm (New York: Holt, Rinehart and Winston, 1941), pp. 50, 51.
10. *Ibid.*
11. *Ibid.*, pp. 57-60.
12. *Ibid.*
13. *Ibid.*
14. *Ibid.*
15. *New College Edition: The American Heritage Dictionary of the English Language* (Boston: Houghton Mifflin, 1978).
16. Fromm did favor Marxism as a theory, while viewing the Soviet system as both a fraud and a failure. Fromm did not believe any society had put Marx's theories into practice as he meant them to be. On the other hand, Fromm viewed capitalism not as a failure, but as a system that needs to be used in a more positive, fulfilling manner.

Capitalism has brought "enormous progress," Fromm said, going so far as to charge that any critical appraisal which neglected the progress "is rooted in irrational romanticism" and suspect of criticizing for "the sake of destruction . . . one of the most important achievements of man in modern history."

17. *Political Pilgrims*, by Paul Hollander (New York: Harper-Colophon Books, 1981), p. 401.
18. *Ibid.*, quoting from "On the Disaffection of Western Intellectuals," by Richard Lowenthal, *Encounter*, July 1977, p. 412 of *Political Pilgrims*.
19. *Op. cit.*, *Democracy in America*, by Alexis de Tocqueville, p. 152.
20. *Op. cit.*, *Escape from Freedom*, by Eric Fromm, pp. 48, 162.
21. *The Undiscovered Self*, by Carl Jung (New York: Mentor, 1957), p. 12.
22. *Ibid.*
23. "Ethics and the New Class," by Peter Berger, Ethics and Public Policy reprint, September 1978, Ethics and Public Policy Center, Washington, D.C.
24. *Op. cit.*, *Political Pilgrims*, by Paul Hollander,, p. 408, quoting from Stephen Whitfield's *Scott Nearing: Apostle of American Radicalism* (New York: Columbia University Press, 1974), p. 192.
25. *The Heart of Man*, by Erich Fromm (New York: Harper Colophon Books, 1964), p. 38.
26. *Op. cit.*, *Escape from Freedom*, by Erich Fromm, p. 117.
27. *Ibid.*, quoting from *History and American Society*, by David Potter.
28. The Gospel of Matthew, chapter 22, verse 50, *The New Testament in Modern English*, translated by J.B. Phillips (New York: Macmillan, 1960).
29. *Op. cit.*, *Political Pilgrims*, by Paul Hollander, p. 406.
30. *Ibid*, p. 410.
31. "Roots of a Revolution: The Influence on Tomás Borgé," by Merle Linda Wolin, *Los Angeles Herald Examiner*, Thursday, May 9, 1985.
32. *Ibid.*
33. "The Sandinistas," *Playboy*, September 1983.
34. *Ibid.*
35. "Ortega: Reluctant Ruler," by Merle Linda Wolin, *Los Angeles Herald Examiner*, May 10, 1985.
36. *Ibid.*
37. *Ibid.*
38. *The God That Failed*, edited by Richard Crossman (Chicago: Regnery Gateway, 1983), pp. 15, 16.
39. *Ibid*, pp. 18, 19.
40. "Strange People, These Americans," by Yuji Aida, *Houston Chronicle*, Outlook page, January 29, 1986.
41. "A Political Pilgrimage," by Clark Pinnock, *Eternity*, October 1984.
42. *Ibid.*
43. *Ibid.*
44. "Why the Conciliar Movement Is Facing a Crisis of Credibility," by

Isaac Rottenberg, executive director of the National Christian Leadership Conference for Israel, and personal interview, Fall 1984.

45. *Ibid.*
46. *Ibid.*
47. *Ibid.*

Chapter Eleven

1. "That Extraordinary Synod: A Report From Rome," from *The Religion and Society Report*, Special Report, March 1986, published by The Rockford Institute, Rockford, Illinois. Taken from a discussion of what occurred at the 1986 Extraordinary Synod called by Pope John Paul II to discuss the Second Vatican Council.
2. *Ibid.*
3. Romans 8:37, Holy Bible, *Revised Standard Version*.

Appendix

1. "Grassroots Church Lobby Network Attracts New Notice in Congress," by William Bole, *Religious News Service*, April 12, 1983.
2. *Ibid.*
3. "A Defection in the Family," by Kai Bird and Max Holland, *The Nation*, November 30, 1985.
4. Personal interview, February 1986.
5. "Contra Atrocities, or a Covert Propaganda War?" by Jim Denton, *The Wall Street Journal*, April 23, 1985.
6. *Ibid.*
7. *Ibid.*
8. *Ibid.*
9. "The Sandinista Lobby," by Fred Barnes, *The New Republic*, January 20, 1986.
10. "CISPES: A Terrorist Propaganda Network," by J. Michael Waller, *Special Report* of the Council for InterAmerican Security, Washington, D.C.; *KGB Today—The Hidden Hand*, by John Barron (New York: Reader's Digest Press, 1983), pp. 245-248; "Who Really Lobbies Against Aid to El Salvador," a speech by the Honorable Jack Fields of Texas, in the House of Representatives, April 28, 1981, published in the *Congressional Record*, p. E1890-91.

11. *Ibid.*
12. *Ibid.*
13. *Ibid.*
14. *Ibid.*
15. *Ibid.*
16. "CISPES: A Terrorist Propaganda Network," by J. Michael Waller, *Special Report* of the Council for Inter-American Security.
17. *Ibid.*
18. *Ibid.*
19. Quoted in the *Congressional Record*, "The Center For Constitutional Rights: Activists In The Struggle Against Our Republic," remarks by Hon. Larry McDonald of Georgia, in the House of Representatives, Wednesday, September 10, 1975.
20. "America the Enemy, Profile of a Revolutionary Think Tank," by Rael Jean Isaac, an Ethics and Public Policy (Center) reprint, July 1980.

Index